W9-AUS-008

FAIR PAY

FAIR PAY

HOW TO GET A RAISE, CLOSE THE WAGE GAP, AND BUILD STRONGER BUSINESSES

DAVID BUCKMASTER

HARPER
BUSINESS

An Imprint of HarperCollins*Publishers*

HarperCollins books may be purchased for educational, business, or sales promotional use. For information, please email the Special Markets Department at SPsales@harpercollins.com.

FIRST EDITION

Designed by Kyle O'Brien

Library of Congress Cataloging-in-Publication Data
Names: Buckmaster, David, author.
Title: Fair pay: how to get a raise, close the wage gap, and build stronger businesses / David Buckmaster.
Description: First edition. | New York, NY: Harper Business, [2021] | Includes bibliographical references and index. | Summary: "The American worker is suffering, and fewer and fewer individuals are earning a living wage. In *Fair Pay*, compensation expert David Buckmaster diagnoses the problems with our current compensation model, demystifies pay practices, and gives readers practical information for negotiating their salaries."—Provided by publisher.
Identifiers: LCCN 2021002285 (print) | LCCN 2021002286 (ebook) | ISBN 9780062998279 (hardcover) | ISBN 9780062998293 (ebook)
Subjects: LCSH: Wages—United States. | Wage payment systems—United States. | Compensation management—United States.
Classification: LCC HD4975 .B795 2021 (print) | LCC HD4975 (ebook) | DDC 331.2/973—dc23
LC record available at https://lccn.loc.gov/2021002285
LC ebook record available at https://lccn.loc.gov/2021002286

21 22 23 24 25 LSC 10 9 8 7 6 5 4 3 2 1

For Tova. May you grow up to find this book outdated.

Contents

PART I

PAY AS WE KNOW IT

CHAPTER 1

What We Know about Pay Is Wrong

On a weekday evening in south Seattle, a crowd formed outside an old Sears warehouse. Local labor organizers gathered with service industry workers against a backdrop of container ships floating toward the city's port. A few had microphones and led chants of "Fight for $15!" while the rest waved signs at the passing office workers as they left the building and headed home for the day. As many as five thousand people would see the protest. The old warehouse was no longer being used to fulfill department store catalog orders. Now it was the global headquarters of Starbucks.

The crowd wanted higher pay, not only for the coffee chain's baristas but for all service workers. They said that $15 an hour was the minimum amount workers needed to live a life of dignity. This was 60 percent more than the Washington State minimum wage, which at the time in 2014 was $9.32 an hour. Seattle's city council wouldn't pass its own minimum wage until the next year, with a series of increases starting at $11. The new Seattle minimum wage would be one of the highest in the nation, far above the federal rate of $7.25, which was set in 2009 and hasn't been touched since. It still was not enough to provide workers a basic standard of independent living, and the rent problem would get worse with time. By 2018, a national study found a one-bedroom apartment to be affordable for minimum-wage employees in only twenty-two counties across five states: Arizona, California, Colorado, Oregon, and Washington. In each of these states, the local minimum wage exceeded the federal minimum wage by at least 40 percent. King County, home of the Seattle metropolitan area, was not on this list.

This livability question has focused much of the public debate about pay on minimum wage. Minimum-wage jobs are usually described in the most literal sense—as a minimum amount of pay provided to a minimum number of workers with minimum skill for a minimum amount of time. We tend to think of minimum-wage earners in nostalgic terms, as if they are temporarily working for low wages at the soda fountain, just students on summer break who need basic work experience before graduating and taking "real" jobs in corporate offices. We downplay the skills required to do minimum-wage work (which often include intensive customer service and physically demanding tasks), and so we mentally disconnect these jobs from an expectation of sustained livelihood.

Estimates from the Bureau of Labor Statistics show minimum-wage workers are neither few in number nor temporary in status. They are also older than the narrative suggests. About 2 million people in the United States are paid at or below the federal minimum wage. More than half are over age twenty-five, and about 80 percent are at least twenty. The majority work in food service. About a third are parents and face increasing barriers to upward mobility for their families, like a lack of affordable childcare or predictable shift scheduling. On a percentage basis, 2 million is only 1 percent of the overall workforce, so critics of minimum-wage increases suggest the laws are therefore unimportant. They underestimate the impact because they fail to look the slightest bit up the income distribution, where we uncover a much larger problem—almost half the nation's workforce at the time of the protests were paid below the $15 threshold.

Starbucks was a smart place to protest. The company was then and remains now well ahead of the retail and food service industry in caring for its people, as its mission statement *to inspire and nurture the human spirit* suggests. Starbucks had, a few months prior, added to its long-standing health insurance and stock programs for all employees by launching a new university degree program in partnership with Arizona State University. The company received fawning news coverage for the innovative program, including a cover story in *The Atlantic* that showed a barista holding a diploma and the headline "Can Starbucks Save the Middle Class?" Though the protesters didn't know it at the time, the company had already started planning some of its biggest employee investments yet.

I was part of the Starbucks corporate team working on this project. My job was to set the pay rates for every Starbucks store employee, including its hundred thousand–plus baristas in the United States, who on average were about my age. The plan was to improve the pay, benefits, and working conditions for store "partners," as all employees at the company are called. Significant starting pay increases, free food while on shift, greater visibility into scheduling, enhanced career development opportunities, and a long-awaited relaxation of the dress code would all be rolled out together in a grand celebration called Partner Experience Investments. Our team felt great about the initiative, but $15 per hour was not on our menu, and in most cities, we would be far from that ideal. At the time, the Fight for $15 movement was considered fringe, if known about at all, as the protests had not yet broken through to the nationwide public consciousness. There was no precedent for that much of a wage increase, and we couldn't point to any other company of similar size paying anywhere close as a comparison.

In my more optimistic moments, I might have thought that for all our efforts and Starbucks' history of incremental corporate benevolence, we would usher in a new era of economic fairness and goodwill just like *The Atlantic* had predicted. Over time the company's efforts would bend back the arc of inequality, setting off a chain of corporate awakening with cascading wage and benefit increases across the economy that would take society back to the days when a middle-income earner could own a house, support a family, see a doctor without risking bankruptcy, and send children off to college on the steady path to an equally stable livelihood. We would Make America Great Again before anyone thought to print the idea on a red hat. In my more grounded moments, I at least knew Starbucks would stand out even further from the competition in the coming year.

What I soon learned was that while increased pay would make a difference in many places around the country, where the economic pressures of affordable housing, childcare, and transportation were not extreme, in most urban centers, our initiatives had no chance of resonating with the daily lives of baristas, including those I walked past working in the store attached to the headquarters, steps away from the protest outside.

I hadn't seen the crowd until I left work that day. Weaving through the signs, I walked toward my car parked on a battered street several blocks from campus, figuratively and literally on the other side of the railroad tracks. At the time, the corporate parking garage had a four-year waiting list, so faraway street parking let me experience a small slice of the city's worsening real estate burden, caused in part by Amazon, which took up an increasing share of square footage in unmarked buildings all over town and untethered housing prices from incomes along with it. This was years before Jeff Bezos would erect a not-so-subtle phallic-shaped building in the middle of downtown to symbolize his public dominance over the city.

On the busiest days, when the Seattle Mariners had an afternoon baseball game next door and street parking filled up early, I parked on the side of the street with the car campers, people whose only option of housing was their vehicle. Eighty years prior, the same land was a Hooverville, named mockingly after President Herbert Hoover as one of the hundreds of makeshift communities around the country where destitute families lived during the Great Depression. Prospects for the people who lived here now were not much better. Most days, I didn't think much about the circumstances that put them in this situation. I'm not proud of my apathy, but I got used to the sight, and I was usually too busy thinking about how to organize my calendar around getting to the third-floor cafeteria in time for the day's fresh salmon. The corporate chefs never seemed to make enough, and by 12:15, it would be gone.

I was only a middling analyst at the company, but I was already insulated by my own financial bubble and career ambition. I failed to see the needs of those directly around me and my own power to advocate for them. Later, I would learn of research showing a tie between a person's wealth and the brain reactions of seeing marginalized people— simply put, the richer you are, the less you tend to physically notice the poverty around you. My middling analyst salary was nearly double the median wage for the city, and more than four times the barista wage, yet I was already treating the working poor next to me as if they were invisible. I was living in the richest country in history, but for an increasing share of its people, fresh salmon was never on the menu. Worse still, in my job I was directly contributing to the problem.

The protesters did not know I was among the handful of passersby who could increase service industry pay—who could make $15 an hour happen—though not without first convincing more senior people it was a good idea. My team was responsible for knowing the trends and amounts that our competitors paid their workers everywhere in the world, in as granular detail as possible, and for recommending the appropriate "market rate" of pay for every job in the company. Traditionally, people in jobs like mine have understood their role to be trackers of market trends. We pay less attention to how we can influence the trajectory of the marketplace itself. The market, in its all-knowing wisdom, would tell us what to do.

Every large company has a group in their Human Resources Department that does this type of work, which, for lack of a more charismatic name, we will refer to as the compensation team. We usually sit in an unglamorously titled group called Total Rewards. Internationally, the standard nomenclature is even blander; we're called Total Remuneration. As a party trick, this work can be fun. By knowing a few details about your job, I can tell you within a few percentage points how much money you currently (or should) earn. If I get it wrong, I can deflect and say there's both an art and a science to the job, and that perhaps I leaned too heavily on the science and didn't properly calibrate for your company's compensation artist. This is all sort of true but mostly a convenient excuse people like me use to maintain a black box around our work and dodge questions or accountability.

After leaving Starbucks, I still played an indirect role in setting barista pay, not as a formal part of the company but in consulting with international franchisee conglomerates that operate brands owned by many companies. My new employer was Yum! Brands, which owns KFC, Pizza Hut, and Taco Bell, and has many of the same franchise (or license) partners as Starbucks. We'll return to how these arrangements work and how they can be problematic for fair-pay outcomes by limiting market competition in Chapter 8. After the restaurant world, I returned to the Pacific Northwest and joined Nike, where I work as I write this book.

For disclosure purposes, I should say a few things about this book's relationship to the brands I have been associated with. I am writing on my own behalf, not on behalf of any company. In these pages I don't share any proprietary company information, warts, or practices, and in the few spots where I do tell stories from my day job, I have changed enough of the details to make my point without exposing the inner workings or mistakes of any company or person (except my own). Sharing specific company details would add little to my reason for writing, which is to explain and improve upon a system that can be changed to bring fair pay to everyone. I am interested in bettering the systemic, corporate view of pay in which most of us work, and any improvements to the overall ecosystem will affect all companies in the same ways. As we'll see, this is because pay design at the world's largest companies is done by a small group of people who are well connected to each other and who use the same proprietary data sets. You can think of us as the world's least-interesting Illuminati. Our field is not well known, and that becomes an advantage we have over you.

Returning to our protest, you should also know I did not volunteer any of my professional expertise to the demonstrators. Had I shared any information about the pay plans we were working on at the time, I would have risked my job and put my own family in the neo-Hooverville. There were proper, legally vetted corporate channels to discuss such things at the right time, through the right messenger, using the right, focus-grouped phrasing, and I concentrated on that. Until then, I had a black box to protect.

MORE MONEY, DIFFERENT PROBLEMS

Across town from the Fight for $15 protests, a different kind of experiment in pay was underway. Dan Price, CEO of Seattle-based credit-card processing company Gravity Payments, announced a new minimum wage at his company. It wasn't $15 per hour, but $70,000 per year, which for full-time employees works out to almost $34 per hour. The number wasn't pulled out of the ether; it was based on a headline-grabbing study that found people's emotional well-being climbs with their income but plateaus once their annual pay reaches $75,000, enough to provide the necessities of life in most places plus a cushion to cover emergencies. As expected, Price's actions also made headlines. He hadn't only raised his company's minimum wage significantly, but funded the move by cutting his own salary from $1 million to $70,000. The Gravity Payments story generated hundreds of global news clippings and its own magazine covers. Among his most flattering was a cover story from *Inc. Magazine* titled "Is This the Best Boss in America?" High expectations for a guy most people had not yet heard of.

Price describes, in his book *Worth It*, being shaped by his childhood experiences—family financial struggles and religious convictions among them. Price's business intentions were also clear, as Gravity Payments would need to position itself to compete in the rarefied evergreen Seattle air alongside local household names like Jeff Bezos and Bill Gates. In the tech industry, where Gravity Payments competes, notoriety is often the only way to attract top-tier talent, and therefore survive. Industry observers know that the difference in work quality between the average tech worker and the top tech talent can be dramatic, even in already niche fields like artificial intelligence or machine learning. The pursuit of "10x engineers"—the engineers who are ten times as productive as their peers—has led to a corporate arms race to find and pay for top tech talent, especially in Seattle. This quest has brought wages up for the entire tech industry and generated a mythology of twenty-something engineers saying no to million-dollar job offer packages. In the early 2000s, competition got so fierce that many tech heavyweights found themselves caught up in a class-action complaint for having established "no-poach" arrangements with one another, in a coordinated effort alleged to have been designed explicitly to suppress pay. In one email to Google cofounder Sergey Brin, released in court filings, Apple icon Steve Jobs warned that "if you hire a single one of these people, that means war." Google's Eric Schmidt, also over email, said, "Google is the talk of the valley because we are driving up salaries across the board. People are just waiting for us to fall and get back at us for our 'unfair' pay practices." Recruiters who crossed the demilitarized zone were fired for their insubordination.

By design, Gravity Payments' minimum-wage pledge gave the company the strategic differentiation it was looking for compared to their better-known peers. Gravity Payments was a different kind of company. The pitch seems to have worked well enough to attract top talent, including Tammi Kroll, the company's chief operating officer, who was reported to have taken an 80 percent pay cut to join from Yahoo. It didn't matter if Gravity and all the other tech companies were already paying well above the legal minimum wage just as a factor of the industry and the kinds of jobs they employed, or that most of Price's earnings potential lay in the long-term equity ownership of the company, not in his annual base salary. Price was now a hero. Today, Gravity Payments continues to be successful. In a January 2020 tweet, Price said that since he put the company minimum-wage plan in place, revenue at Gravity Payments had grown 200 percent.

The Gravity Payments experiment wouldn't affect the service-level workers at the Fight for $15 protests. Price's argument, however, was identical to what the Fight for $15 group had been saying: The current system of pay we accept to be a normal and natural result of the free market is, for most workers, neither normal nor natural, and this market failure is putting the entire economic system at risk.

As we've watched the fallout of the global COVID-19 pandemic, it's undeniable most workers are living in a state of pay precarity that hadn't matched the headline fervor of a humming economy immediately prior to the outbreak. As measured by a stock market that recovered quickly, half of all Americans hadn't participated at all, and 90 percent of Americans owned only 12 percent of the total value gained. As comedian Russell Brand says, "People who say the system works, work for the system." Well, I work for the system, and I *also* say that for many people, it is not working. For some, like elite tech workers, the system pays well (extraordinarily so in some cases), but unfair pay still exists because there is little accountability for businesses that seek to limit the competitive marketplace for pay or that take performative (or no) steps to ensure equal pay for equal work. For most, the system is failing, and understanding how to make pay work better for everyone, so we can all prosper, is the reason for this book.

WHAT HAPPENS WHEN WE ASSUME

Until the Fight for $15 movement entrenched itself across the country, we had little data to show what could happen to local economies under a sudden, large shift in minimum wages. Instead, most people (including me) made assumptions based on their existing biases. The predominant view was that as minimum wages increased, so would unemployment and prices. Therefore, minimum-wage increases were bad and immoral and would backfire. This was Economics 101, we would hear. In fact, maybe we didn't even *need* a minimum wage. Denmark doesn't have a minimum wage, so why do we? The answer is that we also don't have a robust social safety net or broad collective bargaining coverage to absorb economic shocks or to balance power dynamics between employers and employees, but that's a lot to fit on a protest sign or a hat.

With the gift of hindsight, we see that despite the largest movement in minimum wage in modern history, (pre-pandemic) unemployment rates fell, prices didn't spiral out of control, and robots didn't counteract all job growth. Seattle, the epicenter of the minimum-wage movement, outpaced most of America across many employment measures, including a lower unemployment rate than the national average, and was named America's fastest-growing major city for the decade ending in 2017.

Though it wouldn't be fair to say the increase in minimum wage alone caused these results, it does show that economic growth and bold worker investments are not opposing choices. As economist John Kenneth Galbraith said many decades ago, "The conflict between security and progress, once billed as the social conflict of the century, doesn't exist." Seattle has major economic challenges ahead, most visibly in the lack of affordable housing that has pushed many out of the city or into the streets, but it is safe to say minimum-wage increases have not brought the end of economic growth and employment opportunity. In the language of the conservative American Enterprise Institute, Seattle was supposed to be among a growing list of cities with an "economic death wish" for its market interference in wage setting. But in the restaurant and service industry in particular, expected to be hardest hit by the minimum-wage increase, job growth through 2019 was stronger than ever. To again quote Galbraith, "The most impressive increases in output in the history of both the United States and other Western countries have occurred since men began to concern themselves with reducing the risks of the competitive system."

In summary, the worries about spending more on wages and benefits at the detriment of business were wrong, and it's clear that companies have room to be more generous toward their lowest-paid workers. This isn't to say there is no hypothetical breaking point where a high minimum wage reduces employment, only that we have not yet reached that point. Surely there would be affordability problems if the $15-per-hour minimum were raised to $100 overnight, but proposing such hypothetical and extreme positions is often the tactic of those looking to oversimplify and marginalize debates over making even incremental improvements. Though I am not an economist, I will play one briefly to illustrate my point that pay decisions are not usually binary with absolute true and false answers. Instead, getting to right answers about pay often falls on the spectrum from "it depends" to "who knows?"

At a certain point, mandating stark increases in pay (through legislation), or enabling stagnation (through market collusion and suppression), will reduce the number of people employed, either because workers don't make enough to justify the effort of putting pants on in the morning, or because the business can't charge enough for their product or service to afford the increased wages. Rather than being "over the hump" and generating more unemployment, as many predicted, an increased minimum wage of $15 per hour ended up being still below the top of the curve for Seattle, as shown by rising employment and business growth after the wage increase. Nationally, the same argument can be made for increasing the federal minimum wage of $7.25, as we've seen continued economic growth throughout the country in areas with and without local minimum-wage increases. What we now know is the right minimum wage rate for low-wage workers is "who knows, but definitely more than it is now."

Though so many of us were wrong about raising the minimum wage, it's also true that the disconnect was not formed out of malice or ruthless corporate sociopathy and efficiency seeking. Instead, the panic was largely caused by a combination of two things: fear of the unknown, because there was little to no evidence for what happens under mass nationwide increases in minimum wage; and inertia, because many of our beliefs about pay have historically rested on a handful of common assumptions about the value of jobs and the people who hold them. To make pay fair, we have to reset these assumptions, starting with the belief that supply and demand alone determine what people are paid.

SUPPLY AND DEMAND AND A LOT OF OTHER THINGS

The biggest assumption we make about pay is that the free market sets pay rates based on supply and demand for all people, at all times. We think of pay in the same way that blueberries are expensive to purchase in the winter, since they are harvested in the summertime and now must be shipped to you from an alternate hemisphere. In the case of blueberries, supply and demand is a helpful model for explaining price increases. But we can't apply this thinking directly to increasing prices for ourselves (pay) without also making broad assumptions about the transferability of skills and people across jobs. In other words, the basic model of supply and demand falls apart when we realize people can't be shipped like blueberries, they are not as interchangeable, and they wouldn't tolerate a summertime pay cut each year.

The theory goes that where job skills are definable, hard to get, and have value to others, wages should follow the laws of supply and demand. The physician has a clear, indispensable job and spends years to build the skills and temperament needed to do the work. We understand why physicians are highly paid based on supply and demand, and despite a looming physician shortage, wages for physicians have stagnated in recent years, even though we have had an aging population and a healthy economy. It's less clear that other highly paid jobs like investment bankers and management consultants fit the theory, and yet their wages continue to climb. It seems supply and demand are only part of the story of how wages grow. To see what else is going on, let's consider how wages for two other types of jobs work: commercial airline pilots and hotel cleaners.

Prior to the sudden stop in air travel due to the pandemic, commercial airline pilots were hard to find. The job requires a significant investment of time and expense, often a decade or more and over a hundred thousand dollars for licensing. These barriers reduce the supply of pilots, so it should follow that wages rise alongside increased demand for air travel. The job is definable, hard to get, and has value to others. But that's not the whole story.

Not long ago, low-cost regional airlines routinely paid their entry copilots close to minimum wage. Low pay rates were powered not by a sudden increase in the supply of pilots, a decrease in the quality of their skills or licensing requirements, or by a decrease in demand for air travel. Pay decreases happened mostly through a decrease in employee bargaining power at a time when the industry was struggling after the 9/11 terrorist attacks. Wages decreased not only for new pilots but for experienced pilots, too. Factoring the low possibility for high wages with the expense of time and money to become a pilot, future pilots chose other career options. Now, as a generation of pilots reach their mandatory retirement age, the lack of new pilots has created extreme supply-and-demand conditions for their skills, and a highly experienced pilot can command up to $300,000 a year in salary. That is a lot, enough for inclusion in the top 2 percent of wage earners, but it is only similar in adjusted terms to what pilots made in the 1990s. This means pilots have gained little over three decades. By the standard logic—high demand, low supply, high skills, high barriers to entry— pilots should always be highly paid without interruption. Again, other things get in the way of the standard models working as intended, in this case worker power.

Few people would suggest that the answer to a pilot shortage is to cut their training requirements, as it seems important that pilots should know what they're doing. Even the most ardent free-market libertarian flyer would prefer the pilot with additional safety training if given the choice. But it shows that factors other than the natural supply and demand of the free market can affect wages, like regulation, economic shocks, company choices, and bargaining power. This means we must broaden our thinking about who gets paid what and why.

Now consider pay for hotel cleaners. The barriers to entry for these jobs are low, and success isn't as binary or risky as performing open-heart surgery or landing a plane (though success is far more obvious than for a management consultant). The job skills are definable and have value to others, but the tasks can be learned quickly and are not unique enough to the individuals to let them dictate their own rate of pay. The basic skills are not hard to get, though they are exceptionally hard to do well for sustained periods of time. Only in boomtowns like those recently seen in North Dakota and Texas, where a supply of workers flocked to service newly discovered oil fields, do workers have some ability to name their price. But even then, under the most extreme conditions of low market supply and high market demand, the market rate for service workers like cleaners did not approach the Fight for $15 standard. We wouldn't expect pay for hotel cleaners to be as high as the physician's, but there's still more going on to hold wages back than is explained by our basic model of supply and demand.

Most hotel cleaners operate under outsourcing arrangements, meaning the hotel brands or offices they service have no ability to set wage standards, regardless of how well the person performs. Companies have no idea what these workers are paid (or their names or how they are treated, for that matter). Given the separated nature of the work from the parent company and a limited ability to differentiate on worker quality, companies see their cleaning services as just another office supply to be obtained, not as people they are responsible for providing decent jobs to. The companies that actually employ or contract these cleaners (including through new app-based platforms) therefore have every incentive to keep wage costs down and the people invisible to the end user.

In this case, it's not government interference or bargaining power that's limiting wage growth, but market-based private, structural employment arrangements. The lack of visibility between the company and the worker dampens wage growth opportunity, as these workers are out of sight and out of mind, with no access to the growth and benefits of the companies they service. The fabled story of working one's way from the janitorial floor to the executive suite is in most cases no longer possible, because the janitor is no longer part of the company. In Chapter 8, we will revisit how in our rush to create new types of employment segmentation through much lauded "Future of Work" initiatives, we are making our pay systems worse. In Chapter 7, we'll see how these mistakes are especially problematic for underrepresented groups who already experience significant pay gaps.

When we think about pay only in terms of simple models like supply and demand, or in the talking points of our preferred politics, we run into problems. It turns out there's supply and there's demand and there's a lot of other things going on with pay. We shouldn't minimize the role of supply and demand, but we should account for the other things that get in the way. We can make it easier for people to control the supply and demand of their own skills, as long as we're willing to recognize the need for some types of market interventions and employment protections to help workers promote, protect, or learn new skills. Critically, we have to build corporate and legislative systems that allow those skills and opportunities to grow or transfer to other employers who can offer more pay. This is what it means to make pay fair.

WHAT DOES FAIR PAY MEAN?

To talk about pay being fair, we first need to define what we mean by "pay" and "fair." There are lots of ways to define pay, but "fairness" is a politically loaded word whose meaning is affected by a person's worldview.

I separate wealth from pay for two reasons. The first is that the accumulation of wealth has more to do with long-term structural policies on things like taxes, land, and discrimination than business choices. The second reason is that pay is where I have firsthand expertise leading teams that make these decisions. We'll use the words "pay" and "wage" interchangeably, defined as the amount we earn as employees through our regular paychecks, bonuses, benefits, or stock grants from our companies, and not passive income some might have through a rental property or investment gains. What entrepreneurs pay themselves is not my concern, other than to say that before they decide on an amount, I hope they read this book to make sure they pay their employees fairly.

Though wealth is not my focus, it is worth a quick word, because inequality for wealth is an even bleaker story than inequality for pay. The Federal Reserve found that the wealthiest 10 percent of Americans owned 70 percent of the country's total assets, up from 61 percent in 1989. The bottom 50 percent of American households had almost no net wealth at all—decreasing from 4 percent of total household wealth in 1989 to just 1 percent in 2018. The American wealth story, repeated in many places globally, is like showing up to the family reunion and seeing a distant cousin, the one with the big job who lives in a faraway city and never calls, positioned at the front of the buffet line with to-go boxes. Meanwhile, most of us are left at the back of the line with a small salad plate and diminishing patience. If we can make pay more fair, the wealth gap will diminish over time, assuming the structural policies of wealth accumulation change, too.

By focusing on how companies pay employees, we target an overlooked but vital piece of the inequality puzzle. Research shows that two-thirds of income inequality results from the differences in pay among companies, and one-third from differences within companies. Other studies show that inequality is increasing within countries but decreasing between countries. Putting these findings together, we see where two drivers of inequality overlap: the differences in how companies pay their employees within the same country. If we can understand the decisions companies make about who gets paid what and why, we can effectively target the primary causes to wage inequality. Starting in Chapter 4, we'll see there is much consistency in how companies publicly commit to thinking about pay, but this doesn't translate to consistent outcomes. In one corner are the companies that "get it," choosing the path of paying well and equitably for their industry, even if they are slow to make meaningful changes to ensure all their employees are paid without bias and can afford life's essentials. In the other, much larger, corner are the companies that haven't yet realized how far behind they'll fall by not making changes now, instead continuing to leave their workers anxious and pessimistic toward their own careers and financial futures. This book applies to both types of companies.

It's easy to hate big business, but the company itself is the best organizing unit we have to make pay fair. Through large companies especially, we have an infrastructure to distribute pay through standardized jobs and company practices. These jobs and practices appear in market salary surveys and serve as collective reference points for fairness that create basic standards throughout the economy. We will talk about the many failures of these surveys, and the power imbalances created by large companies that limit our ability to move quickly toward fair pay, but our progress would be much slower without these reference points. The alternative, where pay decisions are made in individual company vacuums, would mean employees are kept further in the dark about their pay and would be less willing to restart their fair-pay journey with a new employer. Transparency, at least between companies, creates competition for pay, and I will argue we need to radically escalate the level of pay transparency available to employees within companies for the same reasons. Large companies also give us enough data to review and relieve unequal-pay outcomes across gender and race, as we'll discuss in detail in Chapter 7.

Concentrating on pay in companies builds on work from French economist Thomas Piketty in his internationally bestselling book *Capital in the Twenty-First Century*. Piketty and his team of researchers found that the rise of what he calls the "supermanager" accounts for much of the increase in pay inequality, particularly in the United States. This finding reflects a prior study in the United States that 60 percent of the increase in national income share between 1979 and 2005 went to executives, managers, supervisors, and the finance industry. Owners and entrepreneurs are an important part of these results, but for our purposes will remain paired with the corporate supermanagers because, ultimately, we are seeking to answer how business leaders should make decisions about how to pay the people they employ, at all levels of the company, and how getting these answers right will help us build stronger businesses for the long term. We will not pin inequality only on members of our supermanager executive class, because in my experience they also have a limited understanding of how to design pay in a way that fosters fairness. We will also not view success as the full elimination of pay inequality, as we can always expect some people to be paid more than others for explainable and desirable reasons like unique skill and effort. A more precise goal is to relieve the systemic anxiety of unfair and unequal pay by building trust in the pay process and putting more money in more people's pockets.

To stay focused on how companies think about pay, I also will only mention the contentious topic of immigration briefly here. Despite its boogeyman status, immigration does not factor at all into the decision-making of a company's compensation strategy. Often, workers on temporary status fall into segmented work arrangements, which we'll discuss more in Chapter 8, and are therefore kept entirely outside the company's pay philosophy and not managed by the formal compensation team. There is mixed evidence to support the idea that immigration depresses wages at all, and much depends on the geographic conditions of the country being studied. Further, 45 percent of Fortune 500 companies were founded by first-generation immigrants to the United States or their families, while 28 percent of patents are held by immigrants, so my assumption is that to make pay fair, we should want more immigration, not less. Immigration helps us build more competitive and innovative companies, which in turn allows us to pay better wages.

I will also assume technology and automation to be an important part of our working lives, but I will not speculate that machines are imminently coming to take all our jobs. This is a story we've seen before, from the tractor that replaced farmworkers as "the most common human occupation for six thousand years," to the automated teller machine (ATM). When the ATM first arrived, it was widely thought bank tellers would be made imminently redundant. Instead, we saw their employment increase as retail banks found new lines of business and ways of servicing accounts. In aggregate, the total number of jobs available now has not yet been reduced by automation, though the quality of these jobs has dramatically decreased based on the choices we make about what the remaining and new jobs are worth. Some jobs will disappear, no doubt, but we can expect new jobs will appear, too. Countries like Germany, Japan, and especially South Korea have far higher ratios of robots to workers than the United States, and each enjoys unemployment rates on par with the United States but with much less income inequality. The choice isn't between robots or humans, but whether robots will enhance or devalue the (mostly service and care) jobs we create, and how we choose to help humans earn a livelihood and transition to new types of work. Cornell professor Louis Hyman, in his book *Temp*, says the "point is not to be better robots than robots, but to have more human work than our ancestors—creative, caring, curious."

Finally, though this is not an economics book, I will do my best to pair the rich body of research on fair pay from the field with insights from the corporate world. I will not make my case through models like the Phillips curve or the Gini index, mostly because many others are better equipped and have already done so, and I assume most readers have no desire to walk their bosses through a chart of historical log changes to nominal wage growth during their next salary review. Instead, I'll use the plain language of our work experiences to reduce the friction we feel about pay for everyday employees and company decision makers.

Now, we need to define what it means for pay to be unfair. Deciding what is fair and what is not fair is controversial and often depends on a person's circumstances. The billionaire (or the aspiring billionaire) entrepreneur might say it's fair to believe that to the victor go the spoils, and therefore fair is a meaningless construct for losers to bring down winners. At the other end are those who could not imagine a scenario whereby a single person could earn a billion dollars through any means other than the unfair exploitation of workers, the Earth, the legal system, or some combination thereof. The future of fairness, to the first person, should be avoided because they believe (and they always quote this story) it will look like Kurt Vonnegut's "Harrison Bergeron," where natural human differences are handicapped by the government—intelligence is zapped through medical implants, strength weighed down with bags of birdshot, and beauty covered with masks. As the story opens, "The year was 2081, and everybody was finally equal." To the second person, fairness looks like a utopia they never expect to see.

Rather than parse the debate this way, with ever-moving goalposts of what amount of pay is and isn't fair, or what potentially dystopian/utopian future we might be building, I suggest we think of fairness as an operating mindset. When pay is fair, there is a shared perception between all parties that the process has been honest, with a nonnegotiable understanding that all people should be paid at least enough for their essentials, including some discretionary income. A World Economic Forum white paper from 2019 said it this way: "The best-performing companies in this area will provide—without discrimination—decent jobs, with fair and living wages and appropriate benefits, sufficient to support a decent livelihood for workers and their families." If the

Davos set, many of whom are victors with plenty of spoils, doesn't shy away from a loaded word like "fair," neither should we. Conceptually agreeing to fairness is the easy part; making it happen is much harder.

We need help talking to one another about pay, and as we've seen, we are not starting from a position of strength. When it comes to fair pay, we have a surplus of branding but a deficit of belief that it can happen. We hear phrases like "pay transparency" and "pay equality," but we're not sure what they mean, and we don't accept that they apply to our company or our paycheck. We worry that if our pay was truly transparent, our peers would question our value—they all saw us tuning out to Instagram during the strategy meeting last week. Or if they found out how little we got paid compared to others, we might be disappointed if they didn't become our personal cheerleader, refusing to work in protest until our personal pay gap was resolved. For the highly paid among us, the worry might be whether our humanity now comes down to a number we have to justify every day, all the while dodging attacks from people out for our job and the resulting paycheck. So instead of having the confidence to make sure everyone is paid fairly, we avoid the topic altogether, leaning into our anxiety and clinging onto the few scraps of information we're allowed (or want) to know about how our pay is determined.

Our reluctance to ask the hard questions about pay is hurting business and killing people, and I do mean killing. According to research led by Stanford professor Jeffrey Pfeffer, an estimated 120,000 deaths in the United States each year can be attributed to conditions associated with workplace anxiety, of which pay and benefits are significant factors. This is four times the number of people who die in car accidents each year. Another study found that a $1 per hour increase in minimum wage equates to lower suicide rates among those with a high school education or less. In the southern states of the United States, where wages are lower in large part because there are fewer state-level minimum-wage laws to intentionally shift the distribution of pay, the effects of income inequality have been attributed to two-thirds of the region's higher homicide rates compared to the rest of the country, according to a study by the Equality Trust. The study found the difference in homicide rates was more influenced by the distribution of pay across workers, compared to the amount of pay itself, though both matter. How many HR departments will start counting the ROI on "lives saved" as an internal company metric?

Ultimately, our decisions about pay, insofar as they accelerate or fail to rein in the anxiety caused by income inequality, contribute to a world in which we can create or prevent great harm. The effects of income inequality on our lives from birth to what we now call "deaths of despair" have become so normalized that we're paralyzed over what to do about it. When it comes to pay, most of us don't know where to begin. Simple models like supply and demand give us simple solutions, which will not help solve the complex problem of unfair pay. There is no magic program that can single-handedly rescue us from the downstream effects of unfair pay, including economic anxiety, wage stagnation, and income inequality. Ideas like Economic Opportunity Zones, where parts of a city are dedicated to revitalization through the elimination of regulations, may be either a catalyst for economic renaissance or a dystopian swampland, depending on your political views and financial connections, but they won't solve the problem of unfair pay. Universal basic income (UBI), a program in which we give people money to fill the gaps in our economy, may or may not work at scale, but it certainly won't address the root cause of these gaps—unfair pay—that still must be solved. No app, or in this case no program, can run effectively if the underlying operating system is faulty. What's clear to me is that we need a new way to process the way we think and talk about pay. The most direct solution is also the best solution: let's help more people earn more money.

We should test every tool in our tool kit for making pay fair. I believe the current state of pay is not irredeemable, and I have seen the lights come on for business leaders and workers all over the world when their companies start to think more critically about the role of fair pay. Maybe it's a lack of understanding, creativity, or political will to do the hard work that keeps us from making progress. Or perhaps it's simply bad-faith arguments from vested interests that hold us back. I would argue that each is true, but more often it's that many of us with the power to make changes are too focused on our cafeteria salmon to get us out of the mess we have created.

The urgency for a better type of conversation about pay is dire. We have grown numb to the headlines of rising income inequality because we have also grown numb to the way we are paid and valued by our employers. Carrying this burden not only hurts us personally, which makes our businesses worse, but also makes it much harder to work up the courage to advocate for someone else. And little by little, many of us have accepted a grim and absolutist view that perhaps this downward spiral is our new normal.

Three-quarters of US jobs created since the 2008 financial crisis pay less than a middle-class income, and let's be clear, this is our choice. Of the twenty-five occupations projected by the Bureau of Labor Statistics to show the most job growth through 2028, the median 2018 wage is $16 per hour, and at least fifteen of these jobs do not typically require a university degree. These jobs are not robot handlers; restaurant and personal-care workers dominate the top ten. We have skipped into what the United Way calls the ALICE era, an acronym for "asset limited, income constrained, and employed," where being employed is no longer an indicator of opportunity or progress but is now a signal of what people *don't* have. This is not sustainable.

We think pay is something that happens to us without our input. We believe executives sit in a boardroom, inventing ways to mire their workers in poverty. It may intrigue us to imagine Starbucks leaders plotting from their perch above Puget Sound while sipping lattes made with secret, unreleased milk alternatives. But the truth is, "the man holding us down" doesn't exist. More often, there is no evil plan, just business leaders who have not chosen to make fair pay a priority, allowing the infrastructure for actual pay decisions to be pushed much further down into the organization in radically inconsistent ways. This means "the man" is less like a supervillain and more like an absentee dad who mails you a check on your birthday but can't name any of your friends. Inertia, not intention, is the most powerful force in deciding pay, and we all get to shape that debate. It's the middling analysts, pounding away on Excel spreadsheets, answering the angry emails from employees who feel underpaid, and Googling what other companies are doing, who end up deciding so much of what happens to people's pay over time. That's the scene replicated in most every office, using the same sets of third-party data, appeasing the accountants, not the advocates. It's all less maniacal than it seems, but this gives me tremendous hope that we can make pay fair much quicker than we realize.

We need business leaders to step into the arena, to set a vision for pay, and to speak about equitable wage growth as an indicator of a healthy business, not just as an expense or euphemistically as a financial headwind. We also need workers to understand how their pay is decided and demand better from their employers through more informed, sharper arguments. We need to make fair pay a two-way pursuit, top down *and* bottom up. Pay is complicated, and it is deeply personal. But pay does not need to be rocket science and especially not alchemy. Our most basic assumptions about who gets paid what and why should be challenged and replaced with a new way of thinking. This book will not seek to prescribe solutions to all our pay problems, but it will serve as a platform for a more empowered and transparent conversation about pay than the current norm. An incomplete path to solving a problem shouldn't mean that we fail to take the first step. Most importantly, I hope this book reminds us all that when we talk about pay, we are talking about people's livelihoods and generational impact. An economy where more babies are born into fiscally stable families is a good thing for everyone and an investment with a high return. We must approach this issue in good faith and with humility that perhaps our starting views, and the views of the loudest voices we hear all around us, are simply wrong.

We will have false starts in making pay fair. Companies will make bad choices. Policies will fail. Your direct reports will make unreasonable requests. You will hear "no" or "not yet" from your bosses about your raise request. But we must be willing to experiment, putting more friction into a pay system that drifts now without new thought. Without change, we will allow our free-market system to fail on its own accord, as if we had no personal or institutional agency in the matter. By shining light into our pay systems and approaching pay with a bias toward equitable change, we can begin to see global pay growth as a metric for global good.

Most books about pay are written by academics and legislators and focus on historical, programmatic, and policy change at the macro level. Those are important books, and I will reference many of them, but I believe the future of pay will be shaped in large part by people like me, the ones who actually make fair or unfair pay decisions every day, and by people like you, who will learn how to make sure your pay is fair throughout your career. Whether you're reading this book to manage your own career, agitate for greater pay transparency in your company, or advocate for public policy changes, my hope is that you will finish feeling a little smarter when talking about pay, and a little bolder in asking for more of it.

CHAPTER 2

A New Way of Pay Sincerity

Some years ago, my wife and I were waiting to pick up our daughter from space camp in Houston. To waste time, we spent the Saturday afternoon touring the Johnson Space Center. We marveled at one of NASA's greatest accomplishments, the Saturn V rocket. It was the heaviest rocket ever flown, built to carry humans to the moon and support the launch of Skylab, America's first space station. As we read about how this new era of space exploration happened with less computing power than exists in a modern iPhone, I felt my own phone buzz in my pocket. I looked down to see a text from a colleague and quickly came back to earth. I couldn't help making the inevitable corny joke—Houston, we had a problem.

My team was not being summoned to launch a space station. Our challenge was more terrestrial and inspired no awe. An executive in our company, working in Southeast Asia, was trying to sell shares of his stock but running into a complex paperwork hurdle. Because it was a Saturday, the corporate advisers, approvers, and clairvoyants needed for our ad hoc mission control were not standing by to resolve the issue. Most were off doing nonwork things like enjoying their families. Practically, because offices were closed, no stock transactions could be completed until Monday, anyway. Unfortunately, the executive was ready for liftoff (the space puns will end shortly), which meant we had to drop everything to initiate our prelaunch checklist (soon, I promise) before the market opened again. One phone call was all it took to ruin a number of people's weekends. It was one small step for an executive, one giant leap for the rest of us (now I'm done).

Regardless of a person's title or how much they earn, I believe we have an obligation to listen and respond when someone feels mistreated over their pay. Executives can be victims of the gender wage gap. Middle managers can be paid well below their market value. And a company's lowest-paid (notice I am not saying lowest-skilled) workers may be falling so far behind they have to choose between furthering their education and having electricity. As a result of a pay system that is kept secret, most people don't trust their companies to make fair decisions about their pay. When your paycheck is the tool by which you survive, the basic expectation is fairness, regardless of whether your grocery budget calls for coq au vin or Cup O'Noodles. Expecting empathy around pay should be universal, because empathy isn't about status or rank, it's a human, instinctual response.

The stakes of fair pay for low-wage workers are much higher than those of executives, who we can assume have money in the bank and more career options to control the price of their labor. From the company's point of view, we can also understand the rationality of a person in my position being willing to cancel their weekend plans to solve the executive's pay problems, no matter how trivial or unmoored. The boss does sign our paychecks, after all. But in the case of the low-wage worker, we rarely act with the same urgency. The executive is thought of as an individual with unique personal problems, while the low-wage worker only in the sense of a system that can be disassociated from the personal. We assume some people are paid low because that's just how the world works and what the market says their job is worth. Or that low starting wages are good because they help keep prices low, and this is good for everyone.

Traditionally, there are three perspectives companies try to reconcile on pay: how much the market says a person should be paid, how employees feel about their pay, and how companies affix people's pay to their strategy, mission, and values. We address market and strategy factors throughout this book, but we can quickly cover the data to show how employees feel about their pay. The results aren't positive. PayScale, a compensation research firm, found that 64 percent of people who are paid competitively believe they are paid below market. When people are asked directly about whether they believe they are paid fairly, PayScale found only 21 percent agreed, regardless of their income or rung on the career ladder. Companies, however, guessed that 43 percent of their own employees would say they are paid fairly.

This perception gulf about fair pay between employees and employers is one problem, because it means employer messaging about pay is not resonating. The absolute numbers, where only one out of five employees believe they are being paid fairly, and only two in five from the company's perspective about their own pay programs, is a much more severe problem. Imagine a company feeling comfortable that four out of five customers felt they had been hoodwinked, even if the company knew they hadn't done anything wrong but had only explained the transaction poorly. How long would that company stay in business? In the same study, 60 percent of people who felt undervalued shared their intent to leave their companies. This is an enormous but often hidden replacement cost to companies of time and talent.

To make pay fair is to solve two problems at once, for everyone: the absolute amount of pay people earn, and the process by which pay is determined. The research is clear that something is broken in the process by which we decide who gets paid what and why, which pay problems we treat compared to those we choose to leave unresolved, and how we communicate the pay decisions we make. Unfair pay, including perceptions of unfair pay, is a problem in everyone's self-interest to overcome. To see what has gone wrong, let's now talk about pay strategy and where it comes from.

AMERICAN INFLUENCE

A lack of trust around pay isn't a uniquely American problem. It is a symptom of global trends and headlines around wage stagnation and income inequality, and we are seeing a burst of new wage laws around the world in response. As of 2019, the top 10 percent of workers receive nearly half of all global pay, according to the International Labour Organization, while the lowest-paid 50 percent receive only 6.4 percent. Though unfair pay is a global problem, our primary focus will be US policy and practice because, counterintuitively, this is how we're most likely to develop global solutions. There are three reasons for this.

MARKET DATA

The largest compensation-consulting firms all originated in the United States. In my first draft of this chapter, I wrote of the "big three": Aon, Mercer, and Willis Towers Watson. By my second draft, Aon announced its acquisition of Willis Towers Watson, leaving only two firms to determine most of the world's pay data gathering and methodology decisions. Also within Aon's stable are Radford, the gold standard consultant for tech industry pay, and McLagan, who leads pay for the financial services industry. Most companies big enough to have a human resources department look to these vendors for guidance, and while each firm has global offices with local expertise, the infrastructure they use to report on pay is US designed but globally applied. There are many boutique firms, especially for executive compensation, but none are as important as the big three, soon to be two.

PROFESSIONAL TRAINING

The academic training ground for compensation professionals, World-atWork, is also based in the United States. Though membership and classes are global, the certification coursework in its certified compensation professional (CCP) program assumes American-style market practices and cultural beliefs around individualism and paying for performance, a topic that we'll cover more starting in Chapter 3.

INTERNAL EFFICIENCY

American companies dominate the list of the world's largest employers, including all the world's ten largest publicly traded companies. For administrative clarity and to make internal technology systems work, global companies tend to set a single compensation philosophy from their headquarters and export many of their practices globally. This means the pay decision models set in the United States have an outsized influence over the rest of the world.

Given the established infrastructure behind global pay methodologies and data collection tools, the influence of the American model is unlikely to change anytime soon. While this centralization limits the market's ability to adapt to local needs, for our purposes the design can work to our advantage. Because we find the same unfair pay outcomes globally, then improvements to the model itself will reverberate far outside the States. In this way we can move quickly by addressing root cause issues rather than work for change on an ad hoc, country-by-country basis. First, we need to better understand the model that limits people's pay.

WHY IT'S HARD TO GET A RAISE

To many observers, myself included, both the $15 per hour protest and the $70,000 company minimum wage seemed preposterous. On the Fox Business network, Dan Price was not hailed as a hero but called the "lunatic of all lunatics," and for a time that may have been the bipartisan view (of people who were paid well already). In the business community, these outlandish wage demands were all a socialist fantasy, untenable and unworthy expenses that would lead to the rise of mass unemployment and robots, as if fully functioning robot replacements had been sitting in the break room all along, waiting for the signal. It seemed reasonable to dismiss $70,000 per year as just another tech stunt and not something that would be widely replicated. But $15 per hour was a shocking figure that felt dangerous because of its potential scale and impact on already low-margin businesses like restaurants. If that idea took off, we thought, then the flames of capitalism would be extinguished forever, and we would all soon be living in government hovels, dependent on handouts for survival.

As someone who has spent too many hours calculating the added payroll costs of wage increases at large companies, I can understand why so many initially leaped into their doomsday bunkers. To see why significant pay increases are so hard for companies to comprehend, let's review the strategic and practical reasons why we would choose *not* to give people more money.

First, we can calculate the cost of the Fight for $15 movement for just one company, using publicly available information and a few basic assumptions. In the case of Starbucks, you might assume the average barista works part-time at twenty-five hours per week. Now, we need to calculate the number of baristas. We can do this by assuming that at each store, fifteen baristas are needed to cover all shifts, and searching Starbucks investor documents we find that in 2019, the company had about 8,500 stores in the United States (we don't include licensed stores like those found in airports, whose workers are not Starbucks employees). For Starbucks to give each barista exactly $1 an hour extra, here's about how much it would cost:

$$(\$1) * (25 \text{ hours per week}) * (52 \text{ weeks per year}) *$$
$$(15 \text{ baristas}) * (8,500 \text{ stores}) = \$165 \text{ million.}$$

This number doesn't include additional employment taxes and benefits costs, which would figure to about 30 percent more. Let's call it $200 million to give all baristas that extra dollar per hour, while remembering that our estimate is conservative, as the actual minimum wage was then much further away than just a dollar from $15 per hour. If we needed to give every barista $2 more to reach our goal, the cost would approach half a billion dollars. If all baristas made $10 per hour, taking them to $15 would cost $1 billion. That is expensive, and we've just scratched the surface of the argument to see how compensation teams think, and why a $15 minimum wage was seen as a nonstarter.

If every worker made at least $15 per hour, we would then have to address pay for the next level supervisors, who earned their place to be higher up the chain and would want to maintain their distinction. This would continue, layer after layer, up through the company. How could a company ever afford that level of cascading increases, and wouldn't a massive pay increase also reset employee expectations about pay for years to come? Compensation teams call this problem "pay compression," meaning that companies want pay to progress gradually and leave enough space between career levels so that a promotional pay increase still feels meaningful and worth taking on the additional responsibilities of the new job. When pay compression becomes too tight, companies tend to eliminate job layers to cut off this progression, rather than increase wages for everyone in the hierarchy.

Next, let's consider geography. Should a business pay $15 per hour in Seattle but more in Manhattan? What about Tuscaloosa? This is one of many areas where compensation teams have an information advantage over employees, to the point where we are looking at entirely different data. To figure out what people should be paid in different parts of a country, compensation professionals use an obscure data point called a "cost-of-labor differential," which shows the differences in job prices across cities as found in formal salary surveys. If the national average cost of labor for a job is indexed to 100 percent, slicing the data may show the cost of labor in Manhattan for the same job is 120 percent, and in Tuscaloosa, 85 percent. These amounts are calculated using actual pay rates in each city, meaning employees can't validate these differences on their own because the data comes from third-party consulting sources.

Cost of labor is often confused with cost of living, like the change in cost of groceries and rent, which is easier to understand and readily searchable online. Cost of living, much to people's surprise, is not considered by most companies in setting pay rates. A day in the life of a compensation professional is to hear from employees about their personal cost of living, usually with detailed budgets attached to show us the error of our ways and the failures of our character. Making a cost-of-living case for more pay will fall on deaf ears at your company; I will teach you to make better arguments. The geography of pay matters, and your company thinks about it differently than you do.

Finally, there are strategic reasons to avoid paying higher wages. If Starbucks decided to increase wages significantly, others could theoretically do the same. If the Starbucks compensation team succeeded in the hard work of convincing their business leaders to make the first move toward higher wages, this would also give competitors an easy case for playing catch-up. Most companies target their pay at the median of the market rate (much more to come on this), so if Starbucks moved the baseline for pay forward, others would be obligated to match, eliminating any unique company advantage in attracting workers and effectively nullifying the investment and, in turn, industry margins.

The strategic argument against increasing wages, therefore, is that it doesn't buy you any long-term sustainable advantage and instead makes your entire industry less profitable. As shown, putting $200 million into wages as a first step to $15 per hour could spiral into half a billion or more in annual cost. This expense could instead easily fund a bigger parking garage at headquarters, with less angst from shareholders as a onetime expense that wouldn't count toward the normal operating expense of selling coffee in stores, a closely watched metric for investors. The tax code even incentivizes this choice—in accounting terms the garage would count as a depreciable capital expense, meaning the garage becomes a tax benefit to the company each year as the normal wear and tear of the structure reduces taxable income. Under the prevailing regime, investing in garages makes more sense than wages.

I could go on explaining the whole spectrum of arguments against increasing pay, from misplaced benevolent paternalism to dispassionately engineered financial projections to a general shrug from people in jobs like mine. But in response to the Fight for $15 movement, the overarching sentiment against increasing pay was that many corporate leaders simply did not see it coming, and fewer thought the idea had any merit or would sustain itself. Until then, we had relied on our market survey data to tell us when to make changes. Minimum wage increases had often been incremental, compromise agreements between political agitators and feet-dragging business leaders to avoid unionization efforts. Most of us assumed this dance would last forever, or at least until a legislative chaperone stepped in.

By 2019, the Fight for $15 had won the debate and set the new goalposts for pay. In the year after I first saw the Fight for $15 protests in Seattle, new minimum-wage laws passed in more than twenty states. Paying $15 per hour, or creating a path to $15 over time, is now the norm throughout the United States. Speaking from firsthand experience as a decision maker on retail industry pay, much of the wage investments that companies have made since 2014 have been directed to jobs affected by minimum-wage increases—and wages are now far higher than they would have been for these jobs had there been no legislative action. Public-shaming campaigns like the Fight for $15 movement, combined with a decreasing unemployment rate, worked together to drive wage increases. States where the minimum wage increased between 2013 and 2018 saw 50 percent faster wage growth than the rest. The natural and invisible hand of the free market, or any particular presidential administration's social media posts, had less effect.

Anticipating the new normal, some brands kick-started their pay approaches and pushed beyond the new legal standards. Few companies want to be seen as an employer of last resort, so pay and benefits have started to become essential tools for good public relations. Even companies like Walmart and McDonald's, never having been known as progressive-minded paragons for the working class, have in recent years made bold pronouncements on wages alongside Target, Gap, and IKEA. Many others are doing so quietly just to keep up. We should celebrate these changes while recognizing we have a long way to go to build trust in our pay systems. How then can we push everyone toward fair pay?

PAY SINCERITY

I believe we can hold companies to account through what I call "pay sincerity." Pay sincerity is a way of operating a business and pursuing a career that elevates our expectations about who gets paid what and why, acknowledging that to pay someone for work is to make an investment in a whole person. It recognizes that people should be paid fairly, because while people should earn their measure of livelihood, they shouldn't need to earn their basic humanity. Operating with pay sincerity means that the way we pay should be thoughtful and sincere, free of deceit and cynicism, because the decisions we make about pay can change both a person's outlook and their possibilities. Pay sincerity is a two-way street; it shifts the control and obligation of equitable pay outcomes from being only top down to also bottom up, so those left out of pay determinations now can assert themselves in the future. Sincerity is a virtue worth pursuing, and when applied to business practices, it becomes a measure of accountability.

Pay sincerity is a way of working that relentlessly pursues equitable and transparent pay, provides for the essentials of a decent life, and helps people seek the full reward of their contributions and potential.

Pay sincerity, at its best, is more than an exercise in branding or a qualification that companies can earn to tick the box, as if it were a onetime exercise. Pay sincerity is an active set of choices companies make to create and sustain an environment in which they welcome the sharing of essential pay information, with continuous, good-faith investment in improvement and trust building over time. When employees make it clear that their companies are getting pay wrong, or at least that pay decisions are not being communicated clearly, companies should embrace the opportunity to have repercussion-free dialogue and respond with changes where necessary.

Pay sincerity goes beyond pay transparency, which is often a highly sanitized, one-way release of basic information from the corporate black box, like pay ranges or aggregate equal-pay results. Pay transparency is important, and we will talk about it often, but it doesn't assign accountability for improvements. Once pay information has been made public, we have to learn what to do with the problems we find. If the information is out there, the idea goes, better decisions will be made naturally because people can self-select into better companies and roles. If only it were that easy—we still need a guide to help us understand what the information means and how we can navigate or improve the pay system itself when it isn't serving us well.

Why the word "sincerity"? People can be sincerely wrong, after all. Oscar Wilde said that "a little sincerity is a dangerous thing, and a great deal of it is absolutely fatal." A cynic, or the "Harrison Bergeron" crowd, might say a risk taken in pursuit of a perceived utopia can cause more harm than good. A lot of companies operate with that mentality, preferring control over conversation and refusing to make themselves vulnerable by sharing pay information. By being so afraid of a revolt, a lawsuit, or embarrassment that may come with making small steps toward improvement, they instead choose the path of least resistance. In the worst cases, companies actively stay away from assessing themselves on pay in any serious way, particularly on gender and race disparities, because they know the work can become legally discoverable and that they'll be held liable for not making changes once pay problems have been found. Pay is the most visible space for improvement in our work lives, and we shouldn't take "don't ask, don't tell" as an acceptable position.

John Donvan, host of the debate series *Intelligence Squared*, gets to the heart of what I want to accomplish by using the word "sincerity." In a January 2020 debate featuring Nobel Prize–winning economist

Joseph Stiglitz, Donvan challenges Stiglitz's assertion that "even our corporate leaders have now agreed" that running a business only for the sake of shareholder value does not create societal well-being. Stiglitz had referenced a decision by an interest group of corporate titans called the Business Roundtable, whom we'll talk more about in the next chapter. The group had recently released a commitment statement to run their companies for the benefit of society as a whole, not only shareholders. Donvan's instinctual response was to say out loud what most of us think when we hear this kind of corporate blather: "You don't think this was a public-relations move, as opposed to a sincere impulse?"

When we hear companies talk about paying people more, most of us won't believe in promises of fair pay until the money shows up in our paychecks. So what does it look like to be sincere in a corporate setting?

I see sincerity as a promise with consequences. Sincerity isn't air cover for being obnoxious or for "telling it like it is," which for some people are synonymous. Sincerity means acting with integrity, without pretense, and accepting accountability when things go poorly. Sincerity in our careers means having both the humility and the corporate infrastructure for changing course when we're wrong. We all play a unique role and are accountable in different ways. For those of us with information about pay, we have an obligation to help others understand how to evaluate their pay and advance their careers. For those who know others can't make ends meet despite working hard and making good choices, we have an obligation to speak up and be their advocates. And for those with power to make change, we have an obligation to listen and to make the hard decisions that pull us all forward toward a fair pay future. Even if it costs us in the short run, even if it takes courage, and even if it humiliates us.

In a declassified document from the Vietnam War, the US assistant secretary of defense John McNaughton wrote that the US objectives for the war were 70 percent to avoid humiliation, 20 percent to contain China and the spread of communism, and 10 percent to help the people of Vietnam enjoy a "better, freer way of life." I find this distribution similar to how most companies think about sharing information on their pay programs—70 percent to avoid humiliation, 20 percent to contain lawsuits or unionization efforts, and 10 percent to help employees plan for a better life. The truth is companies have a long way to go to ensure an equitable baseline of pay opportunity for everyone, and companies need an honest, urgent assessment of how they operate and a willingness to be humiliated. I'm convinced that the best businesses of the future will be the ones to embrace the pay sincerity challenge. In the same way that most successful companies build strategic moats around their product or supply chain strategy, those that hold pay sincerity at their core will build such a deep reservoir of trust with employees that they can withstand any temporary missteps.

The decisions we make now shape the kinds of businesses we want to create and work in. Pay is more consequential than a task list or our ability to tame our in-boxes each day, and when we act only to avoid humiliation, our choices have lasting significance. Corporate sloganeering isn't going to make pay fair. We need a whole new way of working and holding our companies to account.

OVERDUE LIGHT BILLS

There are two competing public narratives about pay, neither of which is promoted by actual compensation professionals. One group says that after decades of stagnation, and prior to the COVID-19 pandemic, wages were growing faster than ever for everyone, especially the most historically disadvantaged groups. They say reporting on wage gaps is overblown, that the real gap is only a few points of difference and can be accounted for entirely by job selection. The second group agrees on the existence of wage stagnation but stresses the gaps between the haves and have-nots are now worse than ever. With a few clicks, both sides arm themselves with data from their respective bubbles, creating a tension that leaves us all feeling totally unsure of what is true and what role, if any, we need to play in advocating change.

As someone with access to actual pay data and practices across the global economy, with direct ability to influence more equitable pay outcomes, I am left wondering how we got here. Nothing has fundamentally changed in the world of compensation management. Neither narrative fully resonates with the decision-making frameworks companies use to make pay decisions. Companies are asking entirely different questions about pay than their employees, and, as a result, we rarely provide satisfactory answers for their most felt needs. If you ask someone in my position to choose a restaurant for dessert, we'll tell you about how rising dairy prices have decreased investment in new ice cream flavors, and, as a result, all ice cream in the area is equivalent and so we should go to the closest location. You wanted an experience, and we gave you an embolism. My people are bad dates.

This tension is illustrated well by a 2019 exchange between two experts in their respective fields, neither of those fields being compensation: Katie Porter, the US Representative for much of Orange County, California, and Jamie Dimon, CEO of banking giant JPMorgan Chase. Congresswoman Porter is also a law professor who wrote a textbook on consumer protection, called *Modern Consumer Law*. Speaking to Dimon in a congressional hearing, she outlined in detail the monthly budget of one of her constituents, a single mother of one child who works full time at one of Dimon's Chase retail bank branches. The woman's budget was beyond modest; she had a one-bedroom apartment where she and her daughter slept in the same room, drove a decade-old car, spent only what was essential to eat, and did not budget for personal expenses, health-care costs, or field trips. Each month, after accounting for the essential expenses of life, her ending budget was negative by more than $500. Porter's question to Dimon, who by nature of his job is one of the world's greatest financial wizards, was to ask what spell the mom should cast to make up the shortfall for her family.

Dimon's response, which he repeated with every follow-up question, was to say he didn't know and would have to think about the answer. I believe him. Few executives have any idea what the lowest-paid people in their company make, nor do they often ask. In a follow-up conference call with reporters, and surely after consulting his own mission control of communications, investor relations, and compensation experts, he indicated that the bank, in fact, felt it took very good care of its entry-level jobs. He said his employees started at $35,000 per year (about $17 per hour) and had access to medical and retirement benefits. He closed by saying that when you look at wages, you better look around at other people, and that the banking industry is pretty good on a relative basis.

Now here's the kicker: both Congresswoman Porter and Mr. Dimon were right. They were just answering different questions. Porter wanted a mom to feel valued, and Dimon wanted his bank to create value. Fair pay is measured by different yardsticks, depending on whose perspectives we choose to see. Congresswoman Porter was right to call out the increasing difficulty of getting ahead. You can be a few steps up the ladder, working full-time and making good life choices, and you'll still need some form of good fortune or subsidy from your family or government to get by. By taking a few more classes (that you can't afford and don't have childcare coverage to attend), learning new skills (that are ill defined by management), staying a little while longer (when your bills are due now), and applying for the big job when it becomes available (that goes to the manager's buddy), predictable and meaningful career growth starts to look more like a bait-and-switch tactic. For those who do make it through the career-building gauntlet, they may still find themselves unable to afford a more stable life.

What Mr. Dimon got right was that the bank's wages were not even close to the bottom of the pay scale for the area. According to the American Community Survey from the US Census Bureau for Irvine, a $35,000-per-year wage put the woman and her child in a better position than about 20 percent of the local population. When factoring medical and retirement benefits, it was fair to say the bank offered what most companies consider to be more than competitive wages for an entry-level job. He was correctly saying there were far more vulturous companies out there, and that his bank was "pretty good" by comparison. But when the baseline standards are too low, this is like trying to brag for selling the can of paint with the least amount of lead in it.

Later, Mr. Dimon would hedge his initial statements, saying on a conference call that "we've got to give people more of a living wage," and "if the federal [minimum wage] maybe raises, then states should do more locally so it doesn't damage the economy too much." In the same call, Dimon would say the bank was not in an "arms race" with their competitors, meaning that his company was not about to unilaterally pay higher wages unless forced to do so. Remember, companies have no strategic reason to compete with each other on pay. Nothing he said was technically wrong or outside standard compensation-management practice. The statements were not exactly a profile in courage, either. The subtext was not dissimilar from a statement attributed to his predecessor, John Pierpont (J. P.) Morgan: "A man always has two reasons for the things he does, a good one and the real one." In the case of pay, the "real one" might be that we haven't asked ourselves if there is a better way to operate.

Here's the point: fair pay is a maintenance activity, like an electric bill. People notice when the payment hasn't been submitted on time and the lights have been switched off. Maintaining fair pay is rarely flashy work; it needs regular attention and occasionally all the wiring should be replaced. Rodd Wagner, in his book *Widgets: The 12 New Rules for Managing Your Employees as if They're Real People*, says this about pay: "Mess it up, let it become an issue, and it will often become *the* issue." The problem is that many companies still treat fair pay like an impulse purchase or even a luxury item, something to take care of after all the other bills (and the occasional shopping spree) have been paid for.

If your company pays people poorly, that expense will return to the company somehow. If your wages are uncompetitive below the point of credibility, people will not work for you. If you have bad internal practices, your time will be spent on employee conflicts and customer complaints, and your core business will atrophy. And if your peers are all paying poorly in the same ways as you, legislation will eventually course correct for everyone in ways that upend the business models of entire industries addicted to underpaid labor. In other words, pay your bills or risk having your lights shut off forever.

WE CAN'T AFFORD NOT TO CHANGE

Expecting businesses to do the right thing on pay might sound naive, and the view held by many that the system is too corrupt or tilted to change toward correction and sustainability is understandable. From where I sit in the pay decision chair, I don't agree. I see rapid change toward fair pay outcomes as not only possible but likely. The idea that pay decisions are best left to a black-box, closed system of a few corporate decision makers like me has engendered little trust and brought literal exhaustion to the system. It's time for a new era of pay sincerity—fair and transparent pay is now an expectation, and businesses have to catch up.

I believe companies will start to see fair pay as a competitive advantage. Pay sincerity is a question not just of cost, but also of character and coordination, and each is essential in reinforcing the other. High-character companies start with purpose and allocate budgets toward maintaining their values. Clear coordination ensures these budgets are spent in a way that achieves desired changes through finely tuned processes. Effective cost managers rely on these processes to create more profit margin and absorb new wage expenses. Business schools teach the idea that functional business models can be better, faster, or cheaper, but to run a successful company, you are supposed to pick only two of the three. Meanwhile, our pay models have triple-clicked on being cheaper and chosen to optimize entirely around that idea. Business schools should teach not only the better, faster, cheaper two-choice trade-off, but also the character, coordination, and cost control fair pay triad. In the latter case, smart businesses pick all three.

Pay is usually the largest expense a company makes each year, and so reluctance toward better pay practices often begins and ends with the affordability question. This argument is somewhere between incomplete and overstated. When pay is viewed only as an expense, we ignore the virtuous top- and bottom-line effects of fair pay. When people have more money to spend, they spend it, creating additional consumer demand. When customers are well served by happy employees, they keep coming back for more. And when employees are happy, they don't leave the company; they become more productive over time and create savings through less employee turnover.

The direct link between pay raises and harmful price increases is, in my experience, misguided fearmongering. The consulting firm McKinsey found a similar result by considering the top- and bottom-line choices a company has in expanding its profit margins. By increasing prices 1 percent, and assuming stable sales, a typical company will also increase its operating profit by 8 percent. The company's other choice, reducing variable costs like wages, by 1 percent, had about half the positive effect on profit.

Price increases are spread thin to all customers equally, whereas wage increases are concentrated. Consider the total effects to the company of increasing pay for the bottom half of employees by 20 percent, a significant pay increase in any country. Let's assume the bottom half of wage earners in total account for 20 percent of the company's payroll expense.

	CALCULATION	RESULT
Total Payroll (A)	-	$10,000,000
Percent of payroll eligible for a pay increase (B)	-	20%
Eligible payroll (C)	(A) * (B)	2,000,000
Pay raise percent (D)	-	20%
Total cost of the pay increase (E)	(C) * (D)	400,000
Total payroll increase (F)	(E) / (A)	4%

The total weighted payroll increase to the company is only 4 percent, not the scary 20 percent number that is more likely to draw the ire of the company's finance department. The point isn't that price or wage increases can be extended to infinity, but that the market for both prices and wages can fall out of balance, and small adjustments to prices are unlikely to affect the purchasing decisions of most customers for most products. This is especially true considering that wage increases are copied from one company to another, so the entire product category will get more expensive across brands and reduce pressure to chase lower prices. A 2015 study from Purdue University found that an increase in the minimum wage to $15 per hour would change the price of the McDonald's Big Mac by less than a quarter, assuming McDonald's didn't take any offsetting cost-savings measures, which they certainly would (and it is far from guaranteed the savings would come through reduced labor hours). I doubt they would sell considerably fewer burgers at the new price. Consider also the added ecological and health benefits of buying fewer but better things.

An affordability-first focus doesn't fit with the realities of our company's balance sheets, either. In 2019, US companies were sitting on nearly $2 trillion of cash reserves, so much that prior to the 2020 pandemic they were openly saying they didn't know what to do with it. About a third of the hoard belongs to a handful of tech companies, so there is room to qualify the result. But for all companies, or at least the publicly traded ones, complex laws make investing in regular business expansion or higher wages less prudent than parking funds offshore, letting accounts grow in the form of financial investments, repurchasing their own stock, or returning the excess to shareholders in the form of dividends. When speaking about these record cash piles and the trade-off decisions companies make in spending it, Neil Shearing, chief economist at Capital Economics, was said to have half-jokingly suggested companies could pay their workers more, but "that would be terrible for the stock market." We'll review how companies make these decisions in Chapter 4, but what is clear is that our core business models work fine (with record profits of $2.3 trillion in 2019), and that a lack of investment in pay has been an active choice. When large companies choose to lead and invest in their employees, this creates space to reset market norms around wages (and prices) for smaller companies, which may have less immediate room in their budgets to invest. This is why it's critical to have our largest companies take the first step toward more fair and equitable pay outcomes.

Progress on pay comes from holding one another accountable for making consistently better choices over time. Changing the pay landscape will take time, and we will need allies. In an annual letter to fellow CEOs, hedge fund titan Larry Fink wrote that "frustration with years of stagnant wages" has helped "fuel enormous anxiety and fear" in the broader population. In the same letter, he would press his peers for a "commitment to the countries, regions, and communities where they operate, particularly on issues central to the world's future prosperity." We could choose to roll our eyes, greeting the letter with the fortitude of an umbrella in a hurricane. I say recognition of the problem (if not acknowledgment of his industry's direct contribution) is an essential first step, and we need to welcome leaders in a position of influence. Every generation must shed practices from its past, however long embedded, and there is no reason to think insincere and unfair pay can't get relegated to the same dark corner where we collectively sent fax machines and cargo shorts.

Like the building of the Saturn V rocket, we can solve large problems with the resources we already have, however meager they may seem against the scale of the challenges before us. We have choices about the kinds of companies we build, and the way people experience work. We will not get it right all the time, but we can get it wrong less of the time.

CHAPTER 3

What's Old Is New Again

Fair pay builds stronger companies. We've said that when employees feel less anxiety about their livelihood and more trust in their employer, they treat customers well and get better at their jobs. When customers are treated better, they spend more money. And when customers spend more money, more can be reinvested in fair pay. The story is simple, and the logic intuitive, but we've lost the plot. To find it again, let's see how pay changed over time, starting with business executives in the 1940s.

If you have a generous worldview toward business executives and their relationship to workers, you might see pay sincerity as an opportunity for leaders to redeem themselves and reset the tone from the top. If you aren't as generous, you'll also look to the top, but only to point out that the fish is rotting from the head. With either framing, it is universally true that companies set their pay strategy from the top down. From there, making decisions about those lower in the company hierarchy becomes a decrescendo of pay and benefits, and for many companies, a decreasing willingness to be responsive to the needs of employees. So to figure out why pay works as it does, we have to start from the top.

In the late 1940s, American business leaders felt a secret shame. William R. Basset was one of these leaders. Basset sat on the boards of companies ranging from household cleaning supplies to industrial chemicals, and he believed one of his company presidents was so underpaid that it was actually unfair. He thought the executive's low pay might be setting an artificially low pay ceiling for the rest of the company. The *Wall Street Journal* had run a series of articles in 1942 outlining the growing plight of executives, with titles like "The New Poor: A Salary Ceiling Story of Mr. Smith and His Fellow Bank Directors." Maybe more executives were being paid below their fair market value, and if so, something had to be done.

To study his hunch, Basset contacted a McKinsey consultant named Arch Patton. The consultant confirmed Basset's suspicion: there had, in fact, been a slowdown in pay growth for executives, and there was now data to show they deserved more of the fruit of their labor. Patton held his own findings in high regard, saying, "The impact of this work on the wall of secrecy that then surrounded executive compensation administration was shattering." He would later release a book on the topic, called *Men, Money, and Motivation*, a title reflective of the times showing how inconceivable it was then for women to be included in debates about fair pay (and, of course, he would have been referring only to white men). In Patton's words, his study was "*the* turning point" for executive compensation, and it set the foundation for its explosive growth later.

Arch Patton had invented the modern salary survey. Today, salary surveys—where a third party is paid to collect actual pay information from a company's competitors—are abundant and an essential compensation practice. Understanding salary surveys is so important that we cover them in depth in Chapter 5. Surveys are now the foundation of all compensation decision-making, and they exist for every type of work possible, from marketing coordinator to marijuana curator. A typical salary survey takes in rosters of employee data from companies and then reports it back to the purchasing company in aggregate terms.

Survey data is organized by characteristics like job description, location, and company size, but masked in accordance with legal guidelines
so it is not directly obvious as to who gets paid what at which company.
For publicly traded companies, the rules are a little different, and top
executive pay isn't masked at all. Instead this data is now required to
be totally public and identifiable, assuming a reader has the patience
to comb through dozens of pages of legalese and insider phrases like
"double-trigger acceleration." What Patton discovered is that even a
minimal level of pay transparency can affect dramatic change in how
pay grows.

The first of Patton's findings were published in the March 1951 issue of the *Harvard Business Review*. According to Patton, growth in
"executive pay had fallen far behind the compensation of hourly and
supervisory employees." Between 1939 and 1950, pay for lowly hourly
employees had doubled. By comparison, middle management pay rose
45 percent, but executive pay increased just 35 percent. After adjustments for taxes and inflation, executive spendable income had actually
fallen 59 percent over the period. Until then, nobody had been thinking of the big guy (always a guy). Now, the secret was out.

In his analysis, Patton used a mathematical concept from an Italian
economist named Vilfredo Pareto. Pareto is best known for his Pareto
principle, which describes how 80 percent of results are often due to
20 percent of the causes. This principle is now a common understanding across many business functions, from finding software bugs to
developing sales funnels to managing talent and performance ratings.
Ironically, the original usage of the 80/20 principle was to demonstrate
the concentration of wealth inequality, where Pareto noticed that 80
percent of Italian land was owned by 20 percent of the people. Patton
inverted the 80/20 principle to show his concern about the plight of the
20 (or even the 2) percent of those at the top. He showed that wages in

an organization should be proportional to those above it, which practically meant that by adding the top salary to the next highest salary, and so on, "the resulting totals plotted geometrically will be a straight line." In Patton's view, any deviations to that line represented jobs or people who were over- or underpaid on a relative basis. Some companies use a similar approach today to set executive pay through regression equations.

Within this approach exists a larger point that most compensation professionals will know all too well, that where the data doesn't match the story you want to tell (or are being asked to tell), you can often make the data fit if you squint at it long enough. The quip attributed to British prime minister Benjamin Disraeli, that arguments can be made better through "lies, damned lies, and statistics," applies to pay as much as to any other field, and as such I will teach you to develop a healthy skepticism about market data in your quest for fair pay.

As can be expected, when a consultant finds a way to get the person who has hired him more money, word begins to spread quickly. Other executives began asking Arch Patton to study their wage woes, too. Juan Trippe, then CEO of Pan American World Airways, asked Patton to work on a study of stock options for his executive team. This wasn't Pan Am's first entry into the history of questionable compensation experimentation. In 1938, the company was believed to have been among the first to reprice its own stock options, a now greatly frowned upon practice that allows a company's executives to purchase stock at a lower price than when the option was first awarded, counteracting the entire purpose of a stock option and therefore guaranteeing a gain. Think of repricing stock options like buying a new pair of pants, but when the store puts the same pants on sale the next week, asking the store not only to price match your purchase, but also to throw in another five sets of pants for your troubles. As Duff McDonald, author of *The*

Golden Passport, describes the Patton Pan Am study, the work to justify executive compensation became a "perpetual motion machine" from there. Executives hired consultants, consultants got more money for (and from) executives, and repeat. We now have to squint much harder for evidence that executives are underpaid, but that hasn't stopped the cycle. We'll return to how executive pay works in Chapter 8.

For some, especially those who lived through the economic swings of the Gilded Age and the Great Depression, falling executive pay in the 1940s might have been the dream scenario. Worker wages were rising and executive wages falling—and after World War II it must have felt like justice for those who experienced the brunt of the downturn during those eras. Now, as income inequality again reaches Gilded Age levels and we react to increasingly violent economic crashes, many are hoping to see something like these results again. The feeling is bipartisan, with nearly two-thirds of Americans believing CEO pay should be capped relative to the average worker. Looking back, let's review the conditions that led to the rise of worker pay compared to executives, and whether we really want history to repeat itself in the same way.

The 1940s were a unique time for compensation that likely can't be replicated in a globally interconnected economy, at least through the means used at the time. This period is often called the Great Compression, due to government measures put in place for wages and a corresponding reduction in the pay gap between top and bottom earners. Much of the compression was due to temporary, heavy-handed tactics made through executive orders to help administer the war effort. A war footing gave the federal government a platform to evoke a sense of patriotism, putting the country's free-market economic system on pause to focus on more existential crises. Some changes from this era would last far beyond the war, including New Deal legislation such as the nation's first minimum-wage and overtime laws, passed in 1938. As we'll see in Chapter 7 when we talk about gender and racial pay gaps, not all workers were included in these provisions.

When the war intensified in 1942, President Roosevelt signed Executive Order 9250 to control levels of inflation "which threaten our military effort and our domestic economic structure, and for the more effective prosecution of the war." In the order, a newly created National War Labor Board was given a mandate to approve pay increases. The order covered "all industries and all employees," and tied raises to correcting only "maladjustments or inequalities, to eliminate substandards of living," and "to correct gross inequities." Any wage increase for those paid over $5,000 (about $80,000 in 2020), was prohibited, unless there was a significant change in job duties. The result was that raises went almost exclusively to the lowest-paid workers, because it was simply too difficult (and sold as unpatriotic) to increase wages for anyone else. Management pay had effectively been capped.

The order was inclusive of all components of pay "in any form or medium whatsoever," including gifts and bonuses, but it explicitly excluded benefits. With no other options to increase worker pay, US employers began offering additional health insurance benefits to their workers, a practice that through today has uniquely tied American health insurance benefits to a person's employer. For those with employer-provided health insurance now, which is most people in the United States, a good portion of your raise each year isn't going toward your salary but is hidden in the form of increasingly expensive healthcare coverage. No conversation about pay stagnation can be complete without recognizing how this historical accident is now an economic albatross, stifling opportunity for innovation, entrepreneurship, and normal wage growth. When workers are afraid of changing companies or starting their own business because they may lose benefits or have to change doctors, a concept economists call "job lock," wages and economic growth sputter and make us all worse off.

Government limitations on executive pay didn't mean that executives had to sit back and take it, however, watching their purchasing power decrease each year through inflation. Instead, executives shifted their focus to the other side of the income equation that they could still influence, by hoping to reduce the tax impact of their existing pay packages. As Arch Patton puts it, after World War II, "the proliferation of compensation devices . . . were conceived for the purposes of reducing taxes on executive income." Attempts at avoiding taxes—where at the time the top marginal rate in the United States was more than 90 percent, compared to 37 percent today—led to more complex pay designs. Today, it can take twenty or more pages of a public company's annual financial disclosure to describe the types of executive compensation packages offered, with perhaps just a few pages given to things like the company's financial performance and perceived business risks. If a serious attempt is to be made at slowing down the disproportionate growth of executive compensation relative to the average worker, much legislative work will be needed to resimplify the types of compensation that companies can provide, and to reduce the tax schemes available as work-arounds. Focusing on the top-line total of compensation alone will not be sufficient to outwit what is now a well-oiled industry of Arch Pattons.

• • •

After President Truman revoked Roosevelt's executive order in 1946, a spirit of wage intervention continued into the 1950s as the country fought a new war in Korea. Truman signed a new executive order on September 6, 1950, that created a governmental Wage Stabilization Board, authorized to control wages for all hourly (low-wage) employees.

The board was to be composed of nine members: three as representatives of the public, three as representatives of labor, and three as representative of business and industry. One of the members representing the public, to be designated by the president, was to chair the board.

Today, many countries have similar arrangements, some also a product of wartime alliances, where the division of accountability among the public, government, and industry acts as a proxy for ensuring trust in the overall pay ecosystem. In Germany, for example, today's companies are made up of two boards in an arrangement called "codetermination": a management board recognizable to Americans as the traditional independent board of directors, and a supervisory board with half of its members being voted into the role by employees. This structure was a compromise agreement meant to repair the trust needed to support a market economy after World War II. During the war, Adolf Hitler had banned labor unions, and many managers and owners of Germany's largest industrial companies who worked on behalf of the Nazi Party were tried for war crimes in Nuremberg. Today, German compensation teams have to get major decisions approved and maintain a positive working relationship with these groups. In Chapter 8, we'll return to these shared-power relationships and their effectiveness. America's brief and limited experiment in codetermination through the Wage Stabilization Board lasted only through 1953, just in time for Arch Patton's study to begin reverberating across the emerging American compensation industry.

WHOSE COMPANY IS IT ANYWAY?

The Great Compression lasted through the 1960s, its end coinciding not with a physical war but a more ideological battle about the purpose of business itself. Since at least the 1910s, the first legal priority of a business was that it had to put the interests of its shareholders ahead of its employees or customers, an idea called "shareholder primacy." The idea is that by looking out for the best interests of shareholders, who are the owners of the company, the managers of the company will through self-preservation act as stewards and do what is best for secondary stakeholders like employees, customers, and the environment. The most critical part of shareholder primacy is that shareholders must come first in all decisions. Relegating workers to second place (at best) meant wage growth hinged on either government fiat or shareholders voluntarily agreeing it was in their best interest.

This hierarchy was given legal credence in the 1919 case of *Dodge v. Ford Motor Company*, after Henry Ford notoriously doubled the rate of pay in his plants to $5 per day. Ford's idea was to pay what are called "efficiency wages," or pay rates that are intentionally above market rates, to increase demand for the jobs he was offering and corresponding productivity from his newly happy and well-compensated workers. Though his vision wasn't entirely rosy—he hired up to two hundred detectives to monitor his workers' private lives for "thrift, cleanliness, sobriety, family values, and good morals in general"—Ford saw his own financial well-being as tied to that of his workers, so he chose to prioritize the interests of his employees more directly than those of shareholders. This did not go over well. Shareholders thought the extra investment in wages was not needed, because nobody else was doing it, and that the extra cash belonged to them in the form of dividends, so they sued Ford. The courts upheld Ford's right to pay the higher wages, but he was forced to pay out a dividend, which the Dodge brothers used to form a competing car company.

By the 1950s, judges had seen enough similar cases to reject the idea of explicit shareholder primacy, where shareholders not only come first but also always and only. Through the ensuing years, the courts continued to soften the edges of shareholder primacy to allow business managers more legally codified discretion over their spending choices. In a notable 1968 case, the Chicago Cubs president and board of directors were sued for refusing to install lights at Wrigley Field. The team's management argued that baseball was meant to be a daytime sport, as opposed to shareholders arguing that they were losing a profit opportunity by not having night games. The court ruled in favor of the team, saying that unless a business is shown to be committing fraud or otherwise acting illegally, managers have wide discretion to run their businesses under what is called the "business judgment rule." The Chicago Cubs wouldn't hold their first night game until 1988, when the league warned the team that they wouldn't be able to host playoff games until lights were installed.

The era's management intelligentsia blessed the business judgment rule approach, agreeing that managers should have leeway to make holistic choices about the companies they have been chosen to run. Peter Drucker, perhaps the most influential management thinker of the last century, took things a step further to say the first priority of a business is not serving the shareholder, but instead saying in his 1954 book *The Practice of Management*, "There is only one valid purpose of a corporation: to create a customer."

To put customers first, Drucker assumed business leaders must have an intrinsic motivation to serve and be trusted by customers. Therefore, it wasn't necessary to formally align their interests through pay. Activities that create customers and serve shareholders should align naturally, and incentives would be seen as an unnecessary conflict of interest that made customers question the motives of the seller. The reverse is true now, where executive pay is almost exclusively based on incentives (salary often makes up 15 percent or less of the total pay package). But for a time, the idea of tying more pay to extra risk in hopes of maximizing shareholder gain was not common or recommended. To quote a management textbook from 1951, "It is usually unwise to have a large proportion of executive pay consist of incentives." With legal protection to apply the business judgment rule in their daily spending choices, business leaders could safely invest in higher pay without much worry. The philosophical case for *how* to pay employees more would come later in the decade, not through the earlier advice of Drucker but with the emerging popularization of the "pay-for-performance" model.

MERITOCRACY IS THE PUNCH LINE

The philosophical underpinning of pay over the last several decades rests on the idea of paying people according to their performance. If one person has more inherent skill or outperforms another, more pay is the prize. This is how the well-functioning workplace as we understand it, the meritocracy, should operate. The word "meritocracy" first came into existence around the same time Drucker and his peers were relitigating the purpose of business itself. In 1958, British politician Michael Young wrote a book called *The Rise of the Meritocracy*, giving us the new word and unintentionally also a foundation that would change business forever. I say unintentionally because Young understood our ability to create a true meritocracy to be a joke.

Young wrote *The Rise of the Meritocracy* as a dystopian satire set in the future world of 2034, where the elite class is considered more deserving of their outsized rewards due to their superior effort and inherent intelligence (the exact formulation being IQ + effort = merit). As the story goes, those in the lower castes are shut out from opportunities to change their station in life, not because of their performance, which is only one half of the equation, but their preordained status according to various IQ tests.

For more than sixty years, the joke has gone over our collective heads. Young said much the same in a refreshed introduction to the book where he suspected some of his readers, "without having read it . . . have neglected, or not noticed, the fact that the book is satirical." Our now sacred and entrenched corporate belief that attaching pay to our perception of merit alone was not meant to be taken as a prescription, despite it *sounding* true and fair, but as a warning of "how sad, and fragile, a meritocratic society could be." Now, in an almost too on-the-nose association, the common language used by nearly all companies for their annual pay increase process is the "merit increase." (In some countries it is more common to say "increment," which I think is a more honest description of the difficulties in equitably assessing employee performance outside of routine production jobs.)

It wasn't just the corporate world that adopted merit language. The US Equal Pay Act of 1964, intended to end gender discrimination in pay, established that pay differences resulting from a merit-based program were acceptable and exempt from the law. As we'll find in Chapter 7, this creates an enormous advantage for employers who can pin acts of what employees perceive to be unfair pay on a merit program that may not be as objective as the company thinks. As Young might have guessed, we're seeing more research now questioning our ability to accurately and equitably link pay and performance. In theory, pay for performance sounds plausible, even prudent, but to work well a lot of planning and maintenance is required. In order for pay for performance to work fairly, it requires the integration of objective, unbiased processes and measurements starting from the time of talent sourcing to hiring and throughout the entire employee life cycle, something that few employers do well or consistently.

By the 1970s, paying people based on perceived merit had triumphed. Merit became not only a popular practice but a moral imperative, and no person was more indirectly important to the pay-for-performance movement than the economist Milton Friedman. All books about modern inequality eventually find their way to Friedman, and this one is no different. Friedman wrote an essay in the *New York Times Magazine* in 1970 titled "The Social Responsibility of Business Is to Increase Its Profits," an evangelistic callback to the gospel of shareholder primacy. Friedman was concerned about the growing desires from business leaders to pursue social ends, similar to the Dodge brothers and shareholders of Ford earlier in the century. It can't be understated how influential this essay would be for global business over decades. To Friedman, social ends included what he called the "catchwords" of eliminating discrimination and avoiding pollution, neither of which warranted rewarding based on performance. Any tactic that achieved anything but the most direct benefit to shareholders was "approaching fraud," the uncrossable standard of the business judgment rule, and those who chose the path of most resistance were "unwitting puppets . . . that have been undermining the basis of a free society" and "preaching pure and unadulterated socialism." Milton Friedman was not subtle, and I can't imagine he was a good party planner.

By Friedman's logic, all profits generated by a business are by definition owned by the shareholders, which is, of course, legally true. To spend profits of the company on social issues "insofar as his actions lower the wages of some employees, he is spending their money." In theory this means that all wage expenses, whether hourly increases to low-wage earners or as perks for an executive's adult children to fly on the corporate jet, should be evaluated as a set of choices in need of prioritization. The worthiest wage expenses should be justified through necessity and performance—not only personal performance but also compared to possible share price performance.

While Friedman's theories may resonate in some corners of academia, they leave no room for practical decisions about how companies determine who gets paid what and why. Actual decisions about pay are not evaluated on equal footing. In my experience, pay decisions follow a hierarchy where the rules are increasingly punitive the lower in the organization you go. This is why there have always been naysayers among the executive ranks who understand that pursuing profit is essential but know better than to fully cosign Friedman's worldview. Jack Welch, former CEO of General Electric, called shareholder primacy "the dumbest idea in the world." Paul Polman, former CEO of Unilever, called the idea "a cult." Giving more pay to more people is never a dispassionate mathematical exercise alone, and the rules are different for those at the top. As we'll see in Chapter 6, making trade-offs on pay depends not only on proximity to power but also the effectiveness of the company's processes, the priorities of the business, and the culture of permission it maintains to talk about pay without repercussion.

Friedman wasn't proposing a libertarian fever dream, exactly. He did say business leaders have a responsibility to "make as much money as possible while conforming to the basic rules of society." I'm unpersuaded. I struggle to see how basic rules of society would exist at all if not meant to imply an inherent level of care and responsibility for the well-being of those around us. Friedman's thinking assumes that everyone has equal power to act in their own best interests and to right their own wrongs, and that we will act rationally to do so at all times. He said the "great virtue of private competitive enterprise is that it forces people to be responsible for their own actions and makes it difficult for them to exploit other people for either selfish or unselfish purposes."

So for Friedman's ideas to work, our starting worldview must be one of inherent justice, or at least one where exploitation exists but is self-correcting, rather than the world we live in with power asymmetry where we regularly have to remove structural barriers to overcome and prevent marginalization.

In Friedman's view, government actions to raise wages were especially problematic. He called the business leaders who promoted these policies "short-sighted and middle-headed." From the perspective of business leaders who applauded government action on pay, their perspective was perfectly logical, especially for pay interventions in the entry ranks, where Friedman accused businesses of acting under "the cloak of social responsibility." Business leaders, in their pursuit of profit, want to avoid an arms race on pay increases, preferring not to compete with one another but instead have a minimal level of government intervention that sets the basic rules of society for a business and its competitors in tandem. For context, Friedman was working at the University of Chicago in 1946; he formed his ideas in the time between FDR's and Truman's executive orders that limited pay increases. Postwar wage controls were no doubt on Friedman's mind, but, contrary to his predictions, no markets were destroyed despite the government intervention.

Friedman's ideas persisted even as he became an adviser to President Nixon, who installed his own temporary wage freeze in 1973. After Friedman, there remains a long line of worrywarts who translate incremental interventions on pay into Chicken Little for the economy. Each generation faces this tension between government and private industry, and it's a difficult balance to get right. Though my generation of millennials has been accused of killing everything from doorbells to divorce, those of us calling for more responsive leadership do not mean to suggest we have the free market on our hit list. While younger generations are often belittled for wanting constant recognition of our achievements, this is exactly the meritocratic system we've been taught and understood to be our only option for success. What if, instead, we were all in on the joke, that we understood how purist meritocracy ideology can't be separated from the realities of our social contexts? It's true that good work should go rewarded, but it takes vigilance (and sometimes intervention) to make sure it happens.

OFF TO THE RACES

With shareholders now holding the spotlight directly over their heads, that didn't mean executives couldn't at least stand on stage with them as backup singers. By tying the well-being of a company first to the well-being of shareholders, companies began to methodically align their executive pay programs with shareholders' prosperity, a concept that compensation designers call "line of sight." We'll revisit this idea in Chapter 4, but for now it's only important to know that for shareholders to gain, and thus fulfill the purpose of the organization under the shareholder primacy model, all executive decision-making must focus on increasing the stock price.

The explicit mindset shift toward shareholders had a near immediate effect on wages. In 1973, three years after Friedman's essay, worker productivity and wage growth began to unlink for the first time, leaving companies more profitable but employee wage growth trailing behind. From 1948 to 1973, productivity rose 96 percent, and wages 91 percent. This means that workers were seeing their pay grow in direct proportion to their added contribution to an organization, as has been the long-held assumption by economists. From 1973 to 2014, worker productivity rose 72 percent and real wages just 9 percent.

There are many ways to parse this data in a more globalized economy with greater automation, and also many ways to define productivity and wages to suit your preferred arguments. But the felt experience of most people is that although they now have cheaper televisions and more expensive versions of the same (or worse) health insurance subsidized by their employers, it's much harder now to put the financial building blocks in place for an upwardly mobile life, including sending kids to college, taking an enriching vacation, or saving money for retirement. We can spin the statistics, but if you're reading this book, the chances are you also feel as if somewhere the deal has broken down, that you're not gaining much as you get more productive in your job. If meritocracy is the model we've been given, and productivity is the measure we assume we're judged against, how can wages grow when that relationship no longer exists in any meaningful way? I know of zero compensation teams who track productivity as part of their pay-planning process.

If the new operating system for business now was to exist explicitly for the benefit of shareholders, then to support this change, the legislative and tax infrastructure had to shift to favor shareholders and the executives who expect to earn what amounts to a commission on the share price. With the new-era shareholder primacy model arguably set in 1970, we now focus on choices made in three particular years: 1982, 1990, and 1993.

Prior to 1982, a company's ability to purchase its own shares, called a "stock buyback" (or "share repurchase"), was rare and operated under murky rules because the action was seen as stock price manipulation. We spend more time on this topic in Chapter 4 to show how companies justify repurchasing their stock instead of reinvesting earnings in their businesses (or employees), but in this section we see the practice as an extension of shareholder primacy. With a stock buyback, a company purchases a portion of its own outstanding stock as a signal to the rest of the market that they think the stock is undervalued. The company has more information than typical investors about its future growth prospects, so buybacks are a way for the company to create demand for the stock and generate a higher price. Executives who are paid mostly in stock and judged by metrics like earnings per share (EPS) have a direct incentive to do everything they can to increase the stock price and reduce the number of shares outstanding, and buybacks are intended to achieve both. In theory, this works great for everyone who owns stock in the company, including most employees in the company retirement plan, and extra great for executives.

From a timing perspective, the evidence shows buybacks do achieve their purpose. Executives have been able to time buybacks at a lower share price than the resulting average market price, especially if buybacks are used infrequently. If the company directive is to act first toward the benefit of the shareholder, and especially if the practice is successful, then none of this is irrational. But until 1982, the mechanics of buybacks weren't easy. The Reagan administration and the Securities and Exchange Commission under John Shad, the first Wall Street executive to hold the title since the 1930s, changed the rules to allow companies greater use of buybacks. The Securities Exchange Act, Rule 10b-18, set the conditions of "safe harbor" that, if followed, would allow companies to repurchase their shares without being subject to fraud charges. With more transparent rules now in place, and the threat of fraud accusation lifted, buybacks took off. By 2019, company buybacks totaled more than $1 trillion a year, with the funds coming not only from company profits but also from debt taken on solely to buy more stock.

The primary counterarguments to buybacks are twofold. First, buybacks are seen as a way for executives to launder their pay into a lower capital-gains tax rate. Most of an executive's pay package is in the form of stock, so they would rather grow this account that is taxed lower than receive a regular base pay increase. The second argument is that buybacks are an irresponsible use of cash, and the money would be better spent on investing in the company itself or workers instead of returning it to shareholders. We saw how quickly many companies ran out of cash during the COVID-19 pandemic, leading reasonable people to wonder why companies didn't have a robust rainy-day fund like families are expected to have. I am sympathetic to these arguments, but I think we need to make a sharper case when comparing buybacks to pay. A more effective argument than railing against buybacks generally is to focus on proportion. When companies say they cannot afford pay increases, we should first ask how they prioritize their other investments. Employee investment has a multigenerational impact on people and families, whereas expenses like share repurchases have limited and temporary impact, even in the best-case scenario, due to systemic and uncontrollable market fluctuations. In the case of stock buybacks, a company is making an active choice to prioritize the hope of a short-term stock price increase over other uses of its money—for example, research and development or employee wages. If a company says no to a $10 million investment that closes its gender or racial pay gap, or $100 million to make sure all employees can pay for life essentials, but has said yes to $1 billion in stock buybacks, employees should rightly question the sincerity and decision-making ability of their leaders.

By 1990, echoes of Arch Patton returned as executives started to worry they weren't getting quite enough love for their efforts. The *Harvard Business Review* again played the role of executive champion, with an article titled "CEO Incentives—It's Not How Much You Pay, But How." The new version of the old idea said that pay was not tied *enough* to performance, meaning that executive achievements were going unrewarded, a mortal sin in the era of meritocracy. The solution was more stock ownership by executives to further align their interests with shareholders. Using the Patton playbook, the article showed how far modern CEOs had fallen behind their 1930s predecessors in their "holdings as a percentage of corporate value," when stock ownership was ten times greater. Again, something had to be done! Further alignment of interests through enhanced grants of stock would allow "big rewards for superior performance and big penalties for poor performance." Naturally, greater percentages of executive pay steadily shifted from base salary and into more performance-based pay vehicles like cash bonuses and especially stock options, together with salary making up what we call a "pay mix." The difference in pay between average employees and executives widened until 1993, when the expanding gap became a yawning abyss.

Until 1993, companies could deduct any amount or type of compensation from their taxes as a normal business expense. Sensing the political winds against climbing CEO-to-worker pay ratios, then presidential candidate Bill Clinton campaigned on using the tax code to go after what the public saw as excessive executive compensation packages. The Clinton administration, in its first year, attempted to put a check on corporate boards by allowing companies to deduct only the first $1 million of compensation for their top executives from the company's tax bill. This rule applied to traditional components of the existing pay package, including base pay, bonus, and regular share grants. The new rules exempted additional performance-based pay, meaning primarily stock-option grants, which had an immediate effect on the market norm of a typical executive's pay mix. Today, for this reason, it's almost universal that large company CEOs earn exactly or close to $1 million in salary, with the bulk of their pay shifted into more tax advantageous incentives.

In 1990, fewer than 1 million employees received company shares in the form of stock options. By 2000, the number was 10 million. Not all stock grants are stock options, though the terms are incorrectly used interchangeably. A stock option is not like a share of stock that is bought and held by a typical investor, where the price can be looked up every day and the amount gained or lost is easily calculable. An option has value only if the selling price is higher than the price originally set when given. As an example, if the given price (the strike price) for an option is $60 per share, and the market value (the exercise price) is $80, employees have the option to buy a share of the stock at $60 and sell it for $80, receiving the difference of $20. But if the market price is $59, then the employees' options are worth zero, because like everyone else, they can purchase a share on the open market for less than their strike price. Therefore, since the value of an option was deemed theoretical until the day it was used, options at first had no direct ability to be priced, and were considered free to the company to distribute. The accounting community had essentially given up trying to preempt the latest executive-pay machination. Businesses had no reason to not give out as many stock options as they could, reasonability be damned. From the company's point of view, stock options aligned the interests of executives and shareholders, tied pay with (perceived) performance, and were free to give away! For the shareholder supremacists, what wasn't to like?

The value of a stock option can accelerate far faster than the types of shares most people hold in their retirement accounts, and so the CEO-to-worker pay ratio exploded. According to Steven Clifford in his book *The CEO Pay Machine*, where the ratio was 20 times in 1965 and 87 times in 1987, between 1994 and 2004 the ratio quadrupled to 376 times the average employee's pay, far more than can be explained by companies getting larger.

By 2006, the jig was up. Under the Bush (43) administration, another rule change now required companies to expense stock options, meaning they could no longer be considered free. The theoretical had been made tangible, with most companies choosing to value their options using a mind-numbingly complex mathematical formula called the Black-Scholes value. This formula was hiding in plain sight, published in 1973 in the same era as Milton Friedman's work, but the business community chose not to use it then. Some, especially those in Silicon Valley, viewed the rule change as a detriment to innovation and business growth. It wasn't, especially for them, as evidenced by the types of companies that have done well since then. Others, like Warren Buffett, said stock options had always been a way for companies to hide their risks and lack of profits. Buffett has been said to stay true to this belief when acquiring a company, typically canceling the options plan and replacing it with an equivalent cash plan, which could not be manipulated. Despite the rule changes, the new baseline for competitive executive pay had already been established. There was no going back.

I PLEDGE ALLEGIANCE, TO NOTHING IN PARTICULAR

Many in the business community have understood the failures of the modern pay system we've chosen to create, where the rules and money flow to the top, and proposed ways to make it more equitable. One model, published in 2011 in the (again) *Harvard Business Review* was called the Big Idea: Creating Shared Value. The authors, Michael E. Porter and Mark R. Kramer, identify that businesses can do well only when they address society's needs not at the periphery (for example, through philanthropy or sustainability), but at the center of their business models. The authors said this way of thinking will "give rise to the next major transformation of business thinking." Economic efficiency and social progress were not mutually exclusive, the argument went, and much of our policy is driven by decades of institutionalized inertia. In their view, "Companies must take the lead in bringing business and society back together," not for redistributing the value already created by firms, but for "expanding the total pool." They recognize not just the importance of company leadership but also government regulation, seeing that "the focus on holding down wage levels, reducing benefits, and offshoring is beginning to give way to an awareness of the positive effects that a living wage, safety, wellness, training, and opportunities for advancement for employees have on productivity." In other words, we can't expand the wage pool by roping off the deep end.

I see a progression from Peter Drucker's belief that the purpose of business is to create a customer, to Porter and Kramer's shared-value model, to newer findings like Zeynep Ton's Good Jobs Strategy. To create a customer (Drucker), employees have to do what's best for the customer (Porter and Kramer), which won't always be in the company's immediate financial interest, and which they will not do unless they are treated fairly and given autonomy by their company (Ton). In each model, an obligation to the other (person) is a prerequisite for the progress of the personal. People can't be taught to fish, and therefore feed themselves, if the stream is polluted and they don't have access to the equipment. Some may find this idea distinctly un-American, too collectivist for the country's character. But the research, especially by Ton and her team at the Good Jobs Institute, is clear that taking care of employees is taking care of business, and that employers who provide good jobs with fair pay and career opportunities outperform their peers. The next step is to figure out how we actually do that in a complex corporate setting, and one reason we haven't made this leap already is that those with the power to make pay decisions haven't had a way to be held accountable. But there is a group that can change that.

The Business Roundtable, a revolving group of CEOs from large US companies, has taken several swings at a more equitable business framework. Most recently in 2019, Jamie Dimon (perhaps still smarting from his run-in with Congresswoman Porter) and his peers released an update to the group's *Statement on the Purpose of a Corporation*, saying, in part: "Each version of that document issued since 1997 has stated that corporations exist principally to serve their shareholders. It has become clear that this language on corporate purpose does not accurately describe the ways in which we and our fellow CEOs endeavor every day to create value for all our stakeholders, whose long-term interests are inseparable." It was a rejection of Friedman thinking, of considering only the shareholder, and an embrace of Porter and Kramer and Ton.

Unfortunately, we've been here before. The 2019 statement was a reversal of a reversal. In 1981, way before Porter and Kramer said it, the Roundtable's thought on the purpose of business was to "consider the impact of its actions on all, from shareholders to society at large." But by 1997, when the expense-free stock option spigot flowed unimpeded, the Roundtable gave stockholders the keys once again, arguing that a company's "paramount duty . . . is to stockholders; the interests of other stakeholders are relevant as a derivative of the duty to stockholders."

Fortunately, unlike previous versions of the Roundtable's code, the 2019 version made five commitments, including one about pay and the importance of investing in employees: "This starts with compensating them fairly and providing important benefits."

To make progress on the commitments, the Business Roundtable needs to agree on how it will hold itself accountable. Otherwise, the five commitments will become the five concepts. To compensate fairly and provide important benefits, we will need to see what specific financial commitments, definitions, methodologies, timelines, sacrifices, trade-offs, and benchmarks are made by its member companies. Though tactics for fair pay will necessarily vary by company, my compensation peers working in Roundtable companies are not explicitly tying their work to any public-facing Roundtable scorecard. Without a transparent and common path to follow, compensation teams are driving without a map or roadside landmarks. If the Roundtable changes its mind again, putting shareholders back in the driver's seat, the decision will mean taking away the fair pay keys midjourney. We are seeing this already. Less than a month after releasing the five commitments, one of the Roundtable's most well-known member companies that signed the pledge publicly announced it was cutting health insurance (surely an "important benefit") for its part-time workers, a significant blow to the worldview of pay sincerity that cares for employee essentials.

These pledges have not just been a US phenomenon. Four days after the Business Roundtable made its latest pledge, a group of global companies with some overlap with the American group signed the Business Pledge Against Inequalities as part of their Organisation for Economic Co-operation and Development (OECD) commitments. This version included a commitment to "good jobs with decent wages" and "progress toward achieving pay equity across all equality areas (e.g., gender, ethnicity, disability, sexual orientation)." Without also agreeing to accountability measures and timelines, it doesn't take a cynic to see these pledges as addressing income inequality only for the sake of brand building. Ian Malcolm, the editor who acquired Thomas Piketty's *Capital in the Twenty-First Century*, is said to have called this the Bismarck approach, after the Prussian chancellor responsible for the unification of Germany. Rather than pursue a world of justice on its own merits, he worries the interests of the elite are more often about maintaining standing in "the world where we were preeminent." In our relentless pursuit of fair pay, our job is to hold businesses accountable to their promises.

MEET THE NEW BOSS, SAME AS THE OLD BOSS

After a several-decade experiment in meritocracy, in holding people's futures and livelihoods hostage only to our perception of their performance and potential (which we now know looks remarkably like their starting social class), we should realize the difficulties of assessing and paying for performance and value in an economy that does more complex work than producing widgets. As one generation retires and the next takes over, we also have to recognize that installing a fresh regime doesn't guarantee solutions. The old pay challenges will compound into pay catastrophes unless we make hard decisions to get pay right. In my view, the next generation of leaders, of which I am a part, is already failing the test.

In the name of technological progress, we are too quick to celebrate what amounts to supercharged models of wealth transfer, from workers who provide their labor to the (mostly white male) founders and executive classes who reap nearly all the benefits. In one example, those employed by the gig economy exist in a legislative no-man's-land status between contractor and employee, receiving none of the benefits, security, or ability to influence their pay outcomes as an employee but 100 percent of the blame for their company's inability to make a profit. We've seen this before. The Fair Labor Standards Act that governs US overtime eligibility, for example, was created in the 1930s with similarly suspect carve-outs, at first exempting whole industries in which women and racial minorities were overrepresented, like restaurants, hotels, and agriculture.

The scale of the challenge ahead, accelerated in an app-based economy, has the potential to reset the entire labor market with no point of return. Established companies will act rationally to be more like those they see getting away with playing by a less-defined rulebook. As I sit in conferences and meetings of my peers across different companies, both new economy and old, I hear firsthand how business leaders intend to staff their companies in the future, and it will not be a net positive for low-wage workers under the existing legal and pay framework. In an environment where many have referred to data as "the new oil," the next business booms will be driven by the pursuit of optimization, as if all societal opportunities and problems can be solved by tinkering with our software code. Fair and equitable pay, however, is not a problem to be optimized but a worldview to be cultivated.

The right operating system, which I argue starts with business leaders embracing a mindset of pay sincerity, builds intentional limits to optimization when it comes to people. This gives us margin to experiment, to get some things wrong, to help others thrive, and to push forward together for the betterment of all stakeholders. Let us take a lesson from the Old Testament, where in Levitical law, Jewish landowners (like Pareto's 20 percent) were allowed to comb through their fields only once, leaving room for others to actively work and receive nourishment. *"When you reap the harvest of your land, do not reap to the very edges of your field or gather the gleanings of your harvest. Leave them for the poor and for the foreigner residing among you."* The landowners were not allowed to use their systemic technological advantage in a way that prevented others from bettering themselves; by design, they could not capture 100 percent of a harvest under the guise of market efficiency, self-determination, or optimization.

Reading Arch Patton's book nearly seventy years later, it is striking how little has changed in the operating mindset or day-to-day work of compensation managers. According to his 1996 obituary, sometime in the late 1980s Patton was asked how he felt about his role in the explosion of executive pay. "Guilty," he said, while also admitting that managers had badly abused his survey because of management "assuming that all of its executives were above-average performers." Over the years, the compensation profession has taken a reactive stance to fair pay, rarely stepping up to accept its role as an advocate, and too often absolving this abuse in particular at the top and bottom of the income scale in the name of the market. Of the industry's fecklessness to change the world of pay as it exists now, Warren Buffett said, "You don't suggest [compensation] consultants who are Dobermans. You get cocker spaniels and make sure their tails are wagging."

I'm not convinced we have to give up on the pay system we have, and I believe it can be redeemed to create a world of fair pay that works for everyone. The economist John Maynard Keynes, who thought worker wages would automatically rise in direct proportion to productivity, said that by the year 2030 we'd all be working fifteen hours per week. We have to assume he meant that we'd not only be so productive we could allow machines to do the heavy lifting, but that we'd also all naturally have access to the benefits of our shared progress, or as he said it, "to spread the bread thin on the butter to make what work there is still to be done to be as widely shared as possible." His contemporary Michael Young, in his satirical writings about meritocracy, also made a prediction about the 2030s, but he saw that we'd have to take a more active approach to ensuring progress for all, given our propensity to associate wealth with worthiness. In the real year 2030, we'll find that technological progress and human decision-making can be a wonderful or a dangerous thing, depending on the set of choices we make now for their integration.

In a 2010 report discussing the ratio of corporate profits to employee wages, the St. Louis Federal Reserve noticed a worrisome trend of corporate profits outpacing wages. They had seen similar trends before, but this time gave us a warning: "The past decade and a half seems to be different. Never have corporate profits outgrown employee compensation so clearly and for so long." The path we are on is not sustainable, but neither are we doomed to walk it. There isn't one best way to run a market economy; it is always a product of our choices. By remembering our history, we can see that markets are resilient to our interventions, no matter how many warnings we hear about interference putting us one step closer to collapse, catastrophe, or communism. We can move quickly to make pay fair, but first we have to open the black box and see how companies think about and plan pay now, how to use that knowledge to determine whether we are being paid fairly, and what our role should be in advocating for a more sincere pay environment that works for everyone.

CHAPTER 4

How Your Company Thinks about Pay

The way companies plan pay feels something like separating an egg by hand. It's an essential, routine kitchen skill, though things don't always go well. The work can't get done without getting your hands messy, and as you watch the egg white slip through your fingers, you focus only on keeping the majority of the egg yolk intact so it can be put to good use. Despite your best efforts, sometimes the yolk breaks or tiny shards of shell slip through and get stuck in the egg white. All is not lost, but all is not well, either.

Nobody is impressed by a well-broken egg, because the task is meant to be routine and achieved with perfection. Nobody is impressed with paying someone fairly, either, because fairness is the baseline expectation. Your delicious hollandaise sauce isn't praised for the essential first steps and classical techniques of egg management, but for what comes next in the recipe. The ratio of lemon and butter and salt and especially your whisking prowess are what gets noticed, unless there's an eggshell left in the sauce, in which case nothing else matters.

Similarly, and hang with me on the analogy here, your company's pay professionals aren't praised for administering an unbiased merit process or performance bonus pool. That is the expectation. The real credit comes when they use the results to equitably identify talent for promotions and professional development, and to create representative leadership teams where the bigger money is found and wage gaps disappear. Whether the company acknowledges and corrects its mistakes or quietly kicks them under the fridge is where the hard choices of pay sincerity are made.

Outside factors, including structural differences and unforeseen events, matter a lot. Room-temperature eggs crack easier than eggs from the fridge. Organic eggs are harder to break because of their natural protective coating, called a "bloom." If the chef didn't wash her hands, other people can get sick. It turns out, separating an egg yolk isn't routine at all—it's a process, and each step matters. With pay, the outside factors are infinite and ever changing:

- Market survey data might show a faster increase for generalists compared to specialists one year, and the reverse the next. Now, you have to decide whether to chase the market and increase pay for specific groups every year, or take no action and see how trends develop over time.
- A dated company policy of limiting raises to a fixed percentage might be holding back your current employees from keeping pace with external hires. Now, you have to decide whether to make a onetime pay increase for those who have been held back, if you can even determine who they are, and, more painfully, whose internal budget pays for it.
- The company might reorganize under a new senior leader and put everyone in different jobs under a new hierarchy. Now, you have to decide whether to dramatically increase or lower some people's pay to preserve order and fairness in the overall pay system.
- A manager may have given a retention bonus to a man because he threatened to quit, but not to the woman who said nothing while taking outside interview calls. Now, when the man quits immediately after his

retention agreement expires and the money has hit his account, you have to decide whether to take this money-granting power away from managers and move it into a centralized team under standardized, equitable criteria.

- The company might reorganize again because someone else is in charge now.
- An acquisition might include new employees on a much higher pay scale despite doing the same work as existing groups. Now, you have to decide if or how long you're willing to tolerate the two-tier pay system while trying to make your newly acquired employees not hate you from the start for lowering their pay opportunity.
- And again, the company reorganizes.

There are no set steps or formulas to ensuring fair pay at all times in all circumstances—the egg shards are unavoidable—so instead people in roles like mine have to resort to frameworks and guidelines for making the best possible decisions despite the impossibilities of getting everything right. We can add a little salt here, a hint of acid there, and whisk our hearts out while hoping it all tastes good in the end. Sometimes we have to throw out the entire sauce and start over.

There is some method to the compensation madness, and I'll explain how pay works at most companies. We'll start by assessing how free the market really is for pay. Then, we'll get into the actual thought processes of companies about pay, starting with the "compensation philosophy," the framework used to guide all pay decisions. Having a whole philosophy dedicated to pay sounds grandiose, but there are no rites or rituals, no shamans or sacred texts. In this chapter, we'll question the usefulness of compensation philosophies and their effect on fair pay. In the next chapter, I'll show you how to find your place within that philosophy, and in Chapter 6, I'll discuss how to identify when your pay is out of step with the philosophy and then ask for a raise. It doesn't matter much if we focus on a particular industry or company size. The same principles apply to companies of all shapes and sizes. For the chefs of the compensation world, the local food carts and Michelin star restaurants are using the same base ingredients, and you only need to learn the classical techniques.

THE FREE-ISH MARKET

Material changes in pay do not always happen naturally, and describing the market for pay as free is, at best, incomplete. In business culture, questioning the freeness of our markets is dangerous thinking, and to right a wrong or rebalance the scales through intervention is to risk being turned into a pillar of salt for our irreverence. Market purists have a point; despite the imperfections of markets, no other economic system has done more to raise living standards or to reduce the percentage of the world's population living in extreme poverty. I am not proposing the outright rejection of free markets, though to make sure pay is fair we have to be honest about where the system is not serving us well in its current state and recognize that oversight and interventions against power imbalances matter in keeping the whole system afloat. As Adam Smith put it in *The Wealth of Nations*, "We have no acts of Parliament against combining to lower the price of work; but many against combining to raise it."

Assuming you also believe in some version of markets, and our shared starting belief is that pay decisions are best left to the free market, then we need to make sure the market is actually free. For a market to be free, and I am oversimplifying here, at least one condition must exist: decentralized decision-making. All actors in a free market should be able to make decisions unilaterally to serve their own best interest, without structural barriers preventing their ability to act. Free markets become less free when this decision-making ability is too concentrated in any one entity. Governments can overstep in their roles and prevent free markets, and so too can individual managers, or entire companies and legal systems. Theoretically, this is also true for the concentration of worker power, though rarely, if ever, do workers hold this amount of employment leverage.

There is a disconnect between what we believe to be true about the tie between pay and free markets, and what actually happens in how companies set pay rates. Compensation is a relentlessly benchmark-driven discipline, and as such pay designs usually conform between companies. This isn't a sign of the decentralized decision-making required of a free market, but of a human tendency around conformity and a lack of accountability to do otherwise. I like the way philosopher Eric Hoffer puts it: "When people are free to do as they please, they usually imitate each other." The primary means of conformity on pay is the salary survey. Think of the salary survey as the best deal in business.

Every spring, compensation professionals submit their company's pay data to a few vendors. Every fall, the data is aggregated and returned back as a snapshot of what we call the market. For a few thousand dollars per survey, a company can find the threshold amount they can credibly call the "market rate." If my company has five hundred software engineers, and each is paid $120,000, I will gladly pay for a $5,000 survey to know I don't have to pay them $125,000 each, a rate that one of my managers said (without evidence) would be more competitive. Purchasing the survey has saved me $2.5 million (the $5,000 pay difference times five hundred people), a return on investment of 500X. Salary surveys, to the extent that your company already pays people market credible rates, then become company insurance against wage increases. To make pay fair, we are going to have to find a way around this compensation-industrial complex of salary surveys where only your company has access to the information.

This makes pay look less like a dynamic Olympic sprint of companies in constant free-market competition, and more like an awkward three-legged race where everyone is strapped together and moving at about the same pace. I will call this the "three-legged race problem" of pay. From the company perspective, this system works brilliantly. We have assurance that our pay rates are competitive and we can spend minimally for that privilege. For employees, not having access to this same quality information discourages truly free market dynamics for pay. Greater transparency and improvements in self-reported pay websites can help balance the scales, especially in holding accountable companies that have not caught up to the slow-moving pack.

Practically, let's see how the three-legged race problem works in real life. In a segment with bond-trader-turned-author Chris Arnade about Arnade's book *Dignity: Seeking Respect in Back Row America*, one of the most popular anchors on cable news parroted the commonly held assumption that companies do whatever they can to compete with one another on pay. As Arnade then described the economic realities of the working poor, told to him directly from the sources he interviewed for the book who were struggling to get by, the host dismissed outright the idea that the free market could possibly not be working as he understands it should: "If Wal-Mart is not paying enough, then Target will. And those market forces work out that way. If Amazon is not paying enough, they will move on. When the economy grows, those salaries grow."

We can put this belief directly to the test using recent actions by these three competitor companies.

In 2019, Walmart's CEO Doug McMillon publicly said the federal minimum wage was too low and called on Congress to "put a thoughtful plan in place" to raise it. This sounds familiar to what we heard Jamie Dimon say in Chapter 2. The year prior, Walmart had raised its internal minimum wage to $11 an hour for workers in the United States, about 50 percent above the federal minimum wage.

Amazon followed a similar pattern, raising wages and using the CEO pulpit to call others to do the same. In his 2018 letter to shareholders, Amazon head Jeff Bezos said this: "Today I challenge our top retail competitors (you know who you are!) to match our employee benefits and our $15 minimum wage. Do it! Better yet, go to $16 and throw the gauntlet back at us. It's a kind of competition that will benefit everyone."

Target was ahead of the curve, announcing it would raise its minimum wage steadily each year from $10 in 2017 to $15 by 2020, a 50 percent increase over the three-year period.

If all three companies began to increase wages in response to each other, isn't that a sign that the free market is working as intended, that wages are growing naturally, and that soon all the problems associated with inequality will be solved if we could just stop meddling with the market? Haven't I proven our cable news guy correct?

No, not really. We know this because Bezos said the quiet part out loud by admitting Amazon would only increase wages if they have to, not because they see it as an investment in a better workforce or as a competitive advantage. No company is better positioned than Amazon to crush its competitors with massive wage increases, and still they do not choose this option. Walmart is no slouch either, as the largest private employer in the world and the third-largest employer overall. The company's soldier count is eclipsed only by the militaries of the United States and China.

What Walmart and Amazon are saying (Target has been less vocal), at their top levels of management, is that even the business superpowers are unwilling to go it alone and materially increase pay. There is a limit to their benevolence, and to go any further with more wage investment, more companies must hold hands and go forth together, either by force through legislation or by some implied cooperation agreement. What was really happening is that all three companies were increasing pay as a response to the flurry of minimum-wage investments sparked by the Fight for $15 movement. I can say with certainty, as someone in the same chair and tasked with planning pay for the retail industry during this time, that the scale (and public relations enthusiasm!) of wage announcements made by most companies then would not have happened without legislation. Natural market growth had little to do with it, except as a trailing, secondary effect.

Big companies have the power to increase wages at any time, but not an inclination or incentive. Big companies can afford pay increases, but they still ask for permission from others to do so. This is an inherent failure of compensation approaches that are too coordinated to be useful, too opaque to be challenged, and too focused on pay relative to one another instead of on the well-being of the employee. Assuming pay operates in a free market, that it will grow and be made fair according to its own timeline and conditions as workers freely move about the labor market looking for the best deal, has never fully been on our shared schedule.

A PHILOSOPHY OF SAMENESS

Before digging into compensation philosophies and how they work, we need to understand why companies feel the need to make their pay worldviews known at all. A compensation philosophy is supposed to set the company's rules for who gets paid what and why. The actual decision-making process of the "what" may be more sophisticated or consistently applied at one company than another, but the intent of the compensation philosophy is to focus on the "why" as a North Star for guiding all pay decisions. A less obvious but, I'll argue, more important reason for having a compensation philosophy is to publicly state how a company will respond to the pay decisions of its competitors. Though no company would say this outright, a compensation philosophy sets the limits of a company's willingness to participate in the free market. Remember, companies see no strategic advantage in competing with one another on pay.

Publicly traded companies make their compensation philosophies, well, public. If you haven't done so for your own company, assuming it is publicly traded (meaning anyone can buy stock in it), put this book down and search for "(your company name) proxy (most recent completed year)." The resulting document will be dense, but in it you'll find a section called something like "Compensation Discussion and Analysis" with the important parts. The wording will focus on the top five executives in the company (the named executive officers) because their pay and the governing principles that set their pay legally have to be disclosed. These principles will apply to all levels of the organization. For small or privately held companies, you may have a similar document on your company intranet page. If you can't find the company compensation philosophy, ask your manager or HR team. If you're nervous to ask HR for something so basic, I recommend you start looking for the exits because the company has serious cultural problems. Without this language to know how your company thinks about pay, you will struggle to hold your company accountable or know whether you are paid fairly according to its own rules.

I will now summarize every compensation philosophy in existence. As you read through your company's philosophy, you will see some version of this sentence: "Our compensation philosophy exists to attract and retain the talent we need to achieve our strategic objectives."

Contain yourself from all the inspiration, but there's not much else to it. Under the prevailing model, all pay programs exist only to make sure people keep showing up to work and are unlikely to find a better deal elsewhere. As we've seen, when companies are all offering the same basic arrangement, the compensation philosophy starts to look less like an aspirational worldview and more like a compliance exercise.

I don't believe companies intentionally set their compensation philosophies as a collusive and defensive plot against fair pay, but as a rational outcome of their asymmetric market power. Basically, no one is forcing them to act any differently, and so the current, ineffective state of compensation philosophies is due to neglect and incentives, not malevolence. Most companies wouldn't call their philosophies defensive at all, but offensive in the sense that the actual wording of the compensation philosophy focuses on the active, transactional parts of employment, attracting and retaining people. What's missing from nearly all compensation philosophies is a clearly articulated prescription for ensuring fair and equitable pay, and the governance principles used to keep things in order. Retention is too indirect a measure to assess fairness or equity, because it gives employees no yardstick to measure themselves against. If a company views "not quitting" the same as "treated fairly," they may want to revisit their employee survey data to see how their people really feel about pay.

Unfortunately, the legal and incentive structure for changing a compensation philosophy makes it hard and inadvisable to make changes and pursue anything but sameness. If a company falls out of step with its peers, even if for good and noble reasons, then it risks public scrutiny to fall back in line. Independent proxy advisers will notice and call your company out for trying to be different. In extreme cases, activist shareholders can use these differences to sue or try to seize control of the company. Some of this is understandable. There are a few places in a company where broad consensus exists against people exercising much creativity. Auditing is a good example. Tax is another, except for recent innovations in the field with fun names like the Double Irish with a Dutch Sandwich, a way of lowering taxes (and mollifying shareholders) by shifting home country profits through one Irish company, to a Dutch company, and back to a second Irish company based in a tax haven like Bermuda or the Isle of Man. Pay sincerity should bring the tax team to the table, too. Eliminating these types of "innovations" would help fund government services that support people hurt by a company's unfair pay practices in the first place.

The standard compensation philosophy language isn't bad or wrong, but incomplete. It leaves out critical benefits of a well-functioning pay environment, including any assurances that the company will provide fair or equitable pay. By limiting ourselves to the same stories about pay, using the same objectives about merit and pay for performance and attracting and retaining talent, we should expect the same pay problems to persist. Reforming pay starts with reforming the compensation philosophy.

The philosophical bar, as we practice it now, is too low. In most cases, existing compensation philosophies take great care to outline generic ethical standards the company will follow. This is fine and necessary, but the duty of companies that practice pay sincerity should be more specific. Many companies have supplemental, detailed language and meticulous internal documents about how they operate to create environments of fair pay. These documents are not usually shared beyond the human resources team, but smart companies should get comfortable sharing these details with all employees and even shareholders. Pay sincerity means expanding this knowledge from "need to know" to "you need to know." Nothing will help companies attract and retain talent more than transforming their generic corporate-speak pay philosophy into tangible promises for the benefit of their employees.

The current model of copying everyone else, of playing it safe, leaves a lot on the table in terms of original thought, progress, and accountability. We should expect some variation across companies as they wrestle with the language—here's a start, combining the standard model with the language of pay sincerity:

"Our compensation philosophy exists to attract and retain the talent we need to achieve our strategic objectives, by ensuring all employees can provide for the essentials of life, access equitable and transparent pay, and receive the full reward of their contributions and potential."

Again, many companies will have shades of this language in their internal documents already, though it hits harder when the board says it in a Securities and Exchange Commission filing. Reformed compensation philosophies will get sharper over time as companies hone what fair pay means to them. On this, we should accept Jeff Bezos's challenge—it's the kind of free-market competition that will benefit everyone.

If the Business Roundtable is sincere about its calls for "good jobs with decent wages" and "progress toward achieving pay equity," reform of the compensation philosophy is where they must start. Each member company should agree to update their public compensation philosophy, together in the same year, holding elements of pay sincerity at the core. Other companies will then have no choice but to imitate them. The three-legged race continues, but together we'll be much farther down the track.

MINIMUM VIABLE PAY

Before building a product, the creators of the online file-sharing tool Dropbox made a short video to explain what the product would be and how it would function. The video was effective enough to help the fledgling company increase its waiting list from five thousand to seventy-five thousand people. Today, Dropbox has a working product that generates over $1 billion in annual sales.

Eric Ries, in his book *The Lean Startup*, helped popularize this story and the importance of validating an idea before spending a lot of effort bringing it to life. According to Ries, companies should try to fail quickly through what is called a minimum viable product (MVP), the video in the case of Dropbox. An MVP is a means to cheaply test market interest in a product you want to sell. A proper MVP should have enough of the final product's essential features to get people excited about its distinction in the marketplace, but leave out any bells and whistles to save money and move on quickly if the product idea is a dud.

Companies view pay in a similar way. Compensation teams like to fail quickly and cheaply, too, which I'll call the "minimum viable pay" approach. We will pay you the minimum amount required to get you into the company (attract), keep you at the company (retain), and performing well while not complaining about your pay. Pay is a Goldilocks problem, where too much money compared to market means you'll be handcuffed to the company and grow complacent, and too little money will make you grow resentful and leave or never join the company in the first place. Your company has a minimum viable number for your job and you personally, though they would have the courtesy never to call it that, and you should know enough about how pay works to make sure they aren't giving you the cold bowl of porridge.

Mike Isaac, in his book *Super Pumped: The Battle for Uber*, shares a less-courteous example. Describing Uber's approach to pay during its ascent, Isaac reported, "The company had designed an algorithm that determined the lowest possible salary a candidate might accept before making an offer to them, a ruthlessly efficient technique that saved Uber millions of dollars in equity grants." I suspect it's more likely the tool was used to calculate job offers against a candidate's previous rate of pay, which is less nefarious though still problematic. Until recently, this was a common practice in the field but in many places is now illegal because companies can no longer ask about salary history. (In Chapter 6, we'll talk more about how to negotiate a job offer in a world built on minimum viable pay.)

Minimum viable pay is the end result of companies choosing not to compete on pay, deferring instead to more ethereal (and less definable and accountable) differentiators such as company culture, meaningful work, and balance. There's value in this approach, and avoiding competition on pay has long been the standard model. George Lucas, in a court case from the 1980s, said it directly: "The rule we had, or the rule that I put down for everybody," was that "we cannot get into a bidding war with other companies because we don't have the margins for that sort of thing." If the mind behind *Star Wars* couldn't imagine a way to compete successfully on pay, don't expect your human resources team to have more creative inclinations.

Pay is the most expensive (and least effective) way for companies to buy affection. The research is clear—when people feel their pay is credible, and the process trustworthy, incremental investments in people are better spent on tactics that offer employees a sense of self-fulfillment, like personal development courses and robust leave policies, instead of above-market wages. Maslow, in a prior life, must have been a compensation professional.

Compensation teams can always choose to pay people more, as long as they can get the funding prioritized (more on that in a bit), but every compensation professional has been burned by their past bouts of generosity. Having to reverse an ineffective pay decision is a nightmare, the most expensive way to fail. We've all seen an incentive program fail but rather than stop the program, the additional dollars are folded into base pay, and now the whole team is noticeably paid more than everyone else. We're used to seeing above-the-pay-range offers given to the next must-have person who turns out to be an average contributor. Or as the saying goes, Hell hath no fury like an executive who has been told he can't keep his former Singaporean housing allowance five years after relocating to the United States. We've all been there.

Avoiding this special kind of pain is unfortunately where many unfair pay decisions get their start. People complain. Counteroffers are extended. Exceptions are made. This happens at all levels of a company based on a person's proximity to power. In environments where the squeaky wheel gets the grease, the whole system will eventually get clogged. This means to create a company culture where fair pay is the norm, fair pay also has to be the company line, embedded in manager behavior through consistent policies and practices. From the company's point of view, saying no to squeaky wheels is often the most effective tool for maintaining a fair pay system. If you're the squeaky wheel, you might be absolutely correct to speak up about your pay, but remember you have a different mandate than your company does. You are trying to optimize pay for yourself, while your company is trying to optimize pay for the system.

After you've asked about your company's compensation philosophy, it's time to determine what your minimum viable pay should be. (Note the following applies mostly to corporate jobs, whereas those in low-wage production or service work will want to follow the strategies outlined in Chapter 6.) Knowing your MVP helps you assess whether you are paid fairly, starting with the following questions:

1. What percentile of market is each pay program benchmarked to?

2. When during the year does the company measure to the market?

3. Which industries or companies does the company benchmark against?

The first question is crucial, but again prepare to be disappointed because you are unlikely to hear anything unique. Philosophically and mathematically, the most common answer is for companies to set their pay program targets against the median of the market, more indication your company is not trying to compete on pay but benchmarking themselves to the same rates as everyone else. The market median, or 50th percentile, is the median actual pay for people in your job at other companies, as shown in salary surveys. When you see the phrase "competitive pay" in a job listing, it almost always means the market median.

Some companies aim higher than the 50th percentile, for example the 60th or 75th percentile, especially when benchmarking incentive programs. A common approach is to pay 50th percentile on base pay, the pay in your regular paycheck, but target a higher market percent for bonus or stock in an effort to drive long-term performance and retention. I've heard of a few companies that seek the 62.5th percent as a halfway measure between the 50th and 75th percentile. Don't let that kind of pedantry fool you. The implied precision is almost certainly superficial, like a used-car salesman whose closing move is to slap the trunk and say, "Yessir, this baby has got everything." Meanwhile, the brake lines are being chewed through by rats.

Netflix, in a widely circulated presentation referred to by Facebook COO and *Lean In* author Sheryl Sandberg as "the most important document ever to come out of the Valley," made waves for saying Netflix's compensation philosophy included paying "all of our people at the top of their personal market," which implies at least a 90th percentile job benchmark. That the document was thought to be so profound speaks to how rare it is for companies to choose a nongeneric approach to pay. It's best to ask directly what percentile of market your company uses, and again, if your HR team refuses to tell you, it's time to refresh your résumé.

The second question concerns timing, specifically what month the company seeks to set their pay ranges to match their chosen market position each year. Market survey data, in most cases, is made available once a year in the fall, so to stay competitive throughout the year the company will "age" its market data by adding a fixed percent. If your company expects the market to increase 3 percent this year for an accounting manager, and they receive market data in October with an effective date of April 1, they now need to decide when to align the data to their desired market position, in this case to January 1 the following year.

Survey market rate on April 1	$90,000
Expected annual market change	3.0%
Number of aging months (April to January)	9
Aging percent (months/12 * annual market change)	2.3%
Estimated market rate on January 1	$92,070

Three tactics exist here: lead the market, lag the market, and lead/lag the market. Under a lead position, the company will set its pay programs to match the projected market rate at the start of their fiscal year. Because pay structures typically are only reviewed once per year, the market will catch up by the end of the year. Companies that care most about attracting new talent, and that have cash to burn, may choose this path. Under a lag strategy, the opposite is true, and to save money pay programs are set to match the desired market position by the end of the year, when it's time for the annual pay increase. Many companies choose the middle option, lead/lag, as the ideal trade-off, setting their market target date to the middle of the fiscal year. The company position matters more in countries with high inflation than in countries with low inflation, but in any case, timing is an important data point when assessing your own market position. (Hold this information for Chapter 6, when we talk about what time of year to ask for a raise.)

Finally, the benchmarked industry and company peer set matter, but not in the ways you might think. In most countries, similarly sized companies pay similarly, with little variation by industry or even (for large companies) by city or region. Similarities exist because companies are participating in the same compensation surveys, and competing for the same people in each career level. For example, an accounting director at a global insurance conglomerate in Dallas won't be paid like the next-door accounting director of the regional audit firm. Rather, she is more likely to be paid like the accounting director at a Denver biotech behemoth. The reason is that accounting skills are largely industry agnostic, and the title "director" is likely to mean the same thing across larger companies, because they are using similar versions of what we call "job-leveling" criteria. The director title at the regional firm is assumed to be a person with a less-developed leadership skill set, who is less willing to relocate across the country, and who is likely closer to what the big companies would call a manager. Companies that operate with pay sincerity should be able to readily supply information about their job levels and titling nomenclature and, even better, a summary of the types of companies they compare themselves against.

At this stage, you likely have more questions than answers, and you can start to see why compensation has historically been such a black-box operation. When you learn to assess your experience and capability against your company's desired market position, its timing, its peer set, and your true job level, there is a narrow range of possibility for what constitutes market-competitive and fair pay. Remember when I said in Chapter 1 that compensation professionals know a neat party trick where we can guess how much you're paid with just a few pieces of information? Once you recognize the standard terms and salary survey patterns, as we are starting to see here, you too can quickly assess whether your company is structured in a way that enables fair pay and, more importantly, whether you are paid fairly. Proper compensation teams know how to measure against these specific criteria. But we'll pay you only the minimum amount needed to achieve it, because anything more offers the company no unique strategic advantage, and it creates new unfair pay scenarios if you'll now be paid more than your peers without any justification other than that you were the one who asked for a raise. Beyond the MVP number, if you ask for more, know that creating an environment of fair pay requires us to regularly tell people no.

No exceptions.

LINE OF SIGHT

If the compensation field had a mantra, which we said to ourselves to rebalance and connect with what we know to be true and noble about life itself, it would be the soft repetition of the phrase "line of sight." In our mirrors in the morning, and on our commutes home each day, we'd tell ourselves the same thing while transcending to a higher plane of consciousness: "Line of sight. Line of sight. Line of sight."

Line of sight is the idea that the interests of the person receiving pay should match the interests of the person paying them. If you pay me to be a roller-coaster operator, my job is to make sure no one dies on my watch according to the things I can control. Therefore, I am going to make sure every safety harness is buckled prior to starting the ride. Everybody wins, especially the people who get to experience both a fun ride and also not dying.

There are still things out of my control, like the number of people who line up for my ride, or the general maintenance of the machinery. If I were to be paid an incentive for either convincing more people to ride who may have otherwise avoided the opportunity for health reasons, or for making isolated judgments about how I could make the ride faster or smoother by changing the mechanical settings, I put the whole system at risk, including the owner of the ride.

Line of sight is an important concept and hard to get right. This idea is the philosophical basis for all bonus plans, the thinking being that with the right design, a company can inspire people to work harder and take new and appropriate risks if the reasons for doing so are also important to the company. Behind the idea of bonus payments is the belief that workers are holding back their best work until they are paid extra to work harder, a questionable assumption, as we'll see. When some portion of people's pay is considered to be at risk if they don't perform that extra effort (and it is underappreciated that all pay is at risk if they're fired), people may do whatever it takes to earn the reward. If you dangle a carrot in front of someone, then what you measure is what you'll get, right? Maybe, and sometimes absolutely not.

The classic (and likely apocryphal) story of incentives gone awry is the Soviet-era nail factory. The story goes that a nail factory was directed by leaders in Moscow, under its government-planned economy, to meet quotas based on the number of nails produced. Because quantity was the only instruction given, the factory workers produced the smallest, most useless nails they could to earn as much money as possible. When the bosses in Moscow wised up to the game, they changed the quota to weight. Naturally, the factory workers started producing equally useless nails, but now they were as big as railroad spikes and as heavy as possible.

We can dismiss this as a silly example from a bygone era, but some of our current market-based versions are worse.

Through at least 2015, Purdue Pharma sales reps were reported to be paid bonuses on the number of doctor visits they made, and were pushed by the most senior executives of the company to recommend unnecessarily high dosage levels for its addictive pain medication, an opioid called OxyContin. In a series of lawsuits that eventually sent the company into bankruptcy, prosecutors argued the company engaged in "frequent acts of deception" to boost its product and also profited from the treatment of the addicts they created.

In 2016, Wells Fargo retail bank branch employees were paid in part according to how well they could cross-sell products—for example, convincing customers to have both a checking account and a mortgage at the bank. Incenting pay on quantity alone led to similar results as our tiny-nail example. Bank employees were found to have opened millions of fake accounts without customer consent, sometimes using their own addresses to do so and setting the new PIN numbers to "0000" for efficiency. Instead of building trust, the ultimate store of value in banking, Wells Fargo lost its CEO and faced a $2.7 billion settlement.

In 2019, Facebook stopped paying commissions to sales staff who sell political ads. Though it's always easier to judge in hindsight, taking payment in the form of Russian rubles for ads in an American election, as happened during the 2016 US presidential election, should have triggered suspicion. Sales staff at Facebook were reported to be given base pay increases for their lost bonus opportunity. I'd be interested to see how these sales staff are paid now relative to other sales groups in the company who didn't have their incentive plan fail, but I'd guess for at least a time, the political sales ad team was paid more. As I said, unwinding a failed compensation program is a nightmare, so it's best to build pay programs carefully.

The most common but unnoticed example of the negative effects of line of sight gone awry is the practice of tipping service workers. The history of tipping (at least in the States, where tipping is the norm) is disputed, but many believe the modern version has roots in the Reconstruction Era. As a way to incorporate newly freed slaves into the post–Civil War economy, some employers chose not to pay direct wages but allowed workers to receive only tips. Freed slaves were still seen structurally as being less than a full person and dependent on those with greater power for survival.

Economists like William R. Scott, writing in his 1916 treatise *The Itching Palm*, saw the practice as a direct assault on the value of human life, going as far as to say that tipping is "what one American is willing to pay to induce another American to acknowledge inferiority" and, in comparison to the country's founding opposition to aristocracy, that "every tip given in the United States is a blow to our experiment in democracy." According to Scott, companies had "fastened the tipping habit on the American people and they used the negro as an instrument to do it with." These companies had also gamed their pay plans under the guise of inducing performance, saying a manager of a hotel "proves his insincerity by adjusting (the employee's) wage scale on the estimate that the guests will pass money to his employees!" Elements of this legacy continue through today, as one study found that restaurant parties of three or more tipped white servers an average of 19.4 percent of the bill, while Black servers were tipped an average of 14.6 percent.

In the United States, eighteen states still participate in the separate but lower federal minimum wage standard of $2.13 for tipped workers, with the expectation that tips must bring these workers to at least the nontipped minimum wage. Unsurprisingly, these states are concentrated in the American South, a reverberating echo from the region's slaveholding history. The next time you eat at a restaurant in one of these states, remember that your benevolence determines whether that person will make the bare minimum required by law of other jobs. Only where you fail to tip these workers is the company then expected to fill the gap; even then, there is no guarantee they will do so adequately or equitably. This doesn't mean we end the practice of tipping entirely, especially for highly paid, elite service professions for whom minimum wage isn't a concern (or for people who are paid according to commissions plans), though I do believe the tipped minimum wage should be eliminated. Recognition of the impact of tipping, and the way our choices integrate into the current system, is essential.

Why then, if bonus plans can go so disastrously wrong, do companies still rely on them when the advantages are comparatively small? Why do we view line of sight as so important? The most brutish fights I've seen in my compensation career are about who gets credit for what in the company incentive plan and, when things go bad, whether the targets were ever realistic or fair to begin with. There is no pay program more effective at breaking the trust between workers and managers than the bonus plan. So why bother?

The endurance of bonus plans rests on the belief that they will drive behavior changes. Behavior change itself, in isolation, is not feasible to measure or prove in a corporate environment. The truth is people in my position have no idea if these plans are driving the right behaviors or not. Is the sales manager planning her pitch differently now that she's paid more for her results, or is she successful because the new product line that another team created is simply more compelling? Is the restaurant supervisor driving profit by thinking he should hide the napkins behind the counter, or just inconveniencing customers who will be less likely to return? No company can measure intent, only the number or weight of the nails we want to pay you for.

It turns out that incentive plans are actually about other factors:

- inertia, because everyone else does it, say the salary surveys
- cost savings, because in a bad year the company can off-load a percentage of its wage base by not paying bonuses (or transfer it to the customer through tipping)
- blame shifting, because incentives allow companies to pass accountability for low pay to the employee who likely had no say in the targets they are asked to hit

Tax savings are also a factor, as seen recently by Netflix, which ended its cash bonus plan for executives after the 2017 Tax Cuts and Jobs Act eliminated the ability of companies to deduct performance-based bonuses for executives paid over $1 million. The target bonus amount was reported to be folded into higher base salaries, which suggests the plan's primary purpose had not been about driving desired behaviors but delivering a market amount of pay. A 2008 bonus plan at Credit Suisse was even stranger; the investment bank paid some of its employees in mortgage derivatives that had been made worthless in the 2008 recession. According to Bloomberg, the effect was mutually beneficial to the bank and the employee: the bank got to off-load toxic assets and improve the company's balance sheet, and in the process employees "made a killing" as the products regained value over time.

Bonus plans have a place in an equitable pay program when carefully designed, especially if bonus pay is based on repetitive and measurable tasks or team goals that decouple personal risk and anxiety from the person's essential livelihood. A poor incentive design stifles pay sincerity, preventing our relentless pursuit of equitable and transparent pay. If you are on a bonus plan now, ask how the targets are set and how payouts have fared across demographics. If you are a manager or compensation designer considering implementing an incentive plan, or if you are in these roles but haven't reviewed the health of your current plans in some time, make sure to establish a calibration step before each target-setting session and payout calculation to monitor for potential bias, and create an effective exception and conflict resolution process. But first, consider whether incentives are worth the hassle, or if your company's plans could be more effectively replaced through additional base pay or a more objective and less personal tool like stock awards.

LAST ON THE LIST

Pay and benefits are, by a wide margin, the largest expense most companies have each year. Mature, stable companies in most industries will spend 15 to 30 percent of their sales on pay and benefits, or up to 50 percent in the service industry. The closest approximation to a personal budget is your monthly rent or mortgage. And like budgeting for a mortgage, the way companies plan for the expense of pay becomes automatic with time, and fresh thought is rarely put into the process. We will have to rethink this automated approach to make pay fair.

To help work through this section, let's imagine you run a successful business selling $1 billion per year in dog food, a highly competitive industry with plenty of uncertainty. After paying for the obvious expenses like ingredients, salaries and benefits, office space and supplies, and advertising, you still have the nonobvious expenses like interest on the loans you've taken out, insurance, and, of course, taxes. Your business is not yet large or global enough to run the Double Dutch with an Irish Sandwich maneuver, so your tax bill is larger than the bigger competitors on a percentage basis. At the end of the year, you have $100 million left over as net income. Congratulations, successful dog food entrepreneur!

What choices do you have for that remaining money? Making these decisions requires a brief primer on corporate finance, which I'll try to keep as painless as possible.

You have two choices: keep the money, or give it back to shareholders. Both start with evaluating "opportunity cost." Opportunity cost is the potential gain you could have had by making a different decision with your money. If seeing a movie provides more personal value to you now than saving that money in an interest-bearing savings account, you should go see the movie. The true cost of the movie ticket will grow over time as you remember you could have saved the money plus gained interest. If in ten years you will still value the expense of having seen the movie at the new, higher cost, then buying the ticket was the rational choice. You might not make daily choices with this mindset, but businesses will always prioritize their biggest spending on investments where the potential returns are more than the opportunity costs.

The first option, and the one that seems most obvious, is to keep the money within the company. But *how* to keep the money creates its own set of choices:

GROW THE BUSINESS: If your dog food is available only online, but next year you would like to put the products in retail grocery stores with all new flavors, that means you need more sales staff, account managers, and chefs. You'll also need legal staff to write the contracts, logistics teams to handle the shipping, and technology systems to keep track of everything. The first years in a new line of business will be the expensive kind of learning, where you won't be able to fail fast.

INVEST IN THE FUTURE: Getting from $1 billion to $10 billion in sales means you may need a new office building and new machinery to make your factories more productive. You'll also need better research labs and test kitchens. These are expensive, multiyear projects that require careful planning. If interest rates happen to be low at the time, a business may choose to take on debt to fund the development instead of paying in cash, assuming the return on the investment of the new buildings is expected to be larger than the interest payments on the loan. Again, all budgeting decisions are about the opportunity cost of your limited resources.

SAVE FOR A RAINY DAY: All companies try to build up reserves—called "retained earnings"—by setting aside money to grow in investment accounts. If next year your dog food company has to weather a food safety scandal, the money set aside now can keep the company solvent and be used as collateral for new loans needed to invest in regaining trust with your customers.

REBALANCE THE BALANCE SHEET: For accounting purposes, all companies maintain what is called a "balance sheet," a snapshot picture of everything the company owns and owes. The balance sheet is like the chief financial officer's report card. Failing grades, like unhealthy levels of debt or inventory, or too much cash on hand not being invested, will be obvious to shareholders. The CFO will be expected to make adjustments. This may include stock buybacks, which will have two effects: making the balance sheet look healthier by putting excess cash to work as an investment, and signaling to the market that the company believes the stock is undervalued and is therefore a good purchase.

Our second option, return the money to shareholders, seems less obvious. When a company pays its shareholders directly, this is called a "dividend," and these regular payments are expected for companies of a certain size. Stock buybacks also function as returning money to shareholders, as the company purchases the stock from shareholders, but for simplicity we'll focus on direct payments of cash dividends only.

Recalling our review of shareholder primacy from Chapter 3, the prevailing business environment operates under the idea that the purpose of the company is to benefit its owners, which means its shareholders. With every dollar spent, then, the company has to think about the opportunity cost of its alternative choices. Will the long-term return on this single dollar be higher if I keep the money, by investing it in the business or addressing a structural opportunity in the balance sheet, or by giving it back to shareholders to invest on their own? Remember, shareholders are the owners, and each dollar belongs to them. Managers are expected to make all decisions on their behalf.

What I didn't tell you is that for some reason, your dog food can be consumed only by labradoodles. All other dogs get sick eating your food. You've tried everything. Now, once you've saturated the labradoodle market and gained as much efficiency as is reasonable (cutting corners led to a food safety scandal), you're realizing the company is unlikely to grow as fast as it did in its run from zero to $1 billion in sales. Investors are spooked, and if at the same time the overall stock market is growing faster than your company, reasonable shareholders may wish to invest elsewhere and want their money back to do so. You'd rather they hold on to your stock instead of selling it, because you have a new kind of food launching in three years that all dogs can consume, and you need their funding to get the new product to market. So you return a portion of the $100 million in cash back to shareholders each year to keep them from abandoning you. Some industries, like utilities, are known for their regular dividend payments. Utility companies themselves grow very little each year, but their profits are constant and the cash they return to shareholders functions as a guaranteed, and liquid, return on investment. Many retirees fund their livelihood on dividends, so cutting payments is not an option because retirees have lots of time to complain and may call for your resignation.

Practically, your dog food company will need to make some combination of the above two choices to make everyone happy, keeping some of the money and redistributing the rest. Running a business is complex and requires trade-offs. The three-year timeline to create new food is the most visible spending need, but the unseen factors matter, too, as in our egg-cracking example. If a competing dog food company is now doing delivery, or if suppliers have filed a joint lawsuit against you for contract infringement over the food safety scandal, your company will need to find a way to respond to everything at once. The last choice you'll make is to invest in pay—there is too much else to do. Considering you make it through the choice gauntlet above, what else is holding pay increases at the back of the line?

Business leaders are judged less on the absolute amount of wage investments they make—how many dollars they are spending—than by quarter-by-quarter, or year-by-year percentage changes. An executive who adds $20 million to the $300 million payroll of her dog food company will show a wage-growth rate of more than 6 percent, twice the recent US market benchmark rate of 3 percent. She'll need to be able to frame this abnormality as a onetime investment, because next year she will be judged on year-over-year percentage growth. If she repeats the above-market investment, investors will start questioning her management ability for not hitting market benchmarks. She has become Henry Ford and the investors are the Dodge brothers. Questions will seldom come up about to whom the $20 million is going (it could be executives, middle managers, or hourly workers), or why the investment is needed. These questions are pushed far lower into the organization, to the middling analysts of the compensation team to figure out. Senior business leaders at large companies, those with power to change investor dynamics, rarely ask to see how wages are distributed in their own companies below their direct reports and in aggregate for large business units. Their concern is the 3 percent benchmark, and they trust others with sorting out the details in a way that isn't illegal and won't make them look bad or put their own jobs at risk.

This percentage bias is why, under existing compensation models, changing pay for low-wage-volume jobs can be so hard. Figuring out how to give one person with a unique leadership job, or who is an extra squeaky wheel, a $50,000 raise per year is easy. The expense will be treated as an exception to the 3 percent internal budget applied to everyone else. The standard compensation philosophy allows the company to spend the money needed to attract and retain that one person without being noticed. This will be a onetime investment the business won't have to keep answering for each year, because that person will not keep asking for equivalent increases, or more likely, will have been promoted or left the company and replaced by a lower-paid person.

Spending the same amount in absolute terms ($50,000) by giving fifty low-wage workers $1,000, as through a 50-cent-per-hour raise, is a harder task. This type of increase will be baked into the financial cake for years, because there is little opportunity to claim it as a one-off event or to reset pay back to the lower rate once increased. This is why many companies fight against minimum-wage increases. The boss will notice that a large group of employees received a pay increase above the 3 percent market benchmark and will want answers that aren't repeated the next year. This is a terrible problem for low-wage workers who have fallen far below living wages, and persistent pay increases above the market benchmark to help these workers catch up will have to be fought for each year. If a majority of a company's workers are paid the US federal minimum wage of $7.25 an hour, they would need a five-year annual growth rate of about 16 percent (five times market) to break the $15 threshold. If they are paid $10 an hour, they would need a five-year growth rate of 9 percent (three times market). This won't happen without the CEO caring enough about the well-being of their lowest-paid workers to explicitly set a wage target, bypassing internal squabbles and dealing with the investor consequences.

Without intervention from business leaders who recognize their role in moving the market rate of pay, who are willing to break free from the three-legged-race-to-the-bottom of unfair pay, companies will continue to treat pay as if they have bought a house (their employees) and are now paying a fixed-rate mortgage. Property taxes on the house may adjust slightly from year to year, and essential upkeep requires some level of regular spending. But generally, investing in a remodel, or in our case significantly raising pay for low-wage workers, is not found in the budget because it has less directly visible returns and is therefore seen as a lower opportunity cost than other investment choices. Making the case for additional pay is hard unless the house clearly needs a new roof, and even then, many companies will expect their employees to get through at least one winter with drip buckets scattered around the kitchen. The alternative, paying people fairly under a reformed and comprehensive pay philosophy, is how smart companies avoid foreclosure.

In a classic episode of *The Simpsons*, Marge tells her family that they can't afford to buy a new television from a (then high-end) store like the Sharper Image. She reasoned, "We can't afford to shop at any store that has a philosophy. We just need a TV." When it comes to your pay, you can't afford to work at a company whose leadership treats pay only as a benchmarking exercise, as just a TV, and that doesn't explain how its compensation philosophy will enable a competitive and fair pay environment for all employees. If you are unsure where your pay stands in relation to what the company says it believes in, the opportunity cost of not asking is too high.

CHAPTER 5

How Much Are You Worth?

Imagine a software engineer friend comes to you with an idea. She's testing whether people have an interest in using something like "the Facebook of pay," an app that syncs to your social media accounts and shows a 100 percent accurate ranking of your friends' incomes. We share everything else about ourselves online, she says, so why not pay? If given the opportunity, would you use an app like this? Who would you look up first? And do you think knowing how much your work was worth relative to others—total pay transparency—would solve the twin problems of stagnant wages and the pay gap?

Norway tried something similar. And no, it didn't solve either problem.

Since at least 1882, tax returns in Norway have been public information. Until 2001, any Norwegian could visit their local tax office and make a formal request to see another person's official income. After 2001, with the arrival of online and searchable databases, the process became much easier, saving the pay lurker a cold bicycle ride to the tax office. For a short time, third-party developers were able to integrate information from these databases with sites like Facebook, generating income rankings of your friends. In peak weeks, these sites were more popular than YouTube, and Norwegians were more likely to search for tax returns than for the weather. The fun lasted through 2011, when the government banned the public usage of these lists for commercial purposes. In 2014, the reins were tightened more when anonymous searches were disallowed. Now, you can still look up your boss's pay, but she will be notified by email that you did so, which might make your next meeting a little awkward.

Norway's long-standing culture of pay transparency, though a point of national pride, helps make pay fairer but has not been enough to eliminate unequal pay. According to data collected by the OECD, Norway's gender pay gap between men and women is 7 percent. The gender pay gap, which we will discuss at length in Chapter 7 as one way among many to measure fair pay, calculates the difference in actual pay between men and women, regardless of their jobs or where they may fall in the company hierarchy. A high pay gap typically means a company also has representation gaps, with more men than women in senior leadership roles. At 7 percent, Norway does a lot better on the measure than places where there is less pay transparency, like the United States, where it is 18 percent. But the link from pay transparency to a lower gender pay gap isn't direct or absolute, as Norway also fares worse than places with less pay transparency, like Romania, which leads the OECD list at under 2 percent.

This means transparency and the gender (or racial or intersectional) pay gap are not the only problems we have to solve to make pay fair. We need people to know how to interpret pay information when made public, and how to build an infrastructure that can correct for and sustain equitable pay. Actual levels of pay and the potential for everyone to earn more of it are as important. For many, being 18 percent underpaid in the United States is preferable to being 2 percent underpaid in Romania, because the higher pay gap in the States comes with higher absolute pay and greater economic opportunity. Once, while on a project in Bucharest, Romania, I worked with a retail business that could not keep their locations staffed. Employees were using their pre-Brexit EU passports to take the same job at the company but in the comparatively unequal UK, where the pay gap is eight times as high, at 16 percent, but where base pay is much higher.

Some use this economic opportunity argument to suggest there are little to no true problems of unfair pay in developed economies like the United States and the UK. They argue that where pay gaps persist, they are a second-order problem that will sort itself out in time, so long as we don't damage the conditions for overall pay growth. Of course, they say, men and women should receive equal pay for equal work, but we need to let the market solve the problem in its own way. People (and by people, I mean the underpaid groups that are overrepresented by women and minorities) should sit down, enjoy the ride, and be thankful for how good life is in these countries.

This hierarchy of choices between markets and equality is unnecessary. We can close the pay gap while creating greater economic opportunity for everyone. As pay transparency initiatives become more popular, and we in turn make the pay gap more visible than ever, we can learn more effective ways to make improvements to the whole system at once.

A world with more pay transparency is inevitable. So is a world without tolerance of wage gaps. Employees at many companies, high payers among them like Google and Microsoft, have taken matters into their own hands by secretly collecting and publishing their own salary spreadsheets. We should expect this trend to continue. Confidential salary-sharing apps like Blind and public sites like Levels.fyi, Salary.com, and Glassdoor, at first dismissible by compensation professionals because of poor data quality, are becoming more sophisticated. Businesses will need to accept this new normal of increased accountability and harder pay conversations. The winners, whether companies or employees (and ideally, both), will be those who are best prepared, who can interpret newly transparent pay data as it is now and raise our collective expectations of fairness. While the rest of this book helps all of us accelerate this transformation, this chapter will at minimum help the secret salary spreadsheet makers out there produce more convincing data points.

UNFAIR ON PURPOSE

Those who oppose fair pay as I describe it—as an activity with both market and structural blind spots in need of correction—often worry that changing the way pay works will limit business innovation, or that business leaders will no longer be able to reward their truly outstanding performers. I see this often in start-up environments and in all companies with ambitious managers, and before we learn to parse the differences in how most companies assess paying most people, I want to address the topic to show how exempting certain types of companies or superstar employees from the ways of fair pay creates more problems than it solves.

Regarding business innovation, I find Paul Graham's 2016 essay titled "Economic Inequality" instructive, though likely not for the reasons he intends. Graham is a guru among founders and in his essay said that "eliminating great variations in wealth would mean eliminating startups." Hyperbole aside, his argument was that business start-ups may, in fact, directly cause inequality, but that on the whole this was a favorable trade-off for a broader economic system that can create new wealth from nothing. Creating new wealth is a good thing, but I wish he would have also created daylight between helpful and harmful start-ups. Not all start-ups (or traditional businesses, for that matter) are built to sustain fair pay outcomes. Some are designed intentionally around the idea, which we'll explore more in Chapter 8.

How can founders make sure they build the kinds of companies that value fair pay? Simply put, they should not write a pitch deck that creates new conditions for low wages and inequality to thrive. Founders, recognize that you get to choose your business model, and you get to decide whether you operate with pay sincerity from the outset. To apply pay sincerity to the mission statements of well-known start-ups (some of which have grown into behemoths), you're not "connecting people with possibility" when you're deducting tips from the base pay of delivery drivers. You're not "igniting opportunity" when you're leading the legal fight against independent contractor classifications that would give people a basic sense of security. And you're not "elevating the world's consciousness" when you're handing the CEO a billion-dollar walkaway package for nearly bankrupting the company.

The same mentality—that innovation trumps fairness—permeates large companies, too. Laszlo Bock, the legendary former head of Google's human resources function (called People Operations), helped the company land on scores of Best Places to Work lists around the world. Untold numbers of copycats have tried to replicate the Google culture and work environment, and I can think of few companies that have done more to influence and enhance the standard offering of pay and benefits for the entire marketplace (at least for office workers). But what Bock is best known for in the compensation world is an idea he admits is provocative, described in his book *Work Rules*, that companies should intentionally "pay unfairly."

To pay unfairly, as Bock describes it, is to acknowledge that "two people doing the same work can have a hundred times difference in their impact, and in their rewards." He takes this literally, saying one person could receive a $10,000 stock award, while another in the same job could receive a $1,000,000 award. In his view, fair pay means being paid according to your contributions, with top performers contributing many multiples more than the average performer. This is meritocracy in its most distilled form, totally aligned to the prevailing views of business discussed in Chapter 3. It's also risky.

To make paying unfairly work, Bock insists that pay programs have both "procedural and distributive justice." In other words, people have to trust the process, the amounts given, and the worthiness of the recipients, or else the company risks breeding "a culture of jealousy and resentment." He's right: even the best companies that believe they can ensure both types of justice create risk with intentionally unfair pay, because for many companies, high performance is confused with frequent presence. Pay is too often associated not with results generated, but with the hours put in physically at the office. There is, of course, a gendered dynamic that results from this pay approach. As long as women are culturally expected to carry the greater physical and mental load of the unpaid work of family life, they risk losing out on the rewards of paid work. If pay sincerity means to help people seek the full rewarding of their contributions and potential, setting after-hours work activities and expectations that unintentionally reward presence and participation over performance will have to go. Men, the easy part of being an ally is to clear the lowest bar ever: leave the office at a reasonable hour and put down your work email until morning.

Paying unfairly assumes a company can accurately measure sustained multiples of outsized contribution in an unbiased way, and that they will be able to communicate these unequal awards to a broader employee population once the rumors start. Good luck. By paying unfairly, you might breed not only resentment but also a biased and potentially illegal pay system. Google, a company with some of the world's smartest minds and that swims in an ocean of data like no other, can likely measure its ability to pay unfairly better than anyone, and yet it has had problems in how its overall pay culture is viewed by employees (despite all the

Best Place to Work awards). In late 2018, Google staff worldwide held a walkout over the company's treatment of women. The second of five demands made by the protesters was for "a commitment to end pay and opportunity inequity." The phrase "opportunity inequity" sounds to me a lot like presence mattered more than performance when setting pay and promotions. I will assume your company is not as good at data collection as Google, which means paying unfairly is unwise.

WHO DO YOU THINK YOU ARE?

A senior human resources leader runs down the stairs, waving a copy of the *New York Times*. He tears into his compensation team, demanding to know why he's just read about another company that pays their retail store managers double. He hasn't spent any part of his human resources career doing compensation work (the path to HR executive rarely includes a meaningful rotation through the field), so he's missing the nuances of what he's reading. A few of the team look at one another, drawing telepathic straws for who would have to tell a person much higher in the company hierarchy what is obvious to them. Finally, someone speaks up. "Their stores are much bigger. Our whole store is like a single department in their store, and each of their stores sells fifty times what our stores do. The managers in the article manage other managers, and our managers do not. The store manager you're reading about is closer to our job of a district manager, and so they are paid more."

At another company, an employee is transferring offices from the United States to Canada. She has been switched to the Canadian payroll, where the market rate of pay is significantly lower than in the US, while her new taxes are significantly higher than what she had in the States. She's getting squeezed at both ends and says she shouldn't be punished for taking a development assignment, especially since she's been labeled a high-potential talent. This has to be gender discrimination, she thinks. Her new boss carefully explains her entire new total rewards package, complete with health insurance she no longer has to pay for and equalization mechanisms to keep her long-term pay intact while she's away from the United States. Altogether, she's coming out ahead, but she's still livid that her base pay, in absolute terms, is now lower. The business is now anxious they've angered a superstar employee. They cave, shuffling some benefits around and keeping her pay the same as in the States but directly converting to Canadian dollars. Now the Canadians are mad (as much as is possible for Canadians) the new person is paid so highly—more than her new boss! She is relieved, and though she has now learned that pay isn't the same in every country, she doesn't feel it was fair she had to fight. Meanwhile, the company regrets creating the assignment and wonders what battles they have ahead to make sure she isn't permanently overpaid after returning to the US office. No doubt, she will want a raise when she's completed the assignment.

Now the assistant for a chief marketing officer asks why his pay is lower than the assistant for the chief operating officer. The two have talked about pay and he knows the two aren't receiving, in his words, "equal pay for equal work." He doesn't realize the differences in their respective places in the company. The CMO's team works mostly with vendors, making his marketing team small compared to operations, who work with a massive group of employees spread throughout the globe. The COO is next in line to run the whole company and is assigned to a higher pay grade than the CMO. Not only is the COO assistant's job much more complex, but she has a decade more experience doing the work than the CMO's assistant. He is completely unaware the entire administrative team is carefully and uniquely reviewed each year, more than any group except executives at the company, because the job has a direct line to senior leaders. The company's compensation leader learned long ago that upsetting the administrative team was a rookie mistake.

Each of these stories represents valid but explainable concerns about pay. This is the kind of pain that takes up the days of compensation teams worldwide. What seems unfair and makes employees feel overlooked can actually be part of a system that had more thought put into it and rigor applied than the employee realizes. Or there could be a serious mistake in need of immediate correction. Knowing this distinction to determine a job's worth, and when to choose your battles for more pay, starts with knowing your peers—to whom and how to compare yourself—across countries, jobs, or teams.

A study on the Norwegian tax system found that relative pay between you and your peers is a more important driver of satisfaction than the amount of pay itself, assuming pay was enough to meet essential human needs. Simply put, if your pay was above those you considered your peers, you were happy and, if below, you were sad. The study found that households with fewer resources were more likely than high-resource households to oppose greater income transparency. When you already have daily reminders that you are not doing well compared to others, like unpaid bill notices and thoughts of dreams unfulfilled, you don't want everyone to ask you about it.

Getting a clear picture of who your pay peers are is hard. Trying to find this information on your own can be problematic, especially when using self-reported pay websites—the kind mentioned before that you find while searching online for your job title plus the word "salary." Two types of these sites exist. The first is run by recruiting firms that have every incentive to overprice their results, creating in you an urgency to find a better job that only they can fulfill. The second type are self-reported, where anyone can submit their own job and pay information. The idea is that the wisdom of the crowds will, given enough information, produce accurate results. At present, the data quality from these sites is not reliable enough to meet the standards of professional compensation teams, and we doth not touch these sites with our un-gloved hands. Self-reported pay sites will get better with time and play a critical role in ensuring fair pay as they become more reliable, but for now it's important to know many compensation teams will not take arguments for pay raises seriously if reliant on this data.

The difference in self-reported website data and the data found in formal compensation surveys used by companies to set pay rates is in how the data is collected. In formal surveys, the level of data available is granular, normalized, and complete. For example, I can find with certainty the competitive range of pay for an expert-level Israeli data scientist. Survey companies are able to provide, in aggregate terms, actual pay data for every expert-level Israeli data scientist at my chosen comparator companies. If you happen to be an expert-level Israeli data scientist, your pay (without your name) was submitted to these survey vendors. Unfortunately, you as an expert-level Israeli data scientist are not allowed to purchase this data about yourself and your peers. The data you find online in self-reported sites will be accurate only where submitters have a common understanding of the word "expert," and who have the self-awareness not to conflate their job with something more advanced, like a data-reporting specialist who thinks he is a data scientist. If the reporting specialist enters his pay information alongside true data scientists, he is bound to think he is underpaid. The task of normalizing people to jobs across companies, of assigning groups of true peers, is difficult and time-consuming, and this is the reason companies are willing to pay vendors for their services.

Companies have an information advantage over employees by having access to more complete data. This is called "information asymmetry." Data you found on the Internet is not on par with data your company has, and so you need something more than Google searches to help you assess your pay and get a raise. If you're struggling to find who your true peers are, or you want to make certain your current understanding is correct, you are going to need some inside help to know the right questions to ask.

AN INSIDE JOB

If your company is not transparent about pay, and you do not have a friend in a role like mine handy (anyone who does this work is constantly called by friends to check on their pay), your next step in finding your true peers is to look for people in the same or substitute jobs. To understand this, we have to define a lot of terms to find out what your job actually is.

This should be straightforward, but at your company and among pedantic compensation professionals, it might not be, especially if it's the kind of place that gives people titles like "Head of," "Customer Experience Rockstar," or "Creative." Job titles with the word "ninja" have increased 140 percent since 2015, though prospects for office samurai are less clear. Cutesy job titling might make companies look hip and nimble and egalitarian, but the practice if not done carefully can work against creating more equitable organizations by confusing people about their job level and true peers. Confusion, whether intentional or not, always works in the company's favor. Vague titling means a company can't be held accountable to a standard—equal pay for equal work—where there is no commonly understood definition of what "equal work" means. Behind the titling curtain, these companies almost always have a shadow job hierarchy that aligns to the same salary survey standards as everyone else.

Knowing your worth (not as a person but in pay under the prevailing model of work in a capitalistic society) starts with knowing what your job is, in the company's eyes. You might view a job as the set of tasks you do, or as that place you go to on weekdays with the coffee that tastes like industrial soap. You might know specifically from your business card that you are the senior manager of marketing operations for the southwest region. If you are unsure, ask to see your job description. A job description is a document that outlines in broad terms what you are expected to do. The document has likely been lost in a file somewhere, neglected and sitting next to the overhead projector. As a general rule, the older your job description looks, the more you have to worry about when it comes to ensuring your pay is fair. You must make sure your job description aligns with the work you are actually doing, because this sets the baseline for your pay. Look at it once a year, and don't count on your boss or HR manager to maintain this document for you. If you can't find or access your job description, consult a job-leveling guide (more on that below) and ask your manager about the expectations for your job. Then, write up a job description yourself to establish shared expectations with your manager and HR. Later, we'll talk about how to enter this conversation without making anyone antsy.

At minimum, your job description should have a few basic identifiers that will help you make sense of your place in the company. The basics are your job title, which differs from your position, your job family, and your job level. Let's work backward from your business card title as senior manager of marketing operations for the southwest region:

POSITION: *". . . southwest region."* A position is the unique headcount spot you fill in the company. A position is different from a job, which many people can be in at once. If your company has a layoff and your position has been eliminated, it means you, not necessarily everyone in that job. A position may have its own tailored job description, called a "position description," and a unique "desk title," which is a secondary title companies let a business unit choose themselves, sometimes in place of pay or to make the person appear more senior to external clients. Early in my career, to account for cultural norms, I would regularly have to exaggerate my desk title in international markets to be allowed into certain meetings, but this didn't mean I was officially ready or should have been paid for the bigger job. A customer experience ninja is an example of a desk title, but the official title the compensation team uses to review pay to salary surveys might be something like "customer support representative 1." Pay is not set based on position, but many companies do apply a geographic adjustment depending on the location—the northeast region position may have a pay range premium 10 percent higher than the southwest region, for example. Above a certain job level, usually first-line executives, these geographic differences will disappear as the talent market for these roles is considered to be national, not regional. You should know whether your company uses these types of premiums, and you should never accept a new title without asking how the change applies to your job level (see below).

JOB: "*. . . of marketing operations . . .*" A job is a core set of duties you are expected to perform. In our example, the marketing operations team might be tasked with preparing marketing campaign logistics or analyzing which campaigns are most effective. Other people may be in the same job and have the same set of job duties as you, but work for a different group in the company. The southwest person and the northeast person are assigned to the same work (job) but different regions or accounts (position). A rule of thumb is that 80 percent of your work should look like what everyone else in the job does. If it doesn't, you are in the wrong job or job level, and your pay may also be wrong.

Now we're getting to how your pay is actually set. Market survey data is organized by a combination of job and standardized job level, which we review next. In our example, this combination is the senior manager (job level) of marketing operations (job). We drop the southwest region part unless we're looking at survey data only from this region. To find your market pay rate in a salary survey, your job duties are pegged to the most similar definition also found in a survey vendor's "job library," a massive catalogue of genericized job summaries used with all their clients. Job libraries are as exciting to read as they sound. Assigning your job to a survey job summary from the job library is called a "job match." The job match is the most critical information you need to gauge whether you are being paid competitively.

Position > Job > Job Level > Job Match > Market Survey Data

Each survey match will be compared to market survey data in one of three ways:

1. BENCHMARKING: Most companies take a subset of core job matches that are important to the company and common in surveys to form "benchmarks" that become the basis of their pay ranges, which we talk about in the next section. Companies like this approach because it is most closely tied to the market, making the explanation of pay rates easier to employees. Every company that participates in the survey and assigns workers to that job match will report its employees' actual pay data. If you feel underpaid, the most likely scenario is that the survey match for your job is not correct. Although companies do not typically share job match information with employees, because it can be such an inexact process, they should at

least be open to your questions as a good-faith measure of shared accountability.

2. SLOTTING: Sometimes, a job is too specific to a company to be compared to the market. An energy drink company might have jobs that do only brand evangelism. A bank might have privacy specialists for specific types of oligarchs. An insurance firm might have actuaries who do only art valuations. Or the survey data simply came back so wonky that it was disregarded by the compensation team as an unusable outlier. When these situations arise, a job is slotted, which means the job is aligned to similar benchmarks based on gut feel in an attempt to create as little noise as possible in the organization. Occasionally, a job will receive a "premium" or a "discount," usually 10 percent up or down, if the job is subjectively viewed to be slightly larger or smaller than a comparable benchmark. Now we're getting into the gray areas of compensation, the art over the science.

3. POINT FACTOR: Point factor systems are based entirely on the subjective assessments of a job by the reviewer. Rather than assign jobs to survey matches, a point factor system scores each job on a Rube Goldberg machine of factors that are proprietary to a specific survey vendor, resulting in a hierarchy where all jobs within a range of points are assigned to a pay range, and the bucket of jobs with the most total points is paid the highest. Under most point factor systems, the results are hard to validate and harder to convince employees of their fairness. One vendor's system might score a job with 175 points and another job 168 points on their secret scale without much clear difference as to why, and as a result they may or may not be placed in the same pay range bucket. Thankfully, this practice is outdated but is still used especially in developing markets as an "easier" way to control for notoriously volatile survey data. Whether the employee has any idea how the system works or is given the right language

to ask questions about their pay are secondary concerns. If your company uses a point-factor methodology as its primary method of setting pay, you have a steep uphill climb ahead to determine if you are paid fairly, because it's unlikely your compensation team can fully explain what the vendor has sold them.

JOB FAMILY: A "job family" is a hierarchy of like jobs that a person can reasonably expect to be available to them in their chosen career path. If you work in the marketing function, a job family might include all jobs and job levels for advertising, social media, brand strategy, and nontechnical product management. Large companies will subdivide families into subfamilies for added clarity about career paths. Some companies have fixed rules about jumping from one job family to the next, and you must know these rules to navigate your fair pay journey. When used as a box-ticking exercise to control for strict professional standards like accountancy or law, these practices are acceptable. When used to preserve "next in line" succession practices, companies that limit career path options through arbitrary job family rules only reinforce their representation gaps. Generally, the tighter the control a company exercises about who can move into a job family, the more likely there are significant (and perhaps undeserved) differences in pay between the groups. Companies should evaluate whether their internal job movement rules are defensible, remembering that pay sincerity *helps people seek the full reward of their contributions and potential.* If the same talent can reasonably move from one job family to another and perform well, significant pay differences are hard to justify.

JOB LEVEL: For example, an "analyst," "senior manager," or "vice president." A job level is a standardized description of the relative capability, hierarchy, and authority of a job. A job level explains the complexity of problems the person is responsible for solving. Of our job description identifiers, job levels are the most opaque, and where misunderstandings create many unfair pay decisions. It's likely that your company has official standards for job levels, but also likely the way jobs are used in practice will vary from one business unit (or one person) to the next. Regular calibration of job expectations to job levels across the company is an essential habit for fair pay.

Every person assigned to a standard job level is expected to contribute to the overall success of the company according to the definition of that job level, regardless of whether the person is in marketing or human resources or management of the corporate jets. Definitions for each level will be written in the company's "job-leveling guide," a Rosetta Stone–like document that gives you specific key phrases to assess whether you are in the right level of job, and to sprinkle into your pay conversations when you are up for that next promotion. Consider these typical differences found in a job-leveling guide between a manager and a senior manager—the distinctions are subtle, but if your work sits in the senior manager category, you should expect to be paid like one:

	MANAGER	SENIOR MANAGER
Who you manage	Individual contributor professionals with a university degree	Other managers or advanced individual contributor professionals
What you manage	Results of the direct team and day-to-day technical guidance	Results of multiple related teams or one significant team within a function. Rarely offers direct technical guidance
How you manage	Adapts plans from function leaders	Develops plans for function leader approval
Your authority	Guided by policy	Guided by budgets

Many companies make this information available, but if yours does not, job-leveling guides are widely searchable online with little variation. Market survey vendors have no incentive to customize a job-leveling guide for themselves or a company, because companies could not easily participate in multiple compensation surveys if they did. Whatever you find online when searching for a generic job-leveling guide, especially if it comes from the "big three" firms mentioned in Chapter 2, is almost certainly close enough to what your company is using, if not the verbatim language.

Within the job-leveling guide you'll find about four basic groups of job levels, regardless of industry: support, professional (jobs that likely require a university degree), management, and executive. Some surveys have additional groups, for example at the support level to distinguish technical support from administrative support, what we think of as "blue-collar" jobs compared to office jobs. Each group has a number of fixed levels sorted as a hierarchy. Large companies may interpolate levels, meaning they take the standard set given in the surveys and insert what they cleverly call a "tweener" level between the two. The groups overlap at certain stages to reflect typical pay levels and to acknowledge the equivalent contributions of technical work and managerial responsibilities: a professional 1 (or P1) might be equivalent to a support 3 (or S3), with corresponding titles like analyst for the P1 and senior technician for the S3. The professional group will be eligible for more career progression and pay, whereas the support jobs might cap out at the equivalent of the professional 2 or 3 job level.

The job-leveling guide at your company will look similar to the table below, where each row has the same or similar pay ranges, and each combination of group and number has its own definition. In the above table, our manager definition is equivalent to the M2 and the senior manager is the M3 (the M1 is a supervisor, the M4 a director, and the M5 a senior director). Remember, knowing your survey job level is what matters in setting your pay rate. Titles are not enough, because they are unique to your company or industry, and smaller companies will not use the most senior levels in each group.

SUPPORT	PROFESSIONAL	MANAGEMENT	EXECUTIVE
			3
			2
			1
	6	5	
	5	4	
	4	3	
	3	2	
4	2	1	
3	1		
2			
1			

We still have more terms to define, but we now know enough to see how everything comes together to determine your pay range.

YOUR HOME ON THE RANGE

If there's one term in the compensation world that resonates outside the black box, it's the "pay grade." In any show about a detective trying to solve a case, at some point he will be accused of withholding information by a lower-level investigator. The detective will then say something like, "I'm sorry, that's above your pay grade," usually while sliding on sunglasses and slamming his car door. When we talk about pay grades, we are talking about both job levels and "pay ranges." Before we determine what fair pay looks like for you specifically, we need to talk more about how pay ranges work.

Pay ranges are the possible rates of pay for a job; they are not determined by the person in the job. A pay range will have a minimum, a midpoint, and a maximum. Pay ranges are stacked on top of one another in a reasonable progression from one job level to the next, called a "pay structure." Often, pay ranges overlap where the maximum of a lower-level pay range extends above the minimum of the range of the level above, which allows a company to hire highly experienced (or promote barely qualified) people for the job. To illustrate, here is an example portion of a pay structure with three pay ranges. Each job level is assigned a generic number or letter, called a "grade" or a "band" (a band-based range merges multiple grade-based ranges so it is usually wider). Large companies may have more than one range per job level.

JOB LEVEL	COMPANY GRADE	MINIMUM	MIDPOINT	MAXIMUM
Professional (P3)	42	56,000	66,000	76,000
Professional (P2)	41	48,500	57,000	65,500
Professional (P1)	40	42,500	50,000	57,500

The range midpoint will be set according to your company's compensation philosophy, which you'll recall usually means the 50th percentile of the market. Some companies offset their midpoints to be slightly above their minimum, leaving a lot of room between the midpoint and the maximum. More often, the midpoint is exactly as described, landing directly between the minimum and maximum. The difference between the minimum and maximum is called the "range spread," which in the table above is about 35 percent. Range spreads determine how much your pay can grow in the job you are in, and the spread will typically get wider as you move up in the organization, perhaps to 60 percent or more for the most senior jobs. Wider pay ranges account for the career expectation that you will move up quickly through the early ranks and settle into more senior roles. Wider ranges also allow more flexibility for businesses that need to hire highly paid senior leaders from outside companies, a practice that, if not managed carefully, is ripe for creating unequal-pay outcomes as legacy employees are often left behind. We will return to this problem in the next chapter.

The "midpoint progression" in the table above is about 15 percent from one grade to the next (the difference between $57,000 and $50,000). The percent will depend on the pace of economic growth for the country, and the cultural expectations around promotion frequency within countries. Pay ranges in China and India might have a high midpoint progression due to rapid economic growth, but manage this pace of change through additional "tweener" levels because there is also a high cultural expectation of frequent promotions. Pay ranges in Denmark, with its steady but lower economic growth and social egalitarianism, would see a lower midpoint progression and the standard set of survey levels. Having a consistent midpoint progression percent that carries through the whole pay structure is important; otherwise, as your career grows, you will need larger annual or promotion percentages to avoid being left behind relative to external hires. Too many companies overlook how this simple change can improve fair pay outcomes.

Every person should be paid within the range according to their job and level, though some companies allow a select group of people to be paid above the maximum or below the minimum. There's always an ill-defined, political story to these exceptions, and it's never favorable to the employee. If you're in this position, you should ask why and for how long your pay will fall outside your pay range. In my view, there are no acceptable reasons to pay someone below the pay range minimum. If your company has said you can do a job, you should be paid to do the job within the pay range they believe is competitive. There are acceptable reasons to pay above the pay range maximum, however, especially if you are uniquely technically gifted and can't be wedged into your company's overall pay design. But it's also possible that by being paid over the maximum, you are actually being underpaid because the next pay grade comes with a higher bonus or stock target that you are now not receiving. In almost all cases, you are being held back from the next level because the organizational design of your team comes with an arbitrary ceiling where you are bumping up against your manager's pay. Most companies don't want to have this fight, where managers are making less than their direct reports, but pay sincerity says no to limiting people's potential. The underpaid individuals shouldn't be punished because the company thinks conflict is yucky. If we can learn how to talk about pay more productively, and the rationale is valid, managers who are paid less than their direct reports will get over it.

When your compensation team creates a pay range, they emphatically believe the entire range can be considered competitive pay. From the minimum to the maximum of the pay range, everyone within those bounds is, from your company's perspective, paid according to market. As we've seen, these bounds can be very wide, and when you find out someone in the same job is earning 40 percent more than you, these assurances are not helpful. A competitive pay range does not mean your personal pay is competitive based on your specific experience and contributions. Remember, your goals and the company's goals are different.

While you are trying to optimize your own pay, your company is trying to optimize pay for the overall system, including those who are more and less experienced in the same job. Where you are placed in the pay range is critical, and now we will talk at length about how to discover and advocate for your appropriate range placement, closing the gap between what you are paid and what you should be paid.

Using the ranges in the table above, let's imagine you manage two people in a P2 job, Amara and Mateo. Let's also assume the company does not make pay ranges visible to employees. Amara is paid $60,000, and Mateo is paid $55,000. Which person is underpaid? Is it possible the answer is Amara?

Yes, absolutely.

When companies submit their pay data to survey vendors, in return they expect to find what the "market person" rate of pay is for each survey job match. Because data is submitted by hundreds (and sometimes thousands) of companies, the results end up looking like a normal distribution, meaning most people are bunched into about the same pay rate and have around the same degree of experience and performance level in the job. Often, this "person" will be someone with three to five years of experience performing in that job and job-level combination. At the ends of the spectrum should be people who were recently promoted or who have settled into the job many years ago without aspirations to move up.

If Amara has been in her job for fifteen years, performing well, and is seen as an irreplaceable expert on the team, then she has a screaming case to be paid more than her current rate of 5 percent over the midpoint of $57,000. There are few people in the marketplace as experienced as Amara. A more appropriate pay rate would be closer to the pay range maximum, about $65,000. An additional $5,000 each year, compounded over a thirty-year career at a market average 7 percent return, would total more than half a million dollars at retirement, a sizable down payment on a beach house. By not adjusting Amara's pay, you as a manager are denying her time in the sun.

If Mateo was recently promoted to the job, we can argue that he is paid too highly for his experience. He is one annual merit cycle away from being paid like the "market person," despite having less experience in the job and job level. However, the company may have known this and made a strategic decision to pay Mateo ahead of schedule to preempt another company enticing him away, especially if he is on the fast track to a senior executive job. If Mateo were to ask for a raise now, he should expect to get rejected. He is paid more than competitively. The right move for the company wouldn't be to increase Mateo's pay but to validate his potential by showing him a thoughtful, long-term talent plan (that will come with pay increases later) the company has designed for him.

Small pay choices in the wrong direction, regardless of intent, create unnecessary headaches for companies. The company assumed Amara's minimum viable pay number was $60,000, but only because she didn't know to ask for $65,000, since pay ranges were not made public. The difference wasn't noticeable enough for her to look for jobs elsewhere, but it was costing her significant life opportunity. Paying Amara and Mateo similarly to minimize the perception of unfair pay looked like a good idea on paper. But when Amara finds out she's been underpaid, she loses trust in the company, and both the company and Amara are worse off for the mismanagement.

How a pay range is created, where a person's pay is placed, and what choices are made in support of their potential and career growth are essential pieces of the fair-pay puzzle. Companies that operate with pay sincerity show their employees how the pieces fit together, explain why employees are paid what they are paid, and create an environment free of consequences when asked to defend pay decisions or to make adjustments when they've gotten it wrong.

DIVIDE AND CONQUER

When setting a pay range, a company can choose to group similar jobs and smooth over the market survey results using regression analysis. This leaves a reduced number of pay ranges (or one) per job level or pay grade. Alternatively, they can take a more granular approach to making pay ranges, called "market pricing." A market pricing approach creates a unique pay range for every job, based explicitly on market survey data. Here are the resulting differences:

BENCHMARKING METHOD:

JOB LEVEL	JOB	MINIMUM	MIDPOINT	MAXIMUM
Manager (M2)	All Company M2 Jobs	75,000	90,000	105,000

MARKET PRICING METHOD:

JOB LEVEL	JOB	MINIMUM	MIDPOINT	MAXIMUM
Manager (M2)	Brand Strategy	83,500	98,000	112,500
Manager (M2)	Social Media	76,500	90,000	103,500
Manager (M2)	Marketing Operations	69,500	82,000	94,500

Creating a unique pay range for each job through market pricing is a recipe for unfair pay, especially when jobs are similar. For a niche group of readers who work in my profession, this will be the most controversial section of the book, because it cuts against orthodoxy. True believers in market pricing *truly believe* in the approach. The reasoning makes intuitive sense—that to be market competitive, pay ranges should reflect only independent market sources and be unimpeachably free of company smoothing and bias, as pure as the driven snow.

In my experience, companies that choose this route put too much faith in the sanctity of their market survey data. They have not asked themselves hard enough questions about the problems market pricing can cause. Many assumptions go into how jobs are matched and the data submitted (by the most junior person on the compensation team), how jobs are maintained (by HR managers who haven't looked at a job description in years), or legacy biases the results may contain (historically male-dominated jobs score higher in part through the magic of compound growth). When jobs are unnecessarily divided, people are unnecessarily conquered.

Under a market pricing approach, the order of operations for assigning pay ranges starts with the market, followed by the company making decisions about fair pay. This is backward. Instead, we should start with fair pay and support these decisions with market data as warranted. We also need to know when to reject market data outright, a skill that becomes easier with practice when you hold fair pay at the center of your pay programs and can learn to more quickly spot problematic differences in the data.

If we want to talk more openly about pay, then companies will do themselves a favor by limiting the number of pay ranges used for each job level. The wonky counterargument, that survey data for jobs at the same job level can have remarkably different pay rates, can absolutely be true. A P4 data privacy specialist's market survey pay rate in 2020 will be materially more than a P4 financial analyst's, despite being at the same job level. But these differences are volatile from one year to the next, which gives you an inconsistent story to tell employees, an administrative nightmare, and an inefficient cost structure as you chase individual job market peaks every year.

The problems with market pricing begin when the data comes off spreadsheets and into people's lives. When, as a manager, you are asked to inform a cross-functional team who have delivered a major project together why historically female-dominated jobs like HR and communications are paid less than finance and IT, you will not be able to have a sincere (or fun) conversation with them. Conversely, if you need to round out a technical wizard for a broad leadership role in the future, will you expect him to take a lower-graded job for the long-term potential gain? In the table above, if a brand strategy manager earns $105,000 because he is highly experienced in the job level and needs to learn social media to lead a larger team later in his career, he will be paid over the pay range maximum by accepting the social media manager job. In many companies, he may now be ineligible for an annual pay increase. The positive professional development opportunity the company had planned is now a problem. Arbitrary complexity of pay ranges makes the compensation black box the high potential employee's career coffin.

The better approach is to batch market-priced job levels or adjacent jobs into a limited number of ranges. The idea of using fewer pay ranges is not a revelation, as many companies operate this way already. Some companies use ultra-wide ranges, called "broad-banding" (or pay bands), which after a certain stretching point makes the idea of a pay range meaningless. A clear strategy of using a consolidated number of meaningful ranges has two major advantages to market pricing: to enable and reinforce pay transparency, and to give a consistent platform for pay-equity initiatives (more on this in Chapter 7). This might mean disregarding the results of market data for jobs that are priced lower on a relative basis, but this should not be a concern if we understand that sometimes market data is wrong and we hold firmly to the idea that our first priority is fair pay. A hot job this year most certainly will not be within three years, so the business also saves the extra expense by choosing not to chase fads for the good of the overall pay system. Remember, most companies are only looking to pay what employees will see as credible, not what is market leading.

This harmonized way of thinking has a successful parallel in the financial community with people who call themselves "Bogleheads," after Jack Bogle, founder of the investment firm Vanguard. A Boglehead is someone who forgoes the intense effort required to pick individual stocks and instead chooses the radically simple strategy of investing using index funds designed to track the ups and downs of the overall market. This approach has been wildly successful for the average investor, keeping their stock-market gains high and their administrative fees low. Warren Buffett famously won a $1 million charity bet against a group of hedge fund managers when he chose an index fund to outperform these wizards of finance over a ten-year period. The results weren't close, as Buffett returned more than 7 percent annually to the hedge fund's 2 percent. When we overestimate our ability to pick winners and losers, or in our case to predict employee performance or the true value of certain jobs over others, we, too, reduce our likelihood of sustained success. Similarly, companies that maintain a fair, steady, and coherent compensation approach will come out ahead in the long run by building trust, reducing anxiety, and producing equitable returns across their "portfolio" of employees. When things go wrong, remember that people are not individual stocks to be dumped at the first sign of underperformance, but will appreciate over the long term as you regularly invest in them.

As many business models move toward hyper-optimized, automated personalization for customers, pay is an area where I believe we will see movement in the opposite direction. Radically simple infrastructures within companies will improve the health and equity of the overall internal system. Across companies, as reformed compensation philosophies emerge, personalization efforts will allow more choice in how people receive pay according to their needs, for example by trading some benefits for others or in the types of stock they are awarded. The baseline total rewards opportunity, however, will not vary much within fixed groupings like job level, pay grade, and (an equitably calibrated) performance rating within companies.

As David Epstein sees it in his coincidentally titled book, *Range*, "The more constrained and repetitive a challenge, the more likely it will be automated, while great rewards will accrue to those who can take conceptual knowledge from one problem or domain and apply it in an entirely new one." Epstein quotes economist Greg Duncan, who says, "Increasingly, jobs that pay well require employees to be able to solve unexpected problems, often while working in groups." In other words, companies that remove artificial pay barriers, like indefensible differences in pay ranges, and that recognize that the definition and contribution of a job itself is becoming more fluid, will be more adept to course correct at scale when necessary. For companies with legacy gender and racial wage gaps, eliminating barriers caused by market pricing can be a catalyst for equitable change.

Understanding the ways your company prices jobs and creates pay ranges is an essential step in developing your personal fair-pay strategy. In the next chapter, we'll apply this thinking to give you a plan tailored to your situation. Before we get there, we need to review one more scenario ripe for pay insincerity: how we talk about your total pay package.

THE TOTAL REWARDS TRAP

Pay decisions are made in the context of what are called "total rewards," the total package of what a company gives you in return for your work. WorldatWork, the compensation field's credentialing body, includes five elements to its total rewards model: compensation, well-being, benefits, development, and recognition. At least prior to the work-from-home revolution instigated by the 2020 pandemic, work environment was important, too. Aaron Dignan, speaking of compounding perks at high-wage employers in his book *Brave New Work*, says that "in the war for talent, the modern workplace looks more and more like an all-expenses-paid trip to Club Bureaucracy." As such, I can rank my last three companies by their employee sauna experiences.

Each element of the total rewards package is important, and high-performing companies create flexibility in their plans to meet both the market's expectations and the employee's personal needs, caring for both the forest and the individual tree. Total rewards, as a holistic unit, matters because pay isn't always the biggest pain point in your career. Sometimes a vacation, an opportunity to lead a big project, or recognition through a "nice job" with a wink and a finger gun from the boss is enough to keep you engaged. When things aren't going well at work, more money can help but isn't always the solution, especially if you already have a healthy savings account.

The idea of total rewards can also be a trap. The "total rewards trap" happens when fair pay is substituted for less tangible levers, like nonmonetary recognition and career development, and then regifted to you as a better deal. Substitution of time for money is a common example, like when new parents are told (or it is implied) that flexibility must come at the expense of their pay and career opportunity, despite working the same number of hours as everyone else. For total rewards to work as a cohesive unit, there is no substitute for starting with fair pay. Any attempt otherwise is a shell game that produces cynicism. As I once heard a San Francisco busker shout to a group of freeloading tourists (including me), while we all clapped along to his music, "Tell my landlord how much you liked the show!"

Those especially vulnerable to the total rewards trap work in jobs that are isolated from comparable peers. As a result, they do not receive the shared benefits of broad or adjacent market pay increases. In a corporate environment, most jobs have a substitute —a job a person can reasonably move into if their personal and professional needs are not being met, or if they hate their current manager. If you are an operational expert, your analytical and change-management skills can transfer into any number of similar back-of-house teams like project management or human resources. When you have substitute job options, your internal market value will be similar across each, because smart companies try to make pay plans simple to lessen noise across employee groups who will move around the organization and talk to each other about pay. Companies that thoughtfully batch jobs (and pay ranges) together are therefore more likely to recognize broad and equitable pay increases for everyone. Culturally, most companies try to avoid segmenting their jobs into "haves" and "have-nots," because they know there will always be a new shiny object vying for attention and higher pay. If one group needs additional pay now, the rest of the organization is not far behind in asking for their turn. Rather than play these perpetual whack-a-mole games, compensation teams will instead take systematic actions like increasing overall pay ranges or loosening the rules on who in the company gets to receive what kind of stock or benefit. Jobs that are left out of this batching game are effectively penalized.

Jobs with more substitutes, you will be shocked to hear, are historically male dominated (a clear racial dynamic also exists). Men through the years have had more career options than women in the corporate world, and therefore a head start working in environments with substitute jobs, moving about from one job to the next in their companies and expecting pay growth with each job change. Because of this substitute job effect, men have benefited through the twin superpowers of process inertia and compound growth, relative to the more limited career options thought appropriate for women.

Jobs without ready substitutes are often "paid" through a sense of deep personal meaning, purpose, or pride, and culturally we assume this to be a good and fair deal without asking too many questions. We should recognize the ingrained level of insincerity in this assumption as the total rewards trap.

In some cases, where you willingly give up one total rewards lever for another, the trade-offs make sense and you can make informed choices based on your personal values. Early in its history, when JCPenney was based in New York, the company was known for capping base pay and instead chose to load employees up with above-market stock as a sign of the company's growth potential. Amazon is known to do this currently, and has minted scores of millionaires in the process. For many years, a rapidly growing stock price meant the trade-off of less base pay but more stock worked great for employees of JCPenney. Now in bankruptcy protection after many years circling the drain, a share of JCPenney stock can be purchased for less than $1. When I lived in Texas, I'd often use the (relocated) JCPenney corporate campus as a running track because it was almost always empty. Times change, and it's important to know what the worst possibilities are for the total rewards trade-offs you are willing to make.

Or consider the total rewards case for the US National Security Agency (NSA). The NSA has to hire the world's best data security professionals but knows it can't compete with the top tech firms on pay because of an inherent expectation of stewardship in using taxpayer funds (some of you will laugh, I'm sure). Instead, the NSA transparently makes its total rewards case to applicants not by low-balling pay but by being "good enough" on pay and supplementing with excellent benefits, job security, intrigue, and a deep feeling of purpose and patriotism. If your personal ambitions and values align with the total rewards trade-offs you'll have to make, and if you have the ability to hold a company to account when that alignment breaks, there is no trap in the deal because your essential needs of fair pay are met, the company (or agency) has been transparent about its practices, and you are making an informed decision based on your values.

Within every total rewards model is also a prescription for either failing or taking advantage of people through the total rewards trap. You should always know what is negotiable and what is not (more on this in the next chapter), and how the company approaches decisions around investments in their workers so you can hold them accountable. This is important as more industries and jobs converge. Mega companies are now poaching whole university academic departments, retailers are starting to look like tech companies, and dramatically different total rewards models are being lumped together for the first time. When taking a job or figuring out how much you are worth, you must think carefully about the definitions your company uses when talking about pay and account fully for your total rewards. Regardless of the company's pay design or philosophy, the basic expectation of sincerity should be the same. Is your company *relentlessly pursuing equitable and transparent pay, providing for the essentials of a decent life, and helping people seek the full reward of their contributions and potential?* You are worth at least that much.

If not, let's put it all together and get you a raise.

PART II

PAY AS IT COULD BE

CHAPTER 6

What to Expect When You're Expecting (a Raise)

Compensation is not secrets-of-the-crystal-skulls kind of stuff; there is no decoder ring I can send you or formula to learn that guarantees you will get a pay raise. When pay is unfair or perceived to be unfair, it's usually because people like me have refused to share basic information with you, which leaves you unable to challenge us or has you sitting in a constant state of uncertainty. Once you learn the language and understand the frameworks that guide pay decisions, you can adapt a strategy unique to your situation to determine how and when to ask for a raise or change your company's practices. Having a good strategy can avoid months of mealymouthed corporate doublespeak from people like me.

Companies need to recognize the outsized role they play in creating fair pay outcomes. When companies help their people bridge information and conversation gaps about pay, they become more competitive because all companies want their people focused on the most value-added tasks as much of the time as possible. Arguing about pay is not helping anyone have more time to do meaningful work. People in jobs like mine need to give you information to make sure your pay is fair, so we, too, can get to more meaningful work.

We need to ask better questions about pay to hold the whole system accountable. We need a more relevant way of assessing who needs a raise to reflect not only their market value but their contributions, potential, and life necessities. We need a new model for thinking and talking about pay.

THE FAIR PAY MIX

In 1960, a marketing professor named E. Jerome McCarthy published a textbook called *Basic Marketing: A Managerial Approach.* The book became one of the best-selling university textbooks ever and is now taught in business schools worldwide. One of McCarthy's most enduring ideas, called the "marketing mix," bridged the gap between practitioners and academics to help companies better serve their customers.

McCarthy saw the need for the marketing profession to mature from a focus on independent activities like buying and selling to a focus on integrated problem solving—a shift from the "functional approach" to what he called the "managerial approach." The marketing mix idea helped managers make decisions using a conceptual framework called the "Four P's": product, price, place, and promotion.

Under the functional approach, if a company has a bottle of soap to sell, it designs a plan for each activity independently. The price might be set according to a standard markup on what it cost to produce or pegged to what other soaps in the store aisle cost. Advertising would be designed for a target market deemed the most likely buyers. And distribution would be managed like any other soap, packed together and sent to every store in the city.

Using the newer managerial approach, the soap would not exist without first studying what customer problem the product would solve.

The marketing team will come up with an integrated understanding of what bottle shape the target market prefers (product), what they are willing to pay (price), which kinds of stores should carry it (place), and whether social media influencers should be conscripted (promotion) to use the new soap on their designer countertops. The managerial approach is why some soaps—like those with minimalist label design and natural ingredients—can only be found at specialty grocers and cost twice the amount of standard soaps, despite having equivalent functional value of making dirty things clean. The customer problem being solved, I suppose, is to serve the kind of person who didn't know how much joy they could spark in feeling superior to others about their soap choices.

The customer problems in making pay fair are similar. Customers (employees) are underserved because company practitioners approach the problem with a functional view, managing pay through independent activities like completing pay surveys and running annual merit processes, all with the goal of paying people the minimum viable amount necessary to attract and retain talent. An integrated understanding of the employee's needs is at best a secondary priority and, more often, never considered at all.

Given the enduring relevance of the marketing mix and my abounding affection for alliteration, I propose the compensation field adapt a similar model, making its own shift away from functional outcomes of independent business activities and toward an integrated framework that considers the needs of both the business and the employee. Pay should be managed to do more than attract and retain people but also to solve employee problems, and businesses should operate with an employee-first mindset instead of maintaining the charade that being market-competitive is the same as being people-relevant. In this model, people know what they are worth and are never paid less because of their gender or race. Full-time workers don't file for government food assistance because their paychecks are too low, and no one is fired for a last-minute shift change they can't manage due to not having childcare coverage. Everyone can provide for the essential needs of themselves and their families, trusting that tomorrow can be better than today because an upwardly mobile career path awaits them. The soaps that don't work fail quickly and those that contain harmful chemicals are legislated off the shelves.

To create and sustain this model, where pay sincerity thrives, the givers (your company) and receivers (you) of pay can approach decisions through our own Four P's, what I'm calling the Fair Pay Mix: process, permission, priority, and power. Each "P" gives us a unique opportunity for solving our pay problems. When asking for more pay or fixing the way your company operates, start with assessing which kind of pay problem you have.

Which Fair Pay Mix P (or P's, plural) fits your situation best?

- The **process** your company uses to set and increase people's pay has left you uninformed, behind, or at a disadvantage.
- You are being hired, promoted, or otherwise have the opportunity to talk about pay, but not sure you have **permission** to do so without risk of retaliation.
- Your company has not made fair pay a **priority** and is falling behind on its promises, values, and pay philosophy.
- Your essential needs are going unmet and you have no **power** to force change.

For each of our Fair Pay Mix P scenarios, I will show how to make a compelling case for more pay. Each P comes with pragmatic guidelines as you decide the right entry point. As we go through each example, consider how multiple P's may apply, and in which order you should make your case. You should have a concise, simple story to tell about your pay, which means initiating the pay conversation with a single P, and reinforcing with the other three P's when possible. In our soap example, the aesthetic case alone is enough for a certain type of customer to make the purchase, as long as the price is within reason and they don't have to drive across town to purchase it. In other cases, like in a deep-clean-before-moving-apartments situation, you may want the cheapest and most powerful soap available to make sure you get your security deposit back, natural ingredients aside. Knowing when and how to use each fair-pay P is critical, and throwing every P at your company at once will muddle your message and overload the argument. Companies, think about your employees being on the other side of these requests and how you can make it easier for them (and therefore yourself) to accommodate their concerns and to navigate the pay conversation.

Before embarking on one or more Fair Pay Mix strategies, first take three steps, in sequential order:

1. Assess your job description to see that the job and job level match the work you actually do.

2. Understand the job's pay range and where your pay is set within the range.

3. Have an open conversation with your manager or HR representative about your career, without mentioning pay.

In companies or work environments where the first two steps are not possible because the company hasn't created formal jobs and pay ranges or the information is under lock and key, start at the third step. When asking for information about steps one and two, keep the focus on career as context, and stay away from pay. Most companies make documenting their employees' career aspirations part of their annual goal-setting process, and this is a natural time to start the conversations that inevitably lead to pay. At other times of the year, one way to enter the career conversation is by asking for help on your long-term personal goals. By detaching a surprise career conversation from an immediate expectation for change, your manager can speak more openly about the various paths they see for you and won't assume you are giving them an ultimatum. Career is a low-risk conversation, and good practice for the harder conversation to come later about pay. If we are trying to fail quickly and cheaply, getting a reality check on your career might help you end up with a different pay strategy than you initially planned. You'll also find your manager is as lost as you are and equally uncomfortable talking about pay. You and your manager have something in common—you are both employees, and you both want to grow in your careers and be paid fairly. Opening up pay conversations in companies where managers do not have unilateral power to make decisions about your pay and career is hard for them, too, because they have the same questions about themselves.

Leading with career—if only as a Trojan horse—is critical. As soon as you mention pay, a host of administrative alarm bells will go off for your manager, who will take a career risk of their own by advocating for more pay on your behalf, assuming they can't make the decision themselves. Budgets must be checked. Approvals must be gained. Forms must be completed. Ultimately, you have to make the case for more pay simple enough that it can be sent up the chain of command without delay or being twisted. Ask for a trivial pay adjustment of a few percentage points, mistime the request, or take the wrong Fair Pay Mix approach, and you've missed your chance for a raise. To paraphrase the comedian Steve Martin, your case for more pay has to be "so good they can't ignore you."

THE FAIR PAY MIX: PROCESS

The first P of the Fair Pay Mix is "process," meaning the ongoing maintenance activities a company performs to set and increase people's pay, like annual reviews and hiring and promotion practices. To make a process case for more pay, you have to successfully identify a gap between your own pay and your company's pay philosophy that is unresolvable by the company's standard pay programs. You are telling your company that their processes are broken and have therefore left your pay behind.

Process cases start with knowing and working your company calendar. Every company has some form of central pay-review process in place. In most cases, this is administered annually by HR immediately after the fiscal year closes. Many companies review pay in the middle of the year, too, but typically use this event to focus on a small percentage of people they deem to be top performers or have high potential for future leadership roles. Almost all companies will review pay on an ad hoc basis as well, as long as the problems are severe and urgent (see the third fair-pay P, priority).

To make a process case, you need basic knowledge of how the pay programs at your company work, and what basic outcome you can expect if you choose not to take any action. Assuming your company has a formal annual process in place, your first expectation is that almost everyone will receive some amount of pay increase and you will benefit from this inertia by simply being employed and performing adequately.

But if your goal is to get a meaningful pay adjustment, you need to know what meaningful looks like beyond what is typically possible in the regular cycle.

Each year, assuming the company is financially steady, a pool of money will be set aside to increase pay. During the annual pay cycle, nearly everyone with a pulse can expect a small pay increase, because companies view this event as automatic, like paying the electricity bill. If you're not only trying to keep the lights on but you want to see your name in neon on the marquee, you need the annual event to mean something special. And by the way, your actual electricity bill probably went up, too, so you need a little more money to keep up.

This pool of money will be determined by the country you work in (or in expat situations, the country where your payroll is based). Some companies allocate more or less to specific groups like executives or technology, but most spread the same budget to everyone (the technical term is "peanut-buttering"). The budget number is generated far in advance of the process, typically in the previous spring, as survey vendors ask participating companies what they expect to spend for the year. Usually, the number is a best guess from one of the more junior members of the compensation team who has absolutely no clue what the business will be able to spend up to a year beyond the submission date. Take note, economists: the way businesses model wage increases is not as robust as you might hope.

The US "market" annual pay increase pool has been a constant 3 percent for at least a decade (while unemployment ranged from less than 4 percent to more than 14 percent), again based more on inertia than market conditions. Things like world events, tax policy, and the political party in power are not considered except as generic sentiment measures. In other parts of the world, the pool can be much higher and far more volatile, especially where inflation is high. While most of Europe has held stable in the 2 to 4 percent range, China has managed between 5 to 8 percent, India is often over 10 percent, and survey companies have given up reporting for Venezuela, where hyperinflation has crossed the 1 million percent barrier. Your company is unlikely to give you this number if you ask, because they don't want to have appeared committed to the expense if business turns sour, but it's not hard to figure out. Generally, the reported market budget will be a touch higher than inflation to allow the employee to experience a minimum viable amount of real wage growth each year. Knowing the budget amount functions as your basic expectation of saying nothing about your pay and letting the process run its course. From there, you can also estimate the maximum amount.

The traditional model for distributing pay in the annual cycle is through a matrix that factors in your pay range position and your performance rating, if applicable. Your "range position" is a ratio showing how your pay fits into the job's pay range. The calculation is your pay divided by your pay range midpoint. If you are paid $105,000 and the pay range midpoint is $100,000, your range position is 105 percent. The semantics may differ, and your company might call this number a "compa-ratio," or calculate it in a slightly different way called "range penetration" on a 0 to 100 scale, with 50 representing the midpoint. No matter, the idea is the same: how your pay compares to an internal reference point.

YOUR PAY

ANNUAL PAY	RANGE MINIMUM	RANGE MIDPOINT	RANGE MAXIMUM
105,000	80,000	100,000	120,000

YOUR PLACEMENT

CALCULATION TYPE	CALCULATION	RESULT
Range Position	(Annual Pay) / (Midpoint)	105.0%
Range Penetration	(Annual Pay – Minimum) / (Maximum – Minimum)	62.5%

Examples of pay matrices are widely searchable online, but in most cases look something like the table below. In the example, we assume your company has to distribute a 3 percent total budget using a three-point (high, average, below average) performance rating scale:

YOUR RANGE POSITION

YOUR PERFORMANCE	BOTTOM THIRD	MIDDLE THIRD	TOP THIRD
High	6%	5%	4%
Average	4%	3%	2%
Below Average	2%	1%	0%

Your company may divide the sections not into thirds, but fourths or fifths, or not at all (more on that in a bit). The top left cell, reserved for people who are top performers and positioned low in the pay range, is shown here as 6 percent, or twice the budget amount, but all sorts of multiples are possible. Using our example, a range position of 105 percent (or 62.5 percent range penetration) would probably put you in the middle third, so according to the table your annual increase will be 1, 3, or 5 percent depending on your performance. Managers are often given discretion in the award, so these values could be merely a recommendation. However individual increases are determined, the distribution is a zero-sum game, where for you to get 5 percent, another person will have to get 1 percent to balance the budget. Each year, a matrix like this will be developed for every country, with the total expense rolling up to senior leaders for approval. As long as it all sums up to the 3 percent, the boss won't look at much else.

As you look over the matrix, see how the highest possible pay increase is only 6 percent. This may not feel like much, especially if it means for you to receive more, others have to receive less. That's not where the challenges stop. If you are promoted at the same time as the annual process, your 6 percent is likely to be rolled into your total promotional increase, effectively nullifying the annual increase event for you. Or if your company pay strategy is to lag market, as discussed in Chapter 4, your range position will be at its highest point during the annual process, again limiting your pay increase. Here is a good technique: to get the biggest pay increase possible, always try to get promoted or ask for a raise at the exact opposite time of year as your annual pay increase, assuming your company doesn't hold rigid windows during the year when they allow promotions. If your fiscal year ends in December, ask in June. Come too close to the annual review, and you'll be shortchanged like a child whose birthday comes a week before Christmas.

As you progress through your pay range, notice how your pay increase actually gets smaller—if you are a high performer and in the bottom third of your range, your expected pay increase is 6 percent, but it is only 4 percent if you are in the top third. Or notice how an average performer can get the same as a high performer, assuming the average performer is lower in the pay range. These observations are without doubt the most commonly asked questions to people in my profession, and for good reason. It looks odd, and it seems unfair. But these distinctions are essential.

In Chapter 5, we talked about the "market person," where the market rate of pay is assumed to be what a typical person who has worked in a job for a few years should make. Annual increases follow the same idea. If you are low in the range and performing like the market person, the matrix will accelerate your pay to catch up in acknowledgment that you are contributing ahead of schedule. For those who are high in the range and are already paid ahead of the market person, outcontributing the market person is the expectation. What you want to avoid is being high in the range and a low performer. If that's you, brush up your résumé because your employment situation is tenuous.

If you wait for the formal annual process to address your pay, your increase will be capped at 6 percent. In China, a matrix with a budget of 6 percent may earn you up to a 12 percent pay increase. Most years, this will be enough, assuming you have made a strong permission case and asked for the right amount of pay when you were hired and last promoted, as described in the next section. But sometimes this system doesn't work well, especially when you are far behind where you should be or where annual pay increases are not managed in a differentiated way through pay ranges, and instead the same percentage amount is given out for everyone through flat increases. In these situations, your pay will fall behind market over time, and you will need to make an explicit process case for more pay outside your annual pay cycle because your company's processes are broken.

Companies that make flat increases, through the annual cycle or at time of promotion, do so with the best of intentions. Flat increases look fair by eliminating different treatment within the same level of job performance. This is an easy story for companies to tell, but it harms companies and employees in their pursuit of fair and equitable pay by compounding bad pay decisions over time.

To demonstrate, let's see how a financial analyst named Alex will see her pay grow through a program that gives her annual pay increases of 3 percent each year. We'll assume her pay range has a midpoint of $60,000 that grows by 2 percent each year, a common amount in the United States, as market-based pay ranges tend to track slightly below the market budget amount:

YEAR	PAY	RANGE MIDPOINT	RANGE POSITION
New Hire	50,000	60,000	83%
Year 1	51,500	61,200	84%
Year 2	53,000	62,400	85%
Year 3	54,600	63,600	86%
Year 4	56,200	64,900	87%
Year 5	57,900	66,200	88%

After five years in the same job, Alex's experience should put her at the upper end of being the "market person." She should be excellent at her job by now and paid as such. Sadly, something has gone wrong, as her pay is at 88 percent, well below the expected market midpoint. Normally, we'd expect an 88 percent range position for someone who has been recently promoted or hired and who is learning the skills it takes to do the job. That's not Alex anymore.

The merit matrix won't solve the problem for her. If she were given a 6 percent increase each year, which is double the market rate and the maximum amount possible in our sample matrix, her range position would only be 101 percent. Because of the compounding effects of poor decision-making by her company, though made with "fair" intentions, she is now materially underpaid relative to her true market value. If a company down the street has a similar job at her level available, she could easily take her experience there and expect to be paid $70,000 or more for the same work. Alex should take this argument to her manager and ask why she isn't placed at her appropriate range position. If the company declines to adjust her pay, then congratulations to Alex on her immediate 20 percent pay raise at the new company.

Making a process case for more pay starts with knowing your company calendar and programs and assessing how your pay will fare over time without your speaking up. For low-wage work, the same effect demonstrates the importance of a legislative process, like automatically indexing minimum wage increases to a measure like inflation. If due to the failures of the company's processes, you can show a meaningful gap (10 percent or more) between what you are paid and what you should be paid, you can inspire your company to both increase your pay and fix their processes. If that doesn't work, you have three remaining P's in the Fair Pay Mix arsenal.

THE FAIR PAY MIX: PERMISSION

The next P in the Fair Pay Mix is "permission." Opportunities to build a permission case for more pay are event-based, like when you are hired, promoted, or otherwise have been asked about your pay, but you are not sure what to say without risk of loss or retaliation. When power, our final P, is not shared between the givers and receivers of pay, you as an employee are often starting these pay conversations at a disadvantage. There are rare opportunities where this power dynamic is in your favor, and where you are expected to ask for more money. A missed permission opportunity can follow you for years, forcing you to make a much riskier process case later in your employment after you've fallen behind. Had Alex been hired at $55,000 instead of $50,000, and paid according to a range position matrix with 5 percent average increases, her pay would be $70,000 after five years instead of $57,900. She may not have returned the recruiter's call.

The most common permission opportunities are when you are promoted and when you are hired. This is the time your company expects you to speak up. They've already made the decision to invest in your career, and you shouldn't waste the opportunity to insist on fair pay. In both events, your new pay should be based on your range position. With promotions, you should always ask where the new job places you in the pay range. When you're new to a job level, a range placement below the midpoint and "market person" is appropriate, but you need to make sure your pay isn't so low that you will never hit the top part of the pay range through your company's normal pay processes, as shown in the last section. Frequently, companies set pay increases for promotions as a fixed maximum percentage, usually 10 or 15 percent, and again we see fixed increases as visually appearing fair, and problematic in practice. If you've rapidly moved up the ranks, you may need a large "catch-up" pay increase far above the policy limit.

Taking a new job at an outside company is a special type of permission case, and one you must get right. A lot has been written about salary negotiations from the view of the job seeker; most of it essentially has you guessing what the employer is thinking and gives you tips to Jedi mind trick your way around their traps. Let me tell you what we really are thinking, and how to game us without using The Force.

Knowing your minimum viable pay number is important at all times, but especially so at time of hire. In our earlier example, our underpaid expert Alex would never have known to ask for a pay increase or at what value she should be seeking. Let's now assume her process case for more pay was either rejected or she was too afraid to ask, and she has to return a call from a recruiter at another company for a lateral job change at the same job level.

At some point in the recruiter conversation—and perhaps very early on as a screening tool—the recruiter will ask about salary expectations. This is your time to shine, and I want you to imagine the next sentences being read through a series of connected megaphones to make it as loud as possible.

Do not share your MVP number before you have received an offer. Do not give a range you are comfortable with. Even then, only share your number if necessary because the offer has come back too low.

You have no obligation to share your desired pay number. If a recruiter says they require a number to push your application forward, this is a sign they have bad or lazy processes in place. Think carefully about what that means for the quality of their human resources department and, therefore, your future pay and career growth at the company. There is no upside for you in giving away your pay number. It is not insincere to withhold your pay needs at time of hire, because pay transparency should not be a one-way street where only you have to give up the goods. The ultimate accountability for making sure a company pays fairly rests with the givers of pay, not you as the receiver. To see why, let's continue with our process case example and Alex. She knows she is worth $70,000, and for ease let's assume she also knows her current company's compensation philosophy sets pay at the 50th percentile, as most companies do. There are three potential outcomes from the recruiter call.

First, the offer could come back underwhelming, in this case $60,000. Alex makes $57,900 now, and unless the new company is more exciting, or she hates her current boss, or the proposed total rewards package is more compelling with a higher bonus target, a stock grant, or greater career opportunity, she is unlikely to change jobs. Alex's current company may not respond to a counteroffer at $60,000, because it doesn't pass our 10 percent significance test, or if they do, they will wonder why she went to so much trouble for such little reward. They are not thinking about her future retirement beach house.

The new company could be low-balling Alex, an insincere pay strategy, but it's more likely their pay ranges are either poorly designed or they have set their desired pay position lower on purpose to account for something else in the total rewards package, like a higher bonus target. In either case, Alex knows her number is $70,000 and she should feel confident asking for it. If they don't agree, she's lost nothing, and she can wait for her company to wise up or the next opportunity to come along.

The second option is that the offer comes back much higher than Alex could have imagined. Companies don't advertise their desired pay positioning, and therefore she doesn't want to limit her opportunity if she's unexpectedly found a company that positions itself higher than the market median. If the new company has offered Alex more than her MVP number, she is not done. Alex should still ask her prospective employer where this places her in the new range. If Alex is well above the "market-person" in experience, her expectation should be to get placed high in *their* range, as she will surely be working alongside people paid this way with equivalent experience. If the new company doesn't agree to revising their offer, then congratulations to Alex because she has already exceeded her MVP number. After a couple years working at the new company, once she's established credibility, Alex can then make an effective process case to show she is paid too low according to the company's ranges and her contributions.

The third option exists only if you've shared your current rate of pay or MVP expectations (whoops!), and the company has simply added a percentage to that amount. Any company that operates this way is a company you should assume is rife with pay inequity. Again, fixed percentage pay increases often seem fair at first, but the practice creates risk by importing the pay philosophies and positioning of other companies. If a tech company wants to sell physical products in addition to its software, and they begin recruiting from the majority female consumer goods industry alongside majority male technology companies for similar jobs, a fixed percentage approach may lead to higher starting salaries and sign-on bonuses for men. The two industries also have different norms for an employee's pay mix, where top technology companies rely heavily on stock as a part of the pay package. The recruiting tech company, by using a fixed increase approach, will be excited to find it can cheaply recruit talented workers from other industries, but the inequities these practices create are paid for later in lack of trust and engagement (and maybe literally through lawsuits). Alternatively, when companies are unaware of a person's total compensation package, or when they've made their pay programs transparent from the start, it forces them to design consistent pay guidelines for all candidates.

To prevent this third option, where the employee is forced to carry the mistakes or differences of their past employers forever, many governments have passed laws limiting a company's ability to ask about salary history. States as politically and socially opposite as California and Alabama have recognized how important this practice is in establishing fair pay, and that the burden of pay transparency shouldn't sit only with the receivers.

From a company point of view, prohibitions against asking about salary history are the kind of law that some call onerous regulation, an undue barrier preventing the free(ish) hand of the market from operating with efficiency. This is short-term thinking, usually from people who are nowhere near the arena of making job offers, or who have a mental tic against all regulation generally. Salary history laws might make the lives of recruiters harder in the short run, especially if the recruiter is measured on volume or time-to-fulfill metrics. It is true that a recruiter will have duplicate work when their initial offer is well below the person's MVP. But in the long run, after the company has taken the time to review their recruitment practices and compensation programs with a bent toward pay sincerity, not asking for salary history makes life much easier and more efficient for everyone.

To recap, don't share your MVP number until you have to. When pressed by the recruiter, say something like this: "I'm excited at the thought of working with you, and I trust you will make a fair offer based on your compensation philosophy and my significant experience at this job level." Be sure to hint to the new company exactly where you expect to be positioned within their ranges, assuming that position is high.

Once companies have made the internal changes necessary in their shift toward pay sincerity, they can eliminate pay negotiations in most cases. For most job offers, there will be no need to negotiate, as givers and receivers begin to operate with the same information and in good faith. What was a negotiation is now a transaction. You know exactly what kind of soap you are buying, and you select accordingly. Companies that successfully make the transition will still have pay problems to placate and exceptions to approve, as human behavior makes the compensation field imperfect, but I'd argue that less negotiation can be a good thing.

A common trope about salary negotiation, and equal pay generally, is that women don't receive raises because they don't ask as often as men. Recent research, however, suggests women do ask as often as men, but receive a raise only 15 percent of the time, compared to 20 percent for men. If pay sincerity *helps people seek the full reward of their contributions and potential,* then reducing the need for salary negotiations that work in men's favor relative to women is an important goal. In either case, the chances of winning a negotiation with your employer are not good, so this is a practice you shouldn't come to rely on in making sure your pay is fair.

Until the day comes when the way we pay is transformed and workers trust their employers fully, making salary negotiation irrelevant, we can at least make salary negotiation better. This starts with helping you focus your energy on what matters, by understanding what is negotiable and what is not at most companies. Typically, the larger a company is, or the lower in the organization you are, the less negotiation ability you have. A helpful way to think about pay negotiation at large companies is whether a software system can be designed to reliably keep track of all the little customization choices the company has made over time. Unfortunately, most company software systems, and especially the ones at large companies, are about as flexible as a pair of eyeglasses.

Things like bonus and stock targets or employee benefits are not generally negotiable unless you are an executive. The systems administration of these programs requires as little variation as possible, and in some cases requires legal or board approval to make exceptions. Instead, focus your negotiation energy into your base pay and sign-on pay, which are onetime events and do not need to be specially tracked and maintained in a system across multiple years.

While base pay negotiations should follow your MVP strategy, sign-on cash or stock is where you can exercise leverage. A common approach companies take is to make sure you don't lose anything from your last job over the next twelve months, what we'd call "keeping you whole." By offering to pay you in cash or stock for the next twelve months of lost payouts, companies understand and will try to acknowledge that by leaving your current employer, you will forfeit your current company bonus target and unvested stock. When taking a new job, you should expect at a minimum to be kept whole, on a total rewards basis, unless you've made the mistake of sharing your current pay package and the new company already knows they are offering you a major pay increase.

Beyond twelve months, the company will expect their own programs to be a comparable substitute. This is where you need to assess the total rewards trap, especially with any vesting schedule trade-offs you are making, meaning how many months or years it will take for you to receive the full value of the cash or stock being promised. I know of one major company that gives eye-popping new-hire stock grants but designs them to vest only 5 percent in each of the first two years of employment. This is much slower than typical market practice, where awards vest in equal amounts over three to four years. This means you will receive the promise of a lot of money during the first two years, but not actually receive much of anything. The company, knowing they have this advantage and a line of people willing to work for them, is well known for making every effort to burn people out before they receive any real value from the stock award. From a shareholder primacy lens, it's honestly brilliant if not pathological.

When you are changing employers, you have to be direct and clear about what you are giving up and what you need, and at time of hire you have permission to ask. You only get one shot at this. Unless you are an executive, only onetime changes like base pay, sign-on cash or stock, and special reimbursements for relocation or health coverage waiting periods are on the table. Beyond these opportunities, don't expect to hear yes to much else.

The permission P is your best, least-risky chance to make sure your pay is fair. When you know your numbers, you don't need a secret script to persuade the other side. Take a cue from compensation pros when we decide to change companies—we don't negotiate because we know what we're worth. When you join a new company or are offered a promotion, don't miss the opportunity to ask for what you need.

THE FAIR PAY MIX: PRIORITY

The "priority" case in the Fair Pay Mix exists when your company needs to be shaken up. In these situations, we need to convince your company to do some self-reflection and to make fair pay a priority. Your managers will not only have to be brought into the idea of fair pay, but prosecute the case themselves with their leaders and initiate hard changes that may take years to bear fruit. You'll know you need to make a priority case when you see the following indicators:

- People leave to take lateral or reduced jobs.
- Full-time employees struggle to pay their bills.
- The company has no pay philosophy or other means of being held accountable.
- The finance team has more control over your pay than your manager.
- Executives are the only ones receiving meaningful pay increases.
- No one from your team is getting promoted but more external hires are coming in.
- Employees are never asked for feedback about their pay.
- There is no evidence an equal-pay analysis has ever been run.
- Pay transparency is nonexistent.

Priority cases require bold leadership; this work cannot be delegated or outsourced. These are voluntary actions where the company's leaders, through either goodwill and benevolence or exhaustion and submission, decide to make material investments in their employees. When companies make fair pay a priority, they either catch up to or opt out of our three-legged-race problem of what they see as being market competitive. With a priority case, the company must put pay higher in the budgeting hierarchy and as a result forgo some other investment, like a new parking garage or dividends, which they will not want to do. Based on our shareholder primacy model, wages are a last-resort investment opportunity. To gain approval for pay increases, then, executives must be able to make the case to shareholders, who would prefer to keep the money for themselves.

Brian Cornell, CEO of Target, made a clear and public priority case in talking about the company's multiyear plan to raise minimum pay to $15 an hour, which the company announced ahead of its peers Walmart and Amazon. When pay rates make the news, it is because these companies are outliers to the market. There was no market survey data telling the compensation team at Target this was the right thing to do, and even today (years later!) these rates do not show up in the standard surveys as the market norm. In his explanation, Cornell tied the pay increase directly to the company's seasonal hiring goals that would allow stores to service customers during the busiest time of year: "I think that investment we made in wages had made us an employer of choice, so we are seeing a great reaction to our offering, we're getting a great response from team members. They recognize we're investing in their futures."

Fair pay has to be made a priority at the most senior levels, because in some situations, pay decisions have to be dictated and made collectively. Individual managers making good pay decisions will not be enough to make fair pay work at scale. This is true across the income spectrum. If one person who has made an individual process case—correctly arguing his pay has atrophied due to the company's poorly designed processes—triggers a review of the whole team, and the business becomes paralyzed after realizing many people are not paid appropriately for the same reasons, senior leaders will be expected to step in to dictate a solution. As an employee, if you have made a clear process case, and it's unclear why the business is dragging its feet on raising your pay, this multiple-person problem is the culprit. In these situations, especially in large companies, the business will look for an unrelated opportunity as a cover for increasing pay. It might take the form of a supplemental budget in the annual pay process, or a company restructuring, or an ad hoc, generic "job evaluation" project, so nobody thinks too hard about whether they've been underpaid the whole time. This is not operating with pay sincerity, but self-preservation is a condition most companies will insist upon to make large-scale pay increases happen. Always remember the 70/20/10 rule: the pay insincere think about sharing pay information in a ratio that is 70 percent to avoid humiliation, 20 percent to prevent legal action, and 10 percent to help employees plan for a better life.

The obvious situation for a priority case, and where many businesses need fundamental change, is for low-wage work where a large volume of people are doing the same job next to one another. Retail, restaurants, call centers, manufacturing firms, and distribution centers are all examples. The pay environment for these jobs looks different than pay for professional, corporate jobs, where people are expected to stay employed for much longer and where the variance in skill within a job is perceived to be much wider. For corporate jobs, direct managers have more discretion to make pay decisions, like through the use of pay ranges. For volume jobs, market practice is for pay to be more formulaic and fixed, with strict variations based on something more objective, like time in job.

For volume jobs, companies rely on automatic forms of pay through fixed, objective formulas like *(Hire Rate + $1)* for every year of service, or perhaps modified through a performance rating. Automation of pay for volume jobs guarantees equal pay for equal work, and is the only way to equitably administer pay in environments where entire staffs can turn over each year and the whole crew is affected by minimum-wage or collective bargaining increases. Some small companies, like software maker Buffer, have extended this automatic pay approach to all jobs and made their salary formulas publicly available online. As of this writing, Buffer also makes its job-leveling guide public, based on a widely used system from the consulting firm Radford. Though no large company, to my knowledge, has taken a full automation of pay approach, there is no reason why they couldn't do so assuming they had fair and effective performance- and talent-management processes. Formulaic automation of pay will not be right for every company, and, in fact, most would never consider this approach because they feel it would hurt their ability to attract and retain unique talent. But every company *will* need to wrestle with the tension of how to pay people in a more transparent, less subjective way, because this is the future of the field, and we'll get there by choice or by legislation.

The problem, then, isn't how volume jobs are paid, which is solvable through automation. The real problem is how much these jobs are paid. How can we help business leaders make low-wage work a priority? In my experience, this influence slog is incredibly hard, and it takes years to make progress because change has to come from company leadership who would prefer to do other things with their time and budgets. Around the world, where I've seen priority cases for low-wage workers prosecuted successfully, each of the following is true: increasing pay is directly tied to an organizational strategic initiative, ignoring the problem creates an explicit gap in the company's stated values, senior executives champion the cause, an influential human resources team repeatedly presses the issue, and there is a little luck in the timing. The last two are worth explaining in detail.

Here I must make a quick aside and speak directly to my peers in the human resources field. In our quest to be seen as strategic, to earn a seat at the big kids' table, many of us have frankly not learned how to be influential business partners. In a blistering *Fast Company* article titled "Why We Hate HR," which is as applicable today as it was when published in 2005, Keith H. Hammonds said it this way: "HR is the corporate function with the greatest potential—the key driver, in theory, of business performance—and also the one that most consistently underdelivers."

I once worked with an HR leader who proudly viewed the function as the company's liver, whose only mission was to filter and extract waste from the body. What a grim and boring way to spend your career. True to form, the company had a habit of hiring without discipline and laying off people when it realized it overspent, in the process running out of money to maintain pay at competitive levels for those who remained. For HR leaders, the messy bits of human behavior and business changes will always be an unfortunate part of the job, but if you work in human resources, remind yourself that you aren't the company cops but an advocate for the betterment of your employees and your business. What you neglect or mistreat will in time radiate through the whole body.

As an HR leader, you are competing for scarce resources and prioritization of projects, and this is a competition where everyone else has a head start. Due to no fault of your own, you are last on the list for budgetary consideration. There will always be a brighter, shinier object that your CEO and shareholders prefer to invest in more than things like pay and job training and internal systems. To get more money for your people, your business acumen must be strong enough to understand the company financials and to relentlessly shape a story of the trade-offs and returns to the business for the programs you espouse. Here you have an advantage as the owners of the largest cost item in your business, your payroll. If you delegate your compensation knowledge to a dedicated team because you are not a "math person," you are missing important stories about the health of your company, and you will be of limited use to your people and your business. Step it up or move aside.

Even the most persuasive human resources leader benefits from fortunate timing. Every business will have a part of the year dedicated to reviewing investment requests for the coming year. Usually, this is in the third quarter. Most companies also do long-term strategic planning at this time, which means if you have a major investment to make in people, as we saw with Target, you must come in with a multiyear plan tied to overall strategic initiatives and a multiyear business outlook. Identify opportunities of potential financial luck that could bolster your plan, like an unexpected hit product, a special tax break, or currency favorability, allowing you to frame the pay increase to business leaders as a low-risk, timely investment. It is on you to create the business case and a sense of urgency, to align senior leaders, and to act as an advocate for the whole body. In our triad of cost, coordination, and character, you are accountable for all three. You are more than a liver.

What if your HR team is ineffective *and* the CEO isn't willing or able to take fair pay seriously? Individuals have limited ability to influence the priorities of their companies, so now, it's up to the masses (of employees and voters). This is where power, our final P, comes in.

THE FAIR PAY MIX: POWER

The final P in the Fair Pay Mix is "power." In situations where group dynamics drive collective pay decisions, but business leaders refuse to take meaningful steps toward fair pay (for you or the company), we have to assess how power works at the company or in the industry and demand change. Though employment power now is highly imbalanced in favor of companies, especially in the States, there is no reason things have to stay the same forever, and we'd all be better off if they didn't. As management pioneer Mary Parker Follet is often quoted, "Neither working for someone nor paying someone's wages ought to give you power over them."

I suspect many readers will at this stage throw their hands up in frustration, believing it's hopelessly naive to think employees have any power over their pay in a post-union world. They will scoff at hearing a midgrade, self-interested businessperson say things like, "But if we all start to be sincere about pay, things will get better!" Point taken. There are countless examples of businesses acting in nasty ways to prevent fair pay, and for many, the level of trust is so broken between businesses and employees that they understandably view fair pay as an impossibility. If you've made it this far in the book, I also suspect I've earned some level of your trust, and that I've convinced you that people like me are also the same people you have to convince to get a raise. I'm telling you as directly as I am able that companies *are* able to make these pay transformations, because I have seen them do so firsthand. We should not dismiss the past, but let it act as a prologue in a better story about pay.

The power case for fair pay is complex and presents unique structural issues. In Chapter 7, we will focus on unfair pay associated with gender and race, and in Chapter 8 we will work through the power dynamics of segmented employment cohorts like executives, franchise workers, gig economy contractors, and professional artists. For this chapter, we keep our focus on how to wield pay power in the everyday corporate environment, specifically in three situations: when you have questions about pay, when you have an offer from an outside company, and where some form or threat of collective bargaining arrangement exists.

Asking questions gives you power, as long as you are not being manipulative. Modern laws of workplace power start with asking smart questions in search of genuine understanding. Asking questions about pay is important regardless of the Fair Pay Mix tactic, and especially so if your pay decisions are made in a volume jobs environment. For volume jobs, the personal risk is low when asking questions about your pay as long as you can turn attention away from yourself and onto how the pay program is designed for everyone. You want to express a desire to understand what you can expect to earn as your career progresses. Most workers in these volume jobs are not expected to stay at their companies for longer than a year, so a good manager will see your questions as an encouraging sign that you are "one of the good ones," the rare person who wants to stay and build your career with the company. Here are questions you should try (and it's better if many in the company are asking), which are appropriate for people in any job:

- What companies do we compare our pay against?
- Do all locations have the same pay rates?
- Are pay rates set with your input or given to you from corporate?
- How many career steps does it take to get to management?
- What is the usual pay progression from one job to the next?
- Do we typically promote internally or hire from the outside?
- Does pay increase annually or more often? (If less often, run away.)

Often, you'll find that line managers in restaurants, stores, call centers, and on workshop floors do not have the information they need to answer these questions. They haven't been trained on the compensation philosophy or how pay rates and bonus targets are set, only the few administrative tasks they need to hire and fire employees and communicate corporate pay decisions. The questions above, when asked loud and often, force companies to get more introspective about why they pay what they pay, to provide greater pay transparency, and to sharpen their pay programs to be more employee-friendly and to solve employee problems. Employees shouldn't have to bear the weight of pay being complex, because complexity always favors those in power. Asking smart questions forces simplicity and lays the foundation for clarity, transparency, and a path to fairness.

The second situation where you can exercise pay power is when another company has made you a job offer. This situation is a multiple P argument, in our model fitting somewhere between the permission, priority, and process cases. Navigating an outside offer is like a permission case because your company expects you to talk about pay, though they will be blindsided by the timing. It is also like a priority case, because your outside offer creates pay risk for everyone else on a relative basis, and the company must decide if your pay increase is worth upsetting the balance of everyone else's pay. Finally, an outside offer will work best if you reframe the occasion as proof of your process case. For ease, we can categorize outside offers as a power case for fair pay, because it's intuitive that when you have a job offer, you have power to control the negotiation.

I recommend taking outside interview calls occasionally, not to waste another company's time but to make sure you have a valid understanding of your job level, MVP number, and to meet recruiters you may need later in your career. Know that presenting an outside job offer to your current job is a risky, last-resort move, and you should tread carefully. Many managers will react to an outside offer as a form of disloyalty, an unfair attempt at extorting the company for more money, and your reputation will take a hit as a result. The conversation will be emotional, because you did not have a true permission case, in the company's view, and they will take it personally that you didn't trust them to pay you fairly.

Some companies refuse to make counteroffers under any circumstances, and you should do some sleuthing to know if yours is one of them. If true, don't burn your boat on the way out, because the company may have good reason for this policy. From the company's perspective, if the person has gone to the trouble of getting an outside offer, pay is likely not the only problem the person has with the company. Human resources groups consistently put out studies to show that pay doesn't make the top five of reasons why people leave their company—hating your manager is always number one. Companies also have an entrenched belief that 80 percent of people who accept a counteroffer will leave in six months. This is a widely touted statistic that is hard to verify, because few companies track this data. Given these long odds, it's best to use an outside offer first as verification of your MVP to help you make a process case, and show the counteroffer only if needed where your case is being ignored. If you do show the outside offer, you better be ready to take the other job.

SHH (LET'S TALK ABOUT UNIONS)

Finally, we need to talk about the ultimate power case, where a collective bargaining arrangement exists between the company and its employees. To ensure fair pay, there must always be a viable option for employees to make a robust, collective power case for change. If we think of legislation like minimum wage and equal-pay laws as soft power levers, collective bargaining is the hard power, battle-tested version. If you're on the American corporate side of this debate, dim the lights and draw the shutters, because we are here to talk about unions. If you're not American, continue reading in public places under the full sunlight, because you'll struggle to understand what all the fuss is about.

A traditional and formal version of collective bargaining is the union, but modern formats also include things like sectoral bargaining and codetermination arrangements. Sectoral bargaining allows negotiations to be made at the industry level instead of at the company level, bypassing our three-legged-race problem as all competitors are mandated to act at once. All fast-food restaurants would agree to the same baseline standards for wages and worker safety, as an example. Codetermination is a related idea but instead creates opportunities at the company level for employees to have a vote in the decisions of their managers, including on rates of pay and the design of pay programs. By redistributing power within the company, codetermination also reduces the outside influence of politics and the negative financial incentives of traditional unions to concentrate their own power over time through dues collection. Proponents of these new ideas (to Americans) range from progressives like Senator Elizabeth Warren, who made them a plank of her 2020 presidential bid, to the conservative American Compass institute, which in 2020 released a supporting statement for both sectoral bargaining and codetermination, signed by Donald Trump's former US attorney general Jeff Sessions alongside a number of other prominent conservatives. Support even extends into the Silicon Valley set, as Uber CEO Dara Khosrowshahi called codetermination a "cool model" of which he "would be supportive."

Opposition to collective arrangements, as you will not be surprised to hear since it is the theme of this section, comes down to one thing: power. Adam Smith, of invisible-hand free-market fame on which our economic system is based, knew the market was still subject to power discrepancies in favor of the employer, saying it wasn't "difficult to foresee which of the two parties must, upon all ordinary occasions, have the advantage" in setting working conditions.

When the power advantage is level, the data is clear that employees make more money. In the United States, where unionization faces aggressive opposition, union workers are routinely paid more than nonunion workers. According to a 2013 government study from the Bureau of Labor Statistics, "On average, union workers receive larger wage increases than those of nonunion workers and generally earn higher wages and have greater access to most of the common employer-sponsored benefits as well." Union workers are also less likely to be paid unequally for the same work, as women in unions jobs earn 94 cents on the dollar compared to men, versus about 78 cents for nonunion jobs. This makes sense in the context of our fair-pay priority P, as union contracts often remove individual discretion for pay, especially for volume jobs, instead relying on formulaic start rates instead of pay ranges and fixed increases tied to objective measures rather than any unconscious (or conscious) biases of managers.

Outside the United States, in places where collective bargaining is more common, the fair-pay P's still apply. Pay is managed in the same ways, with the same power dynamics in all countries. This is true regardless of the prevailing government system. I've planned pay in capitalist and communist countries, in monarchies and in social democracies, too. The same pay problems exist because fair pay speaks to bigger themes about human nature. And yet, global companies operate in all these environments at once and still see profitable growth throughout the world. Pay tactics will vary slightly from one country to the next to account for local laws and customs, and these nuances can be difficult and bothersome to track, but they are rarely if ever an overwhelming or existential burden to the business community (at least for big companies, as small companies are often exempt from collective bargaining arrangements). My point is that when a global company says they can't possibly survive in a pay environment of enhanced worker power, rest assured the company is already thriving under those same conditions elsewhere. They know how to do the work; they just prefer not to.

Historians acknowledge that progress made in working conditions, like weekends, overtime pay, and safety laws, are in large part owed to the former power of collective bargaining. Steven Greenhouse, in his book *Beaten Down, Worked Up: The Past, Present, and Future of American Labor*, argues the undeniability of the relationship between peak years of union membership and consistent wage growth, and the decline of union membership with the stagnation of wages and growing anxiety about pay. We hear the same conclusion from Martin Luther King Jr. in his 1965 speech to the Illinois AFL-CIO convention, in reference to the landmark Fair Labor Standards Act of 1938:

> The labor movement was the principal force that transformed misery and despair into hope and progress. Out of its bold struggles, economic and social reform gave birth to unemployment insurance, old age pensions, government relief for the destitute, and above all new wage levels that meant not mere survival, but a tolerable life. The captains of industry did not lead this transformation; they resisted it until they were overcome.

Much blood has been spilled in historical fights between management and labor, as is risked every time those with power are forced to relinquish it. In 1914, at the height of the Colorado Coal Wars, the US National Guard was called in to protect the interests of the Colorado Fuel and Iron Company. They fired shots into the tents of striking workers, killing twenty-one people, including wives and children of the coal workers, an event later known as the Ludlow Massacre. The company even built an armored car mounted with a machine gun for their assaults, which they called the Death Special. Three years later came the East St. Louis riots. This time it was the striking union employees of the Aluminum Ore Company who lashed out. After being replaced by cheaper Black workers from the South, the union members retaliated by burning their substitutes' neighborhoods to the ground. There are many stories of this nature.

The Ludlow Massacre helped establish the eight-hour workday and child labor laws, while the East St. Louis riots sparked the civil rights movement. We may no longer have Death Specials or discrimination as obvious as "whites only" job postings and union bylaws, but their legacy no doubt carries through today in terms of generational wealth and corporate representation gaps. Many countries are in the early stages of these battles now. In Bangladesh, a garment factory fire in 2012, with remarkable parallels to the 1911 Triangle Shirtwaist Factory fire in New York, killed more than one hundred people and led to workplace safety reforms. The next year, a garment factory collapse killed more than one thousand people. Much opportunity for progress remains, and we would do well to know more about the fair pay fights of those who came before us, including Martin Luther King Jr. himself, who was assassinated while attending a strike of sanitation workers.

Shared power matters, and the rhetoric of economic impotence claimed by corporations against shared power doesn't match the reality of what happens to business results under these arrangements. Countries without effective worker protections aren't exactly seeing these problems solved by the free market or the inherent compassion of companies. Each year, a report called *The ITUC Global Rights Index: The World's Worst Countries for Workers*, ranks countries on a 1 to 5 scale for workers' rights. The scale doesn't start at "perfect utopia for workers," but assumes the best-case scenario score of 1 represents a "sporadic violation of rights." At the bad end is a score of 5, labeled as "no guarantee of rights due to the breakdown of the law." In the 2019 rankings, the United States earned a 4 for "systematic violations of rights," the same as Venezuela, the unfailing boogeyman of the free-markets-only crowd.

Fifteen years after the Great Depression began in 1929, US union membership hit an all-time high. The generation taking over the management reins now has spent their most formative years in the wake of multiple economic crashes. As children, they watched their parents lose their jobs and, in many cases, their homes due to no fault of their own. As new managers, they have already had to put their staff in the same position. If we follow a similar historical pattern, we should expect to see a shift back toward worker power throughout the 2020s. This may not take the form of unions explicitly, but the desire for more shared power will always roar to life when trust in the employment relationship has broken down. All people want to be in control of their own fates; this is not a radical proposition.

The rumbles for more employee power are everywhere. The Fight for $15 movement sparked mass increases in minimum wages. Nationwide nurse and teacher walkouts increased pay and visibility of under-resourced working conditions. Walkouts at gig economy behemoths Uber and Lyft drew attention to the precarious employment relationships of independent contractors. Strikes at General Motors included fifty thousand workers. Media companies like Vox and Buzzfeed recognized unions for the first time. A flurry of companies saw their salary information shared via employee-created spreadsheets. Authors did the same, giving me a perfect Venn diagram of my interests in writing books and reviewing pay. More than 250 million workers in India undertook the largest general strike in world history in 2020. Consulting firms like IRI, paid to help companies avoid collective bargaining through what they call "union vulnerability assessments," see the trend, too. In a 2019 report describing a resurgence in the labor movement, IRI had a warning for their clients: "unless you are ready, you are already behind."

The resistance to collective bargaining is also strong. While the Fight for $15 movement accelerated in Seattle, their opposition was systematically earning their own trophies in states like Indiana, Michigan, Wisconsin, West Virginia, and Kentucky. In Wisconsin in particular, former governor Scott Walker managed to legally prevent teachers' unions from bargaining about anything except wages, as long as those wage increases remained less than inflation. Mathematically, this effectively lowered teacher pay year over year. For his efforts, Walker faced thousands of citizens storming the capitol building for weeks on end. He also faced a recall vote, which he won with more votes than in his original election.

Politics aside, it's important we see the reasons for why power matters in making pay fair. Making a power case for fair pay is an act of necessity and desperation. Showing power through collective action enforces the other P's, creating effective pay processes, sparking opportunity (and legal protection) for permission to talk about pay without retaliation, and mandating pay fairness as a priority for all people. Our power stories—of violence and spies and "mink-coat brigades" (led by J. P. Morgan's daughter Anne, of all people) need to be told more often. As a new generation of labor and management struggle with issues of pay insincerity, we cannot forget our heritage or forgo the opportunity to learn from our mistakes. We should all want to avoid seeing something like the Georgia Gig Worker Wars of 2025.

Traditional collective bargaining and labor organizing will likely neither dominate the workplace of the future nor go away entirely, but instead take a new shape. Employee pressure and new legislation will create modern methods of mandated power sharing and pay transparency that enable a real free market for wages and make it harder for businesses to manage their pay and working conditions in an unaccountable black box. Companies should not expect to keep information about pay private in a world of encrypted, global social media.

Where we go from here is a choice, initiated by the givers of pay who now have far more power than the receivers. Business leaders, if you can't stomach the idea of shared power and any form of collective bargaining, there is an easy way to avoid it altogether: practice pay sincerity through the Fair Pay Mix, and do so quickly.

CHAPTER 7

Mind the Gap

While a company's compensation team can highlight systemic problems like gender and racial pay iniquities, and contribute to making them better or worse, we are the corporate machine's last fail-safe. If your paycheck is unfair, the problem has been compounded by previous breakdowns in how jobs are valued and how people are selected to fill them. We are less the canary in the coal mine, signaling trouble ahead, than the black lung prognosis found after years of neglect.

To see what broke before your paycheck, we can apply what we've learned so far—the historical choices we've made about pay, the way companies think about and prioritize pay now, and how we can change our experience with pay through the Fair Pay Mix model—to our most persistent and glaring pay challenges.

Because this chapter focuses on gender and race disparities, let me start by sharing my qualifiers. I am not the most compelling avatar on the subject, and, in fact, my background has at least one groan-inducing detail for every reader. I am a white, heterosexual, cisgender, able-bodied man living in deep-blue Portland, Oregon, raised by loving parents with advanced degrees, in a food- and housing-secure environment. I spent the first twenty-five years of my life in the American South (well, Florida, which is at least South-adjacent), in a suburban evangelical megachurch culture where I learned the gospels of Matthew, Mark, Luke, John, and Rush Limbaugh. Every leader I knew was a white man with a similar affect and haircut. In this world, women can hold only limited leadership roles, which exclusively means the nursery, and are barred from preaching, save for Mother's Day. The only nonwhite people on staff, at least in my day, were understudies who held subordinate roles leading music or satellite church campuses far across town. Martin Luther King Jr.'s admonishment of the church on Sunday mornings as "the most segregated hour" still applied to my thrice-weekly assembly decades later.

My experiences and lack of exposure to other communities gave me blind spots on issues of gender and race equality. In my past and through today, I have not suffered an ounce of discrimination, and I am still learning to see the world through the experiences of others. All of us carry some form of these blind spots that create templates, called "unconscious biases," that affect our thoughts and actions. Camille Chang-Gilmore, global chief diversity officer for Boston Scientific, says it succinctly: "If you have a brain, you have a bias." We use these biases as mental shortcuts to make snap judgments of people and situations to assess what might happen next or what roles people are capable of playing. Sometimes, this can be a helpful thing, especially when your safety depends on it. While I may have no worries about going out for a run in my suburban neighborhood at night, a woman may choose to wait for daylight or take a friend with her. A young Black man may choose not to go at all.

Let's try an experiment. Ask a friend who hasn't been primed by reading this chapter to close their eyes and describe to you what a CEO looks like. Now imagine a social worker, and finally a truck driver. What did your friend see first? When I envision a CEO, the first image I see is a white male with a specific haircut, not because I believe they (we) have any inherent and superior capability, but because the template of a white male as leader has been formed by the experiences of my life and at every company that has employed me. Being able to recall examples from your life and apply them as your default setting is called an "availability bias."

I'd bet my experience is not unique, and that our availability biases of a social worker and truck driver are similar, too. At the CEO level, I'd guess our examples are nearly uniform. The annual *Fortune* magazine list of the world's five hundred largest companies consistently shows that more than 90 percent are headed by white men, about triple their share of the population. On a fixed-numbered list like the Fortune 500, representation is a zero-sum game, so if one demographic group is overrepresented, another must be underrepresented. For comparison, how do Black women fare? When I started writing this chapter, exactly one of the Fortune 500 CEO spots was held by a Black woman. Mary A. Winston held the top job for the retailer Bed Bath and Beyond—but only on an interim basis during a search for a new CEO. On a purely representative basis at about 7 percent of the population, we'd expect thirty-five of the Fortune 500 to be helmed by Black women. It's now zero. The company chose a white man for the permanent job.

My experiences and professional training have shaped my understanding of how the realities of unequal pay intersect with the systems that perpetuate it. In my personal community, I know many people who would count themselves among the 46 percent of all men (and 38 percent of people overall) who believe that the gender pay gap is a myth, that it is imagined and perpetuated to serve a political purpose. In my professional community, the problem of unequal pay is clear in the data and widely acknowledged. The goal of this chapter is to connect these two worlds so we can close the pay gap faster.

Intuitively, most readers will agree that we should seek "equal pay for equal work," which I see as an outcome of having a pay sincerity mindset. Unfortunately, we've neutered a noble and desirable goal, to ensure "equal pay for equal work," by turning it into a slogan without defining terms or creating accountability. Now, the phrase carries all the authority of telling someone to "Fight the system" or "Give 'em hell." Consequently, our debates about equal pay result in people talking around one another instead of seeking genuine understanding and solutions. Carrie Gracie, in her book *Equal*, noticed this semantic two-step in her case for equal pay against the BBC, which she felt was unwilling to counter her arguments on equivalent terms. As she recalls, "Managers had avoided the expression 'equal pay' and talked instead of 'fair pay.'" What she was being told was that while "equal pay is a legal right, fair pay is not." Companies use this distinction to stay within a refined legal framework, but as we'll see, neither phrase carries much legal weight for the employee. Both equal pay and fair pay are phrases in need of redemption and in common usage should be thought of as one and the same. I would not have titled this book *Fair Pay* if I thought otherwise.

WHAT'S IN A NAME

When you hear the phrase "equal pay for equal work," which outcome most resonates with you?

- The ratio of pay between similar work groups should be equal.
- The amount of pay between a person and their peers should be equal.

If you answered "both," good job. Loosely defined, the first bullet describes the "wage gap," and the second a more granular approach called "pay equity." We'll talk about the role of performance, experience, and job differences later. Another possibility exists at the margins, where people who answer "neither" fundamentally deny equal pay as a desirable goal in a free-market system. I won't spend much time entertaining this idea other than to say that in my experience, these people are often already paid well, and they were not raised by single mothers.

The wage gap, in its most distilled form, tries to find the ratio of pay between one work group and another—for example, women compared to men. The calculation is simple and often looks like this:

1. Average annual salary of women at the company: $80,000

2. Average annual salary of men at the company: $100,000

3. The company wage gap equals $80,000 divided by $100,000, or 80 percent (commonly shown as cents on the dollar).

When we see statistics that women are paid 80 cents on the dollar compared to men, Black employees are paid 70 cents compared to white, and Black women are paid 61 cents, this is typically how the calculation is run, save for wonky details like exclusions for temporary employment groups. Variations of the calculation exist—for example, instead of dividing average salary, dividing by the median to control for outliers at the top. In the UK, the wage-gap math (or maths, as they'd say) legally has to include bonus payouts. In France, the wage-gap ratio is determined by a 100 point index of five different gaps: a simple wage gap like our calculation above (40 points), individual pay raises (20 points), promotion rates (15 points), pay increases upon return from maternity leave (15 points), and the presence of women in the ten highest-paid jobs (10 points). In Iceland, companies can determine their own methodology but must pass a high government standard, after which the company gets to display a badge that seems destined for tattoo shop walls. The Icelandic government describes it as a "pie-chart, a stamp, runes and the smiling faces of two dissimilar individuals . . . indicating that the individuals portrayed are both assessed at their true worth." I share these nuances because, as we'll see, this void of consistent standards has become a playground for bad ideas and the false idea that the wage gap must be a myth.

Pay equity is a different type of measurement. Instead of starting the calculation at the full company level, like assessing how pay for all employees in a minority group compares to the majority, a company will create initial filters to control for the "equal work" part of our "equal pay for equal work" phrase. Before any math starts, these filters attempt to normalize for what the researcher deems to be acceptable factors for pay differences, like job, job level, hours worked, and experience. Pay-equity calculations take infinite forms, but a competent analysis follows these steps:

STEP ONE: A company defines the factors it sees as unacceptable reasons for pay differences, like gender or race. Theoretically, other factors could include viewpoint diversity, political affiliation, disability, religion, or sexual orientation, assuming you wanted your company to have that kind of information about you and every other employee. In some countries, collecting certain data is illegal. French companies today, as an example, can't track employee data on race in part because of how the data was used to target minority populations in World War II.

STEP TWO: A company defines factors it sees as acceptable reasons for pay differences, like job, performance, experience, location, and hours worked. These lists can be hundreds of factors long at large companies, depending on the complexity of their operations.

STEP THREE: Cohorts of similar employees are determined—for example, full-time employees in jobs at the same level, in the same location, or in the same or similar functions.

STEP FOUR: Each cohort is subjected to a statistical analysis to find a predicted pay value for each person, compared to a baseline of the majority population in the cohort.

STEP FIVE: Statistically significant outliers, if they exist, are found to show which employees' predicted pay is above or below their actual pay.

STEP SIX: The company decides how to increase pay for the outliers who are paid below their predicted value so they are no longer outliers. This does not mean the people considered outliers are now paid the exact same rate as their peers, but that they are now paid within a range of their predicted value that no longer registers as a statistical anomaly.

The pay-equity analysis is then aggregated into a similar ratio as the wage gap for each cohort and for the company overall. Though results will vary for each company, it will almost certainly be a smaller difference than the wage-gap number. This is because pay-equity data has been sanitized to eliminate any skewing caused by the overrepresentation of highly paid, and typically white male, executives. The two calculations are regularly confused, causing our deniability problem and leading people to say things like the "real wage gap" is 98 cents, not 80 cents. Much more on this in the next section.

There are similarities in the calculations, most importantly that they are both based on point-in-time data. A wage gap could show 74 cents one month for Indigenous employees, but 82 cents the following month depending on who was hired or left the company, especially if there are few Indigenous people at the company and therefore the results are prone to volatility. Similarly, a comprehensive pay-equity analysis could show, at that time the data was pulled for the analysis, 98 cents on the dollar for women in P2-level software engineer jobs based in Austin, Texas, and 101 cents the next time, meaning they earn more than the men.

If a company does have a gap, as most do, this doesn't automatically mean they have discriminatory pay practices and should be exiled from the economy. If the business earns most of its sales on a seasonal basis, like a retailer during the holidays or an amusement park in the summer, a temporary surge in staffing may change the demographics of a company at different points throughout the year. If a company has reorganized and shuffled people's jobs or has not yet fully integrated its latest acquisition, the analysis cohorts may not yet be defined enough to accurately group similar employees. There may also be legacy pay issues, where a long-awaited key retirement or ten will allow the company to shuffle leadership seats and pay replacement leaders in a more equitable way. Gauging improvement over time using a consistent methodology is a more appropriate measure of progress and limits point-in-time excuses.

The most important difference between a wage gap and a pay-equity analysis is the ability to determine statistical significance. Statistical significance in this context means a company has exhausted all acceptable excuses for why one person or group is paid more or less than their predicted pay, and they have a high degree of confidence the difference is not random happenstance but due to the unacceptable factor being tested, like a person's gender or race. Statistical significance does not directly prove that discrimination occurred, but it eliminates the other, more acceptable explanations for the variability.

I can't say for sure the reasons behind my inability to dunk a basketball and impress the neighborhood dads, but my diminutive height is a factor I'd consider acceptable and likely to explain almost all the variability in my failures. However, I couldn't *prove* height was the only factor; others in my height cohort could have more skill, years of practice, or any other number of variables that would fairly account for our differences. With enough data, I could build a model of predicted vertical leap inches for each person. If Spud Webb, a retired NBA star, were in the cohort, he would score higher than me even now despite being my same height. I would accept my relative station, unless the model also accounted for a variable like "pre-test rest." If I was among some in the cohort who were forced to run a marathon before charting our leaps, we could rightly call out the unfair barrier and ask for an opportunity to rest up to meet our full potential. I still wouldn't be able to dunk, and Spud Webb would surely still beat me, but I'd know the measurement process was equitable. In the same way, equal pay through a pay-equity analysis is about finding and addressing unfair barriers to a person's potential.

It's tempting to conclude that because of its greater rigor, a pay-equity analysis is superior to a wage-gap calculation. But rigor doesn't always imply accuracy or effectiveness. Many stories exist of surgeons successfully amputating incorrect limbs and of civilian targets being mistaken for enemy bases, both suboptimal results despite rigorous execution. "A theory is only as good as its assumptions," said the French economist and physicist Maurice Allais, which certainly holds true for pay-equity analysis. Before we hide behind the rigor of a formal pay-equity analysis, declaring victory that we've either solved or disproven the problem of unfair pay, let's think about the assumptions that go into a pay-equity model:

- How do we value jobs? Are some jobs paid more because of relevant and true market forces or is at least some of it related to the compounding effects of overt or indirect discrimination, or a boss who whines so much that we've paid his team more?
- What do we mean by equal work? This is where our job leveling and peer selection matters. What's the hierarchy of ninjas to creatives, again?
- Are people in the right jobs to begin with? How long has it been since job descriptions were last reviewed?
- What's happening at the company? Have new lines of business infused significantly different types of talent into the company this year?
- Are the payroll and reporting systems clean and correct? In large, global companies, this is never an obvious or easy answer.

There are many ways to look at unequal pay, but regardless of the analysis design choices we make, our bias should favor transparency and benefit the employee. An open-source model, as much as is possible given the real legal constraints imposed on this type of work, allows others to challenge and improve our assumptions and get to fairness faster. As companies learn to open themselves up to scrutiny about pay, they give greater clarity to employees and create a feedback loop that fosters trust through shared accountability and power.

I see two immediate opportunities for increasing clarity. The first is ending the argument about whether pay differs based on gender or race. It does, full stop. Nobody with access to company employee rosters would say otherwise—and those without access need only look upward in their company org chart to see where it turns male and monochromatic. Small gaps on a pay-equity basis, the 98-cents-to-$1 results, do not nullify the reality of a larger wage gap, the 80-cents-to-$1 results. These are two lenses on the same camera. The second opportunity for clarity is whether the problem can be solved. My answer might surprise you, but no, it can't. There is no single or final solution to the problem of unequal pay—it can only be discovered and constantly managed. But that hasn't stopped many from claiming otherwise.

P.E.T.E.

Let's try another experiment. Go to LinkedIn and search for any post about the appointment of an underrepresented person to a position of authority. The headline should say something like, "General Motors Names First Black CEO." Brace yourself, because now I will ask you to venture into the comments section, against all hygiene protocol for staying sane online. Here is a selection of comments I see in my own experiment, written on a post about the appointment of a woman to head an electronics company, whom I'll call Michelle.

- "Why should it matter?"
- "We shouldn't lower the bar."
- "This is reverse discrimination!"

That's plenty. Sorry, Mike from Sales at Regional Insurance Broker, but you've never met Michelle, let alone worked with her. I'd imagine Michelle could run circles around you professionally. To everyone else, don't be like Mike.

Why are these reactions so predictable? And why are there so many people like Mike, the "well, actually" warriors of the world who take solace in disproving or tearing down the achievements of others by making sweeping assumptions about their capabilities? Surely the intentional, algorithmically enabled filter bubbles of social media and the perceived sense of loss among majority demographics in a changing society contribute to the problem, but both factors are well outside my domain expertise. Generally, I believe most people are open to the idea that unequal pay exists, but simply think we solved the problem long ago, and that any remaining gaps are solely due to the choices made among groups about the number of hours they perform paid work, the specific jobs they choose, or the roles they play in raising children. Any correction, therefore, must be at the expense of people like Mike at the hands of pesky social engineers like me. This is incorrect.

Often, when people argue we've already solved the problem of unequal pay, they lean on legislation like the Equal Pay Act of 1963, the Pregnancy Discrimination Act of 1978, and similar international laws like the UK's Equality Act of 2010 as proof that it's already illegal to differentiate pay on the basis of gender or race, and therefore new solutions are unnecessary. Or they will see the previously mentioned discrepancies in calculation types and conclude no one really knows definitively what's going on with pay. Their lack of understanding doesn't negate the fact that wage gaps are real and they can be calculated through different means. When you hear people confidently assert the "real" pay-gap result (on a pay-equity basis) is something like 98 cents on the dollar, this is a tell that they are not well versed in the topic. Understandably, when people believe the result is already close to parity, they wonder whether this is as good as it can get, and then start to extrapolate warnings from there to take it easy with all this diversity stuff, lest we enable what they see as "reverse discrimination." Here we must distinguish prejudice from discrimination. Prejudice can come from anywhere and anyone, regardless of power dynamics. Discrimination implicates the greater power of one group to act against the interests of another. Just as there is no such thing as reverse power, there is no such thing as reverse discrimination (or its cousin, reverse racism).

The Equal Pay Act, like other laws meant to eliminate discrimination, leaves wide discretion for companies to pay people differently according to performance and merit or the classification of similar jobs. Again, paying high performers more is not a bad thing, and good work should be rewarded. Some jobs really are more complex and important to the company's results than others. This discretion is not inherently wrong in isolation, but cedes all the power to employers. If we've already done all we can to solve the problem of unequal pay through past legislation, then our options for why pay differences still exist are narrow. On a pay-equity basis, with all acceptable factors controlled for, we now have to believe women (or any underrepresented group) are inherent underperformers compared to men or they work in less valuable jobs. Somehow, I bet Mike wouldn't be comfortable saying that to the faces of his female colleagues.

The intellectual figurehead (but not the originator) of the idea of pay discrimination as overblown myth is a Canadian psychologist named Jordan Peterson. Peterson comes with sharp qualifiers; he has been called both the "most influential public intellectual in the Western world" and a fascist. Peterson is one of the world's most popular authors, has millions of views on his YouTube lectures, and sells out large venues of live audiences wherever he travels. Love him or hate him, Jordan Peterson's opinions are undeniably influential for many people.

One of Peterson's self-described "big fans," and an adoptee of the wage gap as myth worldview, is a former Google engineer whom I'll call Pete (or P.E.T.E., my acronym for the kind of person who thinks of themselves as society's "pay-equality truth explainer"). I'll withhold

Pete's real name because he didn't intend to make himself a public figure, and after a season of intense scrutiny for his leaked internal essay, I suspect he would like to get on with his life in private. The point is, we all know a Pete. Some companies are run by a Pete. Every HR professional has met a Pete or has a whole faction of Petes in their company.

Both Peterson and the real Pete are intelligent, highly credentialed people who have reached the heights of their respective fields. But they both fall into the same trap, confusing terms and conflating a superficial understanding of pay equity and the pay gap. As a result, they conclude the whole topic to be irrelevant. I wouldn't dream of explaining the latest research on clinical psychology to Peterson or quality testing Pete's software code, both of which are outside my expertise. In return, I hope they'd recognize the compensation field is outside their own expertise and be receptive to changing their assumptions about how it all works.

Pete, in his infamous Google memo, and among controversial (to put it politely) ideas about the science of gender, lays out a case for why the gender wage gap must be a myth. He says the pay gap is the result of confirmation bias by left-leaning social scientists, who I suppose have laundered their ideas and spreadsheets through people like me at large corporations in a vast conspiracy to hold all Petes down. In his footnotes, Pete carefully hedges his bets by saying, "Yes, in a national aggregate, women have lower salaries than men for a variety of reasons. For the same work, though, women get paid just as much as men." Pete acknowledges the pay gap, attributing it to what he sees as the natural preferences of the average woman compared to the average man, but then falsely implies this translates into an inexistence of pay-equity gaps. Therefore, the issue is either already solved or, if it exists, can't be changed because of the dictates of nature according to his Internet research.

Pete could have saved himself a lot of trouble, and probably kept his job, by simply asking his company's compensation team to validate his assumptions. Google is a leader on pay-equity analyses; the company makes a detailed description of its methodology available to the public, and published an entire guide on its re:Work blog about how companies can design their own pay-equity analysis. If Pete were still at Google, I wonder if he'd feel confident enough in his conclusion to tell the team they were wasting their time, because he had already looked into it and figured out it was a scam.

The Petes of the world are understandably misinformed because my field hasn't done a great job explaining how pay works, and we've been slow in making progress. I don't blame Pete for this, but I'm less forgiving of Peterson, given his academic capability and the scale of his influence. In a tense interview with Cathy Newman of the UK's Channel 4 News, Peterson claimed that "multivariate analysis of the pay gap indicates that it doesn't exist." This sounds like something an intelligent, highly credentialed scholar would say, and it makes for an authoritative sound bite in front of his acolytes. He used a math-y sounding, nine-syllable word combination—how could he be wrong?

Here's how: as the name implies, a multivariate analysis accounts for many factors at once, following the six-step outline described earlier. As we've seen, there is no standard, unified multivariate model that companies use to determine whether they have pay-equity outliers. Each company's result is a product of their assumptions, methodology, data, and strategic goals. A company chooses how to define and account for its own acceptable pay factors. If a person fundamentally believes men are paid more than women because women have more innate, gender-specific characteristics like "agreeableness" that make them worse at salary negotiation, as Pete argues, then our disagreement isn't about what the math shows. Instead, it's about the assumptions we use to determine what makes people successful. These choices feed into hiring and promotion decisions, and therefore into the models we use to account for acceptable differences in pay, and whether a company should participate in certain practices like salary negotiation at all.

Peterson knows better. I'm certain he's run many multivariate analyses himself in his field and is well acquainted with the methodology. He knows a multivariate analysis is not intended to prove or disprove the existence of something, but rather to show with a high degree of confidence whether any particular factor meaningfully drives the result of a particular model. I doubt he's personally run the numbers himself with complete sets of company compensation data in partnership with someone who understands how jobs in a company relate to one another. Here, I find solace in a Tina Fey quote. In talking about her workplace experiences as the head of a major television show, she says, "I realized there was no 'institutionalized sexism' at that place. Sometimes they just literally didn't know what they were talking about."

Compensation, because of its historically black-box nature, will engender some bad ideas and incorrect assumptions. Pay sincerity means creating space for repercussion-free dialogue and education about how we make sure pay is fair for everyone, as long as the dialogue is in good faith. To quote Pete's essay, in a revised version he released after the initial public outcry, "If we can't have an honest discussion about this, we can never truly solve the problem."

On this point, Pete gets it right.

DOLLAR FOR DOLLAR

Knowing the different types of equal-pay analyses is important, as confusion breeds bad arguments and hinders progress. The two methods tell different stories about pay, and companies must learn how to live in this tension and tell multiple stories at once. Under a raw pay-gap analysis, a company may report women are paid 85 cents for every dollar a man earns, while under a pay-equity analysis, they achieve the only result acceptable to say out loud, $1 for $1. When companies let these definitions stay loose in their employees' minds, even if unintentionally, any improvements made toward fair pay outcomes will be seen as not good enough, further diminishing trust in the way people are paid. Now, I will explain why companies prefer to focus their efforts on achieving pay equity, and then try to redeem the pay-gap calculation, which is my personally preferred measure as a more holistic and relatable indicator of progress.

The truth is, a focus on pay equity means no company is explicitly trying to close the pay gap, at least not directly. Let's assume that after running a pay-gap analysis, a company finds results similar to the US economy as a whole, where women are paid 80 cents on the dollar compared to men. To close the remaining 20-cent pay gap directly, the company will find the mechanics are difficult, if not impossible. If the two numbers we have to play with are female pay (or another underrepresented group) as the numerator, and male pay (or any majority group) as the denominator, we have two options to reconcile the ratio:

1. We can lower men's pay.

2. We can increase women's pay.

Option 1, for most companies, is an untenable solution because it will lead to a mass exodus of men from the company (the legality of such a move aside). Unless you're Dan Price, the CEO who lowered his pay to afford increasing the minimum wage of his company to $70,000, and you have built the kind of company that inspires others toward financial sacrifice and the common good, don't count on others to voluntarily sign up for a pay cut. Regardless of how much you pay someone, you can assume that person has pegged their lifestyle to that amount and is unable to accept or afford anything less. Besides, we want everyone to make more money.

We're left with Option 2. But how do we increase women's pay enough to close the gap? Mathematically, if your pay-gap calculation is based on average salary, you could appoint a woman CEO and write her a massive check, but again this isn't a meaningful solution for anyone except the new boss. Alternatively, you can take a targeted approach by increasing pay for all women. Here is where the problems start. What if 15 percent of the male population is Black? If the company also has a similarly sized racial pay gap, spending directly to close the racial pay gap for Black men will make the gender pay gap worse by increasing the denominator for men's pay. You, as a business leader and practitioner of pay sincerity who genuinely wants to do the right thing but has limited funds to spend, are stuck in a loop.

Instead, companies who find they have a pay gap will tease out solutions that address the inputs to pay, like reviewing hiring practices and consistent usage of job levels, that indirectly close the pay gap and allow for targeted pay increases. The first thing companies will notice is representation at the most senior levels. As of 2019, a record number of female CEOs led Fortune 500 companies. Unfortunately, that record was thirty-three out of five hundred, or 6.6 percent. Black CEOs fared worse, at four out of five hundred, or less than 1 percent (as mentioned previously, none were women). Though CEO data is public information, which gives us a near complete picture of diversity in the top spot, a *Fortune* magazine study found only 3 percent of companies on their list shared full diversity data for their management ranks. Having seen plenty of corporate rosters myself, I assume most companies keep this information private because they are not proud of their performance. Closing the pay gap can be done only by closing the representation gap across management levels in the company.

When companies internalize these problems, they start to rationalize their status by cutting their pay-gap data into targeted groups according to factors like job level. Now, the approach is starting to look less like the simple pay-gap analysis I showed at the beginning of this chapter, where average pay is compared across groups, and more like the six-step, statistically controlled pay-equity analysis. The pay-gap problem has not disappeared but is presented in a new way at the company's discretion. Companies famously play similar games with their earnings reports, through standardized GAAP (generally accepted accounting principles) and non-GAAP earnings ("earnings before the bad stuff," as it's often called). In our case, the bad stuff could include favorable (or questionable) choices about its own data, like excluding a group of employees to prevent known problem spots from surfacing, looking at base salaries only while the worst outliers sit off-camera in the bonus or stock pool, or choosing a statistical confidence interval so narrow that only the most egregiously underpaid people would be found as underpaid. There are lots of ways an insincere company can game its pay-equity ratio, because there is no set rulebook.

To prevent these kinds of games, a well-resourced company will initiate a formal pay-equity analysis with an independent vendor. The external consulting team will be made up of equal parts statisticians and lawyers. Smaller companies without the same resources or a large enough employee data set to meet statistical standards don't have this option. They can focus only on the pay-gap method and make sincere choices about how they cut their own data.

A formal pay-equity analysis, under the six-step process, can take months to run. Making things harder, in the time between pulling the data and getting the results back, business doesn't pause. People change jobs, new people come in, and teams restructure, leaving companies unsure that their results will solve the issues they found months prior or that new issues haven't crept in since. Both the big consulting companies and start-ups like Syndio are starting to offer promising, real-time solutions to close these timing gaps. But by definition, any equal-pay study will be a point-in-time analysis, and companies are unlikely to review and adjust pay alongside each new hire or resignation. Instead, they will defer to fixed times of year to make adjustments. As we saw in the last chapter, fair pay requires you to work your company's calendar.

After the consultants find a company's statistically significant pay-equity outliers, the work is far from complete. Consultants do not hand a company a list of employees they need to write checks to with the amounts filled in to make the problem go away. Companies now have to decide *how* they will close their gaps, and this presents a host of new challenges. This isn't as simple as writing larger or more checks. If the company chooses to adjust *all* negative outliers, regardless of whether the person is in an underrepresented group, this raises the overall bar for equal pay. A rising tide is lifting all boats, but the marina's moorage fee is going up. Alternatively, if the company chooses to adjust pay only for those in an underrepresented group, it is spending less money while achieving the same goal of parity. In this case, only a few boats are being repaired by having the holes in their hulls plugged. Both options are valid, one is less expensive, and neither is easy to communicate.

To take equal pay seriously is to realize that eliminating differences isn't a one-off event or achievement, but a continuous process requiring repeated analysis and investment. Marc Benioff, the founder and CEO of Salesforce, said it this way in his book *Trailblazer*: "There's no one single enemy to identify and go head-to-head with, nor is there a simple, universal solution to champion. Instead, it's a pernicious and far-reaching problem that unfolds quietly, everywhere, all the time, behind the closed doors of conference rooms where decisions get made."

He goes on to describe what happened after his company's first equal-pay investment, and his subsequent realization these investments are here to stay: "One year after running that first audit and making that $3 million correction, we'd run the numbers again. Turned out we needed to spend *another* $3 million adjusting the salaries of employees whose salaries had fallen out of whack since the last audit." In describing the reasons for continuous adjustment, he talks about how Salesforce had purchased two dozen companies and had remaining integration work left to do. "We hadn't just inherited their technology, but their pay practices and culture, too."

Salesforce could have excluded the new employees to save money and announce a better result, but all signs suggest they are taking sincere ownership of their responsibility toward fair pay. If the company behind the world's leading business performance software tells you unequal pay exists and that it's a repeating problem, trust them. And yes, your company has the same issue.

Companies committed to equal pay have historically focused on achieving a $1 for $1 pay ratio. We can think of this as the pinnacle of Pay Equity 1.0. The next iteration should come with a new headline. The prize shouldn't be to achieve a ratio, which depends on the sincerity of a company's measurement choices. Rather, companies should report how many people were found to be below their predicted pay value and the dollars spent on this year's remedy. Equal pay, framed as a maintenance activity under a rigorous, consistent, and public methodology, should be the new standard. Instead of a company pronouncing they've achieved equal pay for equal work, they should instead say,

"Here's what we did this year to *maintain* equal pay." Getting to zero (dollars spent and people underpaid) and staying there is a race-to-the-bottom worth running.

ON OPTING OUT AND COPPING OUT

When the 1938 Fair Labor Standards Act introduced the federal minimum wage in the United States, the law excluded sectors where Black workers were overrepresented, like agriculture, hotels, and restaurants. It wasn't until 1967, after segregation ended (on the books, at least), that the minimum wage was finally introduced to these workers. Recent findings have shown 20 percent of the decline in the racial earnings gap since has stemmed from this single reform of the minimum wage.

With decades less of compounding legislated pay increases to support pay growth for these jobs, it isn't surprising to still find them among the lowest-paid jobs in the market. To close the remaining pay gap, companies need to keeping ask tough questions about how their jobs are internally valued, and the history of why that might be. What choices will we make now to recognize whole parts of the economy that are still being left out from meaningful pay growth, that with changes now will eliminate the remaining pay gap over time? In the United States, we could start by extending employment protections to independent contractors, who are now exempt from antidiscrimination laws. We'll find in the next chapter how critical these extensions become in a world more reliant on contractors through gig work.

If we want to build trust in the pay process, we can't make excuses for the remaining pay gap, no matter how carefully we explain the nuances of our calculations of how effectively we cheerlead for the supposedly impartial free market to resolve the problem for us. Though expectations for companies to provide equal pay have never been higher, most companies are by nature risk-averse creatures, and their internal calculation for equal pay will trail the societal calculation. Where a company has a rigorous, perfect $1 for $1 pay-equity ratio but a stubborn 10 percent pay gap, more will be asked of it. These problems will not be solved overnight, but this shouldn't stop companies from making commitments now. I believe most people would rather work for a company that has an imperfect pay ratio but a thoughtful and sincere plan to fix it than a company that mysteriously always has a perfect pay ratio but where the results seem suspect and out of sync with the felt experience of its employees. As an employee myself, I'd rather feel like my imperfect company has my back than wonder what's going on behind my back.

Companies should comb through their pay and career practices data and ask employees whether each is as equitable as it could be, or if there are hidden penalties. At the top of the list will be fixing the so-called motherhood penalty and its corollary, the fatherhood bump. To again quote Tina Fey, "The topic of working moms is a tap dance recital in a minefield," but no talk of fair pay can avoid it.

Studies show that women are penalized by their companies for having children while men are rewarded. Mothers take as much as a 4 percent wage penalty per child, unless they are already in the top 10 percent of leadership in the company, where the penalty disappears. The reverse is true for men, who gain in stature as they have children, adding 6 percent to their pay. Maybe some of this is innocent. Fatherhood should theoretically make men more mature and in turn more responsible workers, which helps them earn pay raises through incremental performance (this would not, of course, explain the decrease in pay for women). More likely, a legacy of men playing the role of breadwinner has created the impression that their pay matters more than women's pay. Historically, this was explicitly the case as (mostly white) men earned "family wages" while women earned "pin money."

Women reach their peak earning potential eleven years before men, at age forty-four compared to age fifty-five. This difference can be indicative of the well-known glass-ceiling effect, where women's careers and pay grow at the same rate as men's but are capped before reaching the leadership ranks. It can also mean the motherhood penalty is cumulative, slowing down women's pay throughout their career if the company has not removed pay increase barriers, like promotion or pay-review eligibility or access to working on the most critical company projects. Women's pay can then fall so far behind men's pay that the gap becomes self-reinforcing, as women are no longer viewed as "ready" for the next big job opening. ("If we're paying Doug so much more, he must be worth it!") More than 70 percent of women with children at home participate in paid work, so there is much more going on here than women simply "opting out" of the workforce to be parents.

Many studies find the pay gap between women and men doesn't start when women hit the career ceiling or have children, but right after graduation, including for highly paid graduates working full-time hours out of law school and MBA programs. There is even some evidence of a gender wage gap in childhood allowances, as shown in a 2011 Charles Schwab survey that found teenage girls earned about 73 cents to every dollar earned by teenage boys through chores and formal jobs. Given that the majority of moms with university degrees will sequence their lives to make school a predecessor to having children, we again see women "opting out" can't explain the initial pay-gap results unless women take jobs at lower-paying companies in anticipation that only those work environments will support them in the future. While an individual company may show no pay gap for its own population of early-career women, in the aggregate it's clear there is some amount of company-enabled sorting effect happening across gender. Either we believe pay discrimination exists, or that women are purposely leaning into the total rewards trap, choosing to sacrifice fair pay at the outset for more flexible work arrangements or benefits. Law graduates would call this an adverse impact. MBAs would call it a "lose-lose."

Business leaders, think carefully about how you can build trust for the new moms in your company. It's your responsibility to make sure no one is penalized for your unexamined operating practices. At your company, are those on parental leave excluded from pay reviews while they are away? Are they pro-rated in the bonus pool? Do they have any paid leave at all? A quarter of (mostly low-wage, mostly minority) US workers do not, as the United States remains the only industrialized country without legislated paid leave. By not implementing paid leave, you are asking women (or any primary caregiver) to take a pay cut (and likely a permanent career hit) at a time when their lives have become much more expensive. No doubt the same women contributed to the development of the team and strategy behind the company's results. Why shouldn't they also participate in the rewards? Excuses about women "opting out" are more often about companies "copping out" of their responsibilities.

Perhaps we should make pregnancy our fifth fair-pay P.

GETTING TO (AND STAYING AT) ZERO

Achieving and then maintaining equal pay aren't the responsibility of the company's compensation team alone. Fair pay needs an integrated approach, and a lot of things have to go right. Legislation can require companies to follow a minimum but meaningful and coherent standard—like making sure pay is reviewed at least annually for statistical outliers, methodologies are made transparent and available to employees, and reporting is disclosed alongside financial results. Companies can take these steps further, making sure all stages of the employee life cycle are equitable, from talent sourcing to hiring to performance management to promotion and, finally, to exit. The P.E.T.E.'s have it the easiest; they only have to keep an open mind.

We put too much faith in companies to unilaterally solve the equal-pay problem. The idea of sharing power will not be met with enthusiasm. As Carrie Gracie says: "Pay is a power relationship and an employee can't help but go into a pay conversation feeling conscious of the immense asymmetry. Your employer controls your job, your income, your professional reputation. It has all the information, the experience, and the lawyers. It knows how to play this game."

She's right, and they do. In a classic twist of the Golden Rule, it's said that he who has the gold makes the rules. For equal pay, companies don't just have the gold and set the rules. They own the mines, the pickaxes, the only copy of the map, and the pen drafting the environmental survey. While much headway has been made by my compensation-management peers behind the scenes, the existing legal framework for equal pay creates disincentives for companies to talk transparently about their progress, for those who are making any at all. To be clear, many companies prefer it this way because it absolves them of accountability. Intent to do better is not enough, and those with power shouldn't get to make all the rules while facing none of the consequences for breaking them. Without collective business leadership enabled by legislation, progress will be slow and pay will remain unequal. As Frederick Douglass said, "Power concedes nothing without a demand."

A more distributed balance of power would break the stigma of talking about pay and in return counteract the P.E.T.E. platoon. By voluntarily recognizing the existing structural imbalance of power and ceding some control, by opening up the black box to explain how pay works and creating space to talk about pay without repercussion, and by not mounting fights to preempt the most basic legal standardization of equal-pay analysis and reporting, we can close the remaining pay gap much faster than we realize.

One longitudinal study found this is exactly what happens when a company introduces organizational accountability and transparency into its pay processes. Using historical pay data, and after controlling for all acceptable reasons for differences in pay, the company's annual pay increases for women were 0.4 percent lower than for men and 0.5 percent lower for Black employees than white. After launching a bundle of accountability and transparency measures, which included establishing formal criteria and processes and installing a committee to calibrate, monitor, and overrule pay decisions, the unexplained gaps disappeared. In summarizing the results, MIT professor Emilio J. Castilla wrote, "When decision makers know they will be held accountable for making fair decisions, less demographic bias is likely to occur."

Only the largest companies can hire academic departments to run controlled studies like this one to gauge the effects of internal policy changes, or vendors to conduct formal, statistically rigorous pay-equity analyses. But all companies can easily put together a pay-gap data table to see what's going on within their ranks. Unequal pay almost never looks like an email saying, "Let's pay Maeve less because she's a woman." It will never be that obvious. More often, pay discrimination comes from an accumulation of bad practices, a lack of internal governance, and the general inability or unwillingness of business leaders to recognize that rattling noise under the company hood. Unmonitored pay practices later show up in salary survey data, creating a perpetual cycle of unfair pay and a false sense of what the market should be, and leaving employees to wonder why things never change.

No matter the size, all companies can use a simple pay-gap analysis as their minimum standard. That's why I am such a supporter of the pay-gap method and think we shouldn't be so quick to dismiss it in favor of adjusted results, which may have only a veneer of rigor. A pay-gap analysis allows comparisons of big companies to small across industries while highlighting similar questions for each. If the majority of the senior team is male, of course, the pay-gap number will be high. Why is the majority of the senior team male, again? If women are working fewer hours then men, what role do the company's scheduling and leave policies play in its compensation choices? Can a company show the men are more productive than the women overall, or do the men simply reap the rewards of participation and proximity to leadership because their spouses are carrying more than their share of the unpaid work of home life? Is the pay gap for minority groups really a "pipeline issue," or is it because of inequitable promotion practices, underresourced development programs, and sourcing bias toward internal referrals and homogenous academic programs? If your high-flying talent in underrepresented groups is leaving the company, assume they experienced the results before you ran the numbers.

To date, most large companies have ignored or actively opposed publishing global pay-gap results. In 2020, Facebook's board of directors published a statement encouraging shareholders to reject a proposal for publishing global median pay-gap data. The board called the idea "unnecessary and not beneficial to our stockholders," while mentioning the company had "rejected similar proposals at each of our last four annual meetings." In a long preamble, the Facebook board walked the reader through each of its initiatives to increase diversity and representation at the company while touting its multiyear 100 percent

($1 for $1) global pay-equity achievement. Facebook demonstrates its legitimate leadership under the current norms of Pay Equity 1.0, but limits what they are willing to share because no one is forcing them to do so. An unspoken reason, I assume, is the results would be embarrassing to the company, not to mention litigious and confusing to the casual reader (but not to you after reading this book). Few companies would voluntarily take a different stance under current conditions.

Here we have another opportunity for the companies of the Business Roundtable to step up and lead, by agreeing on essential components of a global pay-gap methodology and publishing their companies' global results all at once. There will be (mathematical) blood. But by spreading the shame around, the rest of the market will follow and we will create a new baseline to improve upon. From a strictly legal sense of self-interest, by making a sincere commitment to close the pay gap now, companies may avoid more expensive forms of country-level regulations later.

• • •

The easiest job interview I've ever had started when a senior leader realized we both graduated from the University of Florida. We talked Gator basketball and their historic back-to-back championship run for twenty-five minutes, and the technical parts of the work for the remaining five. There was no avoiding it; we were similar in background, mannerisms, and, yes, demographics. I'd like to think I got the job mostly due to competence, but my ability (or luck) in being able to immediately establish a shared experience no doubt helped my case. Most of us got our jobs in a similar way. At least 70 percent of jobs are found through a personal connection, rather than applicants being plucked from a pool of random online submissions.

The research shows that creating shared connections is critical in negotiations, and what else is a job interview if not a negotiation, designed specifically to establish both your competence and the elusive "culture fit"? What's less obvious is that men have an advantage here, also. When men lead a negotiation with small talk, they have been shown to make a more favorable impression compared to those who jump into the business at hand, and are therefore more likely to create terms in their favor. Applied to our example, that means getting the job. Women, the study found, gain little to nothing from the same types of behaviors.

Nonwhite groups face an extra hurdle before getting to the interview stage. Minority job applicants double their chances for an interview if they take steps to "whiten" their résumés before submission, removing references to schools and service organizations that can infer their race. The same effect holds for businesses that take public and progressive diversity stances as those who don't. Another study found that applications with "white-sounding" names like Emily and Greg were 50 percent more likely to receive interview callbacks than when the same application is submitted with the names Lakisha and Jamal at the top. These are the "pre-test marathons" of the corporate world. These problems can be resolved with robust internal sponsorship programs and representative hiring panels to make sure all job candidates are treated equitably, even if it slows the process down. Of female leaders at major companies, 90 percent have formal sponsors at work. Looking back, my basketball-loving informal sponsor may have set up the rest of my career, including this book.

A high wage gap is the last-stage indicator of a company that has gaps in all areas of employment. Pay equity can only come from process equity and career equity, and solutions must be holistic to the full career experience rather than tinkered with through isolated practice changes. Change will come from making sure our companies are representative of the population and customer base, at all levels of leadership. When we have integrated, thoughtfully redundant practices in place to highlight and prevent blind spots in our relentless pursuit of fair pay, we create opportunity for representation. Representation creates power because power comes through numbers.

To see the power of speaking up in numbers, consider Iceland. In 1975, 90 percent of women in Iceland went on strike. Not just from their day jobs and paid work, but also from the unpaid work of home and childcare responsibilities. At the time, women made less than 60 percent of men's wages on a pay-gap basis. The following year, Iceland passed its first equal-pay law. Now, on each anniversary of the protest, women in Iceland stop all work and begin marching at the precise minute of their equivalent paid workday, marking the remaining time in the day they are comparably working for free. They celebrate their progress but also recognize the work left to do. In 2005, the protest began at 2:08 p.m. In 2008, they left at 2:25. And in 2016, the time was 2:38. At this rate, the marches won't end until 2068. In most countries, the last generation to march hasn't yet been born.

Let's be done with the debate about whether the pay gap exists or if it's a problem worth solving. By recognizing the pay gap starts long before the paycheck but tells a story about the entire employment experience, and by reporting our progress in a way that hasn't been sanitized to the point of sterility, we will build more resilient businesses and livelihoods for employees and their families. If we keep at it, we can untie our marching boots much sooner than we once thought possible.

CHAPTER 8

When Your Pay Gets Disrupted

The future of work, we hear, is coming fast and for our jobs specifically. Flashy conferences, government task forces, and consulting firms now exist to help us all navigate a future of foundational workplace change, where artificial intelligence intends to reduce humanity to some hybrid of omniscience and obsolescence. In May 2019, the phrase "future of work" hit a maximum score of 100 on Google Trends, a tool that shows Internet search frequency over time, increasing from a lowly score of 3 in the before times of May 2013.

In the proposed future, our careers will be fully self-actualized: we will work when we want, where we want, and how we want, assuming the boss gives us the power to do so. If that isn't enough freedom, in this future we can be our own boss! The future of work movement isn't a bottom-up revolution only; it has hit the corporate planning ranks, too. Shiny-object-chasing middle managers parade this future as the ultimate solution to "unlock" business agility, while executives quietly calculate the cost-shifting and risk-mitigation opportunity. The trials of this future have been with us for decades. As it happens, the Google Trends score for "future of work" almost hit 100 in April 2004, too. What's different now is that we have the technology to bring the future forth and realistically begin to apply this new future to all jobs, everywhere. The future of work is now the Future of Work™. Keyboards up, we're surrounded.

One vision of the future of work is a celebration, and the other a warning. In the positive version, our future looks like an app-enabled Swiss Family Robinson. We'll spend blissful days painting sunsets and playing with our children while robots monitor our emails and passive income streams. The less positive version is that we'll be overrun, downgraded to something like the fetus farms of the movie *The Matrix*, where humans aren't born to live but grown to be harvested for powering their machine overlords. Maybe both futures exist concurrently. A privileged few will get paintbrushes while the rest get power plugs. Leading us into this brave new world will be a managerial class of Bob Rosses, who, for a consulting fee, will help us graft happy little trees over our existential employment angst.

The Future of Work™ is really about the future of power. When it comes to models of employment power, as moderated through pay, we already know what leads to fair outcomes and what does not. If the future of work means the disaggregation (the disruption!) of employment, where each of us sets our own employment terms in what Daniel Pink long ago referred to as Free Agent Nation, then the disaggregation of pay will follow. For expediency, I'll refer to the true believers of this new way of working as the FOWLs, for Future of Work Leaders. To see if and how their model will work as the rules exist now, and whether we still believe this future is worth pursuing, we can look to the groups who have already been FOWL'ed up.

The future of pay, as with the past and present of pay, is what we make of it. This chapter, like the last, goes deeper into the power factor of our Fair Pay Mix model, where societal and legislative change enables or inhibits the future we want to create. To make sure we don't go down a dystopian path, we will focus on employment groups who are further into the future of work than the rest of us, and where the Fair Pay Mix is already being exploited or undermined: executives, franchise employees, gig economy workers, and artists. Executives will act as our ideal, where each of our P's is working as it should and unabated pay growth has followed. For the other groups, none of the P's are working, because without first establishing a basic standard of power, our attempts to gain fair pay through our process, priority, and permission options will not be effective.

Pay problems that stem from the disaggregation of employment are not new but have long been cast to the margins by a majority of office workers who, as of yet, have not been directly affected. Things are different now, the FOWLs say. The Future of Work™ is here, and there's no going back.

Should they be right, our choice is clear. We can create a future of work that works for the future, with fair pay bundled into the admission price of operating a business; we can use our new technological tools for good by operating with sincerity and transparency to correct our past mistakes, and enabled by modern legislative frameworks to more appropriately distribute power. Or we can pursue a future of work accelerated by unimpeded new technologies that form a deeper power moat between the givers and receivers of pay, disabling all the circuit breakers we've (literally) fought for over the years to give the whole system resiliency, like minimum-wage protections, worker's compensation, paid leave, health care, and retirement contributions.

Ray Dalio, founder of the world's largest hedge fund and author of *Principles*, worries we're already too far gone in the fetus farms direction, that the "system is producing self-reinforcing spirals up for the haves and down for the have-nots." I agree, but I don't believe the system, the "self" in Dalio's view, is producing these spirals on its own. The spirals are a function of what we choose to allow. As Chip Heath says in his book *Upstream*, "Every system is perfectly designed to get the results it gets," including the bad ones. The Future of Work™ will need a better pay system.

I don't mean to dismiss the FOWLs outright, or appear too cynical. Work *is* changing. In the new world, the Luddites will struggle to eat. Technology is accelerating a fundamental shift in the way we all work, and questions once thought hypothetical are now essential. Should we work for only one company at a time? Does the ideal workday occur on fixed days of the week in uniform hours? Should we all be forced to live in cities we may not like, wasting hours in traffic damaging a planet we do not have time to enjoy? Does everyone need a side hustle? Will we work from home but turn our computers into panopticons of spy pixels and pupil-tracking video calls? Can we avoid the dystopian bifurcation between those with power and a new servant class of on-demand housekeepers and delivery drivers and childcare workers? If the future is here now, I have concerns.

Our choices no longer affect only those at the margins, but by fixing the margins we reset the foundation of employment power for everyone. In 2014, Facebook retired its start-up mantra, "move fast and break things," and replaced it with the more resilient "move fast with stable infrastructure." This is the right cue and an idea that should also apply to all employees and their pay. A better model for pay requires a more stable infrastructure, and stability comes through an intentional balance of power. I've had a front-row seat (sometimes in the driver's position) to watch how the future of work is already playing out where power is too unbalanced, and I believe both the future of work and the future of pay can get much better. If we're not careful, it can also get intractably worse, this time for everyone.

WHEN YOUR PAY GETS DISRUPTED

THE CEO'S UNION REP

The history of pay was not set in stone. Through the years, we've capped pay in wartime, uncapped pay in peacetime, restructured pay at the whims of academics, and lost control of pay through the tax code. After years of machination, executives are now paid on a system of line-of-sight performance, on what amounts to a commission from shareholders in accordance with growing the stock price, while some amount of the downside risk is protected. This is the system we've designed, where it pays to be the boss.

Executives get special treatment because we see them as an "other," akin to celebrities and, in some cases, demigods. They are vaunted as job creators, world builders, and mythologized as the true masters of the universe. They are "makers"; the rest are "takers." This creation narrative isn't just rhetorical. A survey from the University of North Carolina at Chapel Hill asked American Christians to picture what they believed God looked like—and instead of seeing a son of working-class parents born in ancient Israel, the resulting composite image was described by *Forbes* in a revealing headline: "Science Reveals the Face of God and It Looks Like Elon Musk."

Some of us see business leaders as modern personal saviors who orchestrate good in our lives according to their higher purposes. Many executives see themselves this way, too. Others take an old-school route and see the gods as demanding untold and random blood sacrifices in exchange for rain to water their crops. These are not symbiotic belief systems. Divisions and tempers about executives are high and absolute, especially with the next generation of business leaders, of which I am a part, who have not experienced the economic stability of our parents. Instead, we've seen rapid economic growth concentrate to a few and the great promises of a better tomorrow punctured by global economic meltdowns far worse than the "normal" historical recession cycle. If current trends continue in many developed countries, we will become the first generation to earn less than our parents over our careers, despite having more education. In response, we've Occupied Wall Street and made an appointment to Cancel Billionaires when we get in charge. As I write these words, we are navigating a global pandemic, Great Depression–era unemployment, and the largest racial unrest in decades, all at once. On the left and the right, many want revolution. Most of us underestimate how unequal things are.

When Americans are asked what they believe CEOs are paid compared to the typical worker, their answer is thirty times as much. This was true, fifty years ago. Now, it's ten times that amount, or about three hundred times the rate of the typical worker. When asked a follow-up question about what the ideal ratio *should be*, the respondents said about seven times would be appropriate. Twenty-first-century Americans are shockingly close to fourth-century BC Athenians; Plato believed top incomes should be no more than five times the bottom. A more modern comparison is Peter Drucker, who said in 1984 that the right ratio should be twenty times. Globally, high ratios of CEO-to-worker pay are common, though they are not quite as extreme as in the United States. Executives who see themselves as globally mobile talent expect that wherever the bar is set (the United States), the rest of the world should follow. For those who already want to eat the rich, what happens when they realize they've seen only the appetizer menu?

While companies are larger and more complex than in the days of Plato or even Drucker, the growth rate of executive pay can't be fully explained by company size, performance, or industry. Pay for named executive officers (NEOs), the five highest-paid people in a US-based publicly traded company whose pay must be disclosed, would be only half its size if those factors alone were determinative. If we can't explain pay by the obvious math, like company and therefore job accountability size, then there must be more variables in the equation. These extra variables are explained by the Fair Pay Mix.

None of my peers who design executive-pay packages for a living are unaware of the problems in the current executive-pay ecosystem, a system that is perfectly calibrated to create the self-replicating spirals Dalio warns against. We all know this is a carousel from which we can't disembark unless every company steps off the ride together. Dismantling the system as it exists is unlikely, so I'm more interested in what lessons we can learn from executive pay that are applicable to the pay of everyone else. This means we won't spend time debating absolutes of what constitutes fair pay for executives, like exactly how much money is enough or what the right CEO-to-worker pay ratio should be (to be clear, it should be lower). For reasons we'll discuss later in this section, these rants fall on deaf ears. Instead, let's focus on how the Fair Pay Mix explains what's unique about executive pay and how it has successfully tamed economic gravity, and then copy those lessons for the rest of us.

A lot has happened since the Arch Patton days of the basic salary survey. Now, not only do we have dedicated salary surveys for executives, complete with predetermined regression equations we can use to calculate exact "market" rates, but we've also established compensation committees, consultancies, and third-party monitors like Glass Lewis and Institutional Shareholder Services (ISS) to keep things in motion. Each of these observers is running its own calculations and will gladly tell a company when it has stepped off the ride too early.

The most important role in executive compensation is played by the compensation committee, a select subset of the company's board members. This group is tasked with setting pay for the named executive officers and the company's overall compensation philosophy. The internal corporate compensation team (employees in jobs like mine) will then use these guardrails to set pay for everyone else. Committee members receive some combination of cash and stock in exchange for their services, but their much more lucrative day job is often in a leadership position at another company (or they are retired from such a position). This means many committee members have an incentive to not question the process too closely, as they are indirectly representing their own interests. Think of a compensation committee working like a union for executives.

Let's see how the Fair Pay Mix applies to compensation committees, and how many of our P's are in play.

PRIORITY: It's right there in the name, compensation committee. The committee has a purpose, and that purpose is compensation. Check.

PERMISSION: When a board settles on a new CEO, compensation is the last hurdle. The courtship between the board and the candidate began long prior, and they are now smitten. Transition plans are in motion and press releases are being written to persuade shareholders how this person will be the company's (next) once and future king (most often) or queen. The candidate will perhaps ask for more pay because it's a risk-free question. Turning back now for something as trivial as money makes both sides look foolish. Poker players call this being pot committed. The board expects the candidate not only to negotiate pay on the way in, including major sign-on pay, but, in a lot of cases, pre-negotiate the terms of their eventual exit. Occasionally, the incoming executive will make personal demands for their physical relocation, too. This has inspired a cottage industry of corporate relocation vendors with expertise shipping wine collections and horses. Message to the executive: ask and you shall receive. Check.

PROCESS: The compensation committee may ultimately be responsible for setting executive pay, but they aren't exactly firing up the spreadsheets themselves. Consultancies are hired (and would like to be rehired) to offer expertise and independence, à la Arch Patton. The company's own compensation team can make recommendations, too. Yes, companies have employees who recommend what their boss's boss's boss's boss should be paid. What could go wrong? Even groups that aren't asked to review pay will do so anyway, like watchdog groups that have their own peer company selection process and will calculate comparisons to companies of similar size and industry. In short, executives get regularly scheduled report cards on their pay from many different sources, and as far as they're concerned, the only passing grade is an A. Check.

POWER: Traditional economic theory says if you put a limit on maximum pay, a person wouldn't feel motivated to accept a promotion or to do their best work. Therefore, by capping pay, nobody would sign up to be the boss, or if their pay report card comes back with a B rating, they won't work as hard as they can. Traditional economists haven't spent much time working with big-shot business leaders—no one takes these jobs reluctantly or without decades of carefully plotting their career. At a certain dollar value, which is approximately $1 more than the next guy, status matters as much (or more) than pay. The top boss also knows that if he were replaced, the board would incur significant change-management work and risk, and it will look bad for having made a hiring mistake. The next CEO would get a say in choosing new board members, which puts their own spots at risk. For everyone directly involved, and unless the CEO is obviously failing, it works in their best interest to keep the executives paid and the power dynamics unquestioned. Check.

We see that when all four Fair Pay Mix P's are checked and operational, pay growth follows. Pay has reached stratospheric levels precisely because each element of the Fair Pay Mix is made visible, with mandated executive-pay transparency acting as an accelerant. I suppose you could argue the inverse, that if executive pay wasn't transparent, it would be much lower. While this logic is likely true, I don't think less transparency is the right solution for any pay problem. We should instead copy the executive-pay model for everyone, working to make pay more transparent and building the right supporting infrastructure to help pay grow from there.

Executives are used to hearing people scoff at their pay, though few of us would turn down a larger paycheck if offered. Good leaders do matter, and they should be rewarded well for their performance. Ineffective checks on power can mean the highest rewards go not only to top performers but also to those who benefit from dumb luck. In all jobs, there are only four job performance scenarios possible: being good and lucky, being good and unlucky, being bad and lucky, and being bad and unlucky. The way executives are paid, with most of their compensation based on a company's stock price, windfalls can come at random in a good overall economic climate, while the downside luck is protected through predetermined exit packages and board discretion. What should we call it when someone is paid no matter what happens? Is it still pay for performance or something like pay for protection? Regardless, I wouldn't call this fair pay unless everyone else got to play by the same rules.

Barring a collective epiphany from capitalism's better angels, the only way to slow executive pay or to redirect funds toward those lower in the company requires legislation to change the opportunity cost math for companies. We'd need punitive tax penalties for companies that choose executives over workers, working in tandem with highly progressive (and enforced) corporate and personal tax rates that remove the incentive to reward high earners' each marginal dollar. These are hard problems, so put down your Cancel Billionaires mug for now. Legislation and tax penalties alone, assuming the political will existed to make these changes, wouldn't do anything to solve the root issue that executives have drawn a Fair Pay Mix flush. Executive pay could be cut in half or down to zero, and for large companies, the total amount saved for redistribution to all workers wouldn't stretch far. By my estimates for most large companies, the top executive team in total earns less than 5 percent of a company's entire payroll budget, or about what the company spends in annual pay raises. There are two lessons here. The first is a reminder that, as we saw in Chapter 2, many companies can dramatically improve the lives of their lowest-paid workers without much effect on their total wage expense (though the sticker price may look high). The second lesson is that to meaningfully increase pay for everyone else, we will need a more comprehensive solution than soaking the rich.

The latest attempts to slow executive pay are "name and shame" laws, meant to make the most grievous executive-pay packages more visible and less palatable to the public. The CEO-to-worker pay ratio is an example of these laws, and though the results make for interesting reading and a trove of annual headlines, they have limited value because the shock value has worn off and the numbers are easily rationalized. Companies with the largest ratios are often also highly distributed global employers. Consider Mattel, the global toy manufacturer. In 2020, the company reported not a 30-to-1 or a 300-to-1 ratio, but nearly 3,000-to-1. This result was driven by the location of the median worker eligible for reporting, who in this case was a manufacturing facility employee in Indonesia. Few readers have a standard heuristic of fair pay for Indonesian factory workers, and so they quickly lose interest.

Say on Pay, another shaming law, is meant to give shareholders a voice in approving executive-pay packages. The value of these laws is equally limited because failing grades are rare, and the votes are nonbinding, giving vote totals the standing of a participation trophy. However, this doesn't mean shaming laws are worthless. Although Say on Pay laws are new, we are already seeing some of the intended results: in countries where Say on Pay laws have passed, CEO pay had declined by about 7 percent on average, while company performance has increased 5 percent. These laws also jolt companies into different routines of thinking, at least internally. Compensation teams do squirm when pulling pay ratio data together, crossing our fingers that we're never called to justify the numbers in the public square. We know our operating system is not designed for any other outcome.

More pay transparency for the rest of us, like we see now with executives, will pressure companies to get their compensation houses in order faster. To accelerate these efforts, we can mimic the "top-five" disclosure approach for the bottom-five paid employees. To my knowledge, no company voluntarily discloses this data now. For the results to resonate with readers, the bottom five should come from the global headquarters country, so if the CEO sits in the United States, the company would have to disclose its bottom-five paid US-based employees' jobs and location (but not names). By reporting bottom-five pay on a full-time-equivalent basis, compensation committees would put their seal of approval on the process, priority, and permission structure of the entire company's pay practices, not only the executives or the company's too-generic-to-be-useful pay philosophy. If pay for the bottom-five stayed the same every year, if there was no annual pay raise process, and if the compensation philosophy wasn't thoughtfully explained in the disclosure, we'd know to hold the committee accountable. The bottom five would almost certainly come from a volume jobs group, like a manufacturing facility or a retail store, which means for practical purposes, companies would increase pay for the bottom five only as part of a more comprehensive process that applies pay increases to everyone in similar jobs. Where many people are paid at the bottom-five rate, reporting should include the number of people at that rate.

By expanding the compensation committee's remit, we'd short-circuit internal prioritization battles about who is deserving of a raise, which too often depends on your place in the hierarchy. Bottom-five pay acts as a company minimum wage and would cascade pay increases up through the organization. While we're at it, let's also require that we share the demographics of the bottom-five paid employees, just to see if we find any problematic trends (we will).

The lesson of executive pay and the effects of pay transparency is clear: if you can't beat them, join them.

THE FRANCHISE WARS

There's a scene in the movie *Demolition Man* where Sylvester Stallone's character, John Spartan, first learns how the world has changed since he was cryogenically frozen in 1996. The year is now 2032, and Spartan has been reanimated from his slumber. When Sandra Bullock's character, Lenina Huxley, takes Spartan out for a night of dinner and dancing, he is surprised to learn they are driving to a Taco Bell, a place not historically known for its fine dining and dance scene. Huxley responds, "You do not realize that Taco Bell was the only restaurant to survive the Franchise Wars. Now, *all* restaurants are Taco Bell."

If only one restaurant existed, in this case Taco Bell, we'd call that having industry monopoly power. Monopoly is a familiar concept most of us learned from the eponymous board game. Similar to monopoly

power is "monopsony." With monopoly power, there is only one restaurant, and so your entire dining budget goes to various types of Taco
Bells. With monopsony power, there is only one employer, and all your
earnings come from various types of Taco Bells. In other words, like
what I saw in Poland.

For a few years, I managed international compensation for Yum!
Brands, the company behind Taco Bell and other mega-brands Pizza
Hut and KFC. I went to Yum (I will drop the brand's exclamation
point because it makes for confusing sentences) after leaving my role at
Starbucks, and in the transition period I took a call with Yum's Eastern
European partner, AmRest (short for American Restaurants). Within
a few weeks, I was sitting at the AmRest offices in Wrocław, Poland,
working with the company's leadership to improve their approach to
restaurant pay. I was an ideal partner because I understood not only
Yum's compensation model but also the Starbucks approach. This was
important because AmRest franchised both Yum and Starbucks stores
in the region, plus the Burger Kings and several smaller brands.

One proposal to manage pay was to design all pay programs at the
corporate level regardless of brand affiliation. The idea, common for
the industry, was to harmonize for nuances in the types of jobs each
brand uses. A Starbucks barista might be paid the same as the KFC
cashier, for example. The administrative work could be managed more
efficiently that way, and a unified approach would limit each brand's
ability to poach each other's workers for more money. To the consumer,
each AmRest restaurant brand was a competitor. To the employee, the
idea was there would only be one paycheck, and that paycheck would
come from AmRest.

Some form of this model is used around the world by conglomerates
that run many brands at once, sometimes not even in the same category.

In the United Arab Emirates, a company called the Americana Group (notice a naming theme?) runs nineteen different restaurant brands. In the United States, Flynn Restaurant Group operates many Taco Bells, Applebees, Paneras, and Arbys. The German firm JAB Holdings manages businesses ranging from Pret A Manger to pet hospitals. Mitsubishi, better known for its engine production, has long run the KFCs in Japan. Oil change chains operate this way, as do tax services and hotels and airport shops. My favorite example, Alshaya Group out of Kuwait, could build its own mall and house you in the process through its ninety separate brands located across the Middle East, North Africa, and Eastern Europe. Like other industries, there is limited to no public information available about any of these groups' pay programs, but my guess is that few run aggressively competing pay programs across their portfolio.

To be clear, I am not saying franchise and licensing conglomerates are inherently antagonistic to fair pay. In recent years, even without harmonized pay programs many franchisee brands have decided (or been pressured) to remove explicit "no-poach" clauses in their agreements that limit wage-depressing effects. Of the groups I've worked with, I've never seen anything nefarious and have found many that take their responsibility toward fair pay seriously. In my experience, the larger the group, the more competent and sincere their desire to improve the employment experience and working conditions in the aggregate. The problems start with the separation of legal structures, where the franchisee and the brand are separate entities, and therefore the employee is not found on the brand's books. Poverty wages and individual stories of wage theft, like a manager who pockets tips or makes workers perform off the clock, are now the problem of the franchisee, not the brand.

Competence and sincerity aren't enough when a structure itself becomes the barrier to fair pay. The reasons for the persistence of low wages in the service industry are not limited to our standard three-legged race problem, but made worse through an added lack of structural market competition. Thomas Philippon, in his book *The Great Reversal: How America Gave Up on Free Markets*, says it plainly: "If potential workers have the choice between only a handful of employers, then the employers have market power over the workers and can offer lower wages." Franchisees may not be lowering wages intentionally, but they are not feeling much pressure to raise them, either.

The vision of an independent franchise as run by local, entrepreneurial families who set wages by the supply and demand of workers in the neighborhood is, for many brands, not accurate. McDonald's, through its restaurants and supply chain, may be correct to say it has created more Black millionaires than any other corporation. This is not usual for the industry, and I would suspect new McMillionaires are now a rare occurrence. Larger conglomerates and increasingly private equity firms have now entered the game, like Brazil's 3G Capital, which owns Burger King, Popeyes Chicken, and Tim Hortons coffee in its brand portfolio. These types of deals create jobs and can generate great wealth for the owners. When that happens, they should not also struggle to pay fair wages.

When the Franchise Wars are over and all employers become Taco Bell (or Pizza Hut, as it was dubbed over to say in the film's international release), wages will not grow because workers have nowhere else to go. Arguably, we are already in this future. Where there is no meaningful competition, market increases can come only from a different source of pay power, like minimum-wage legislation or collective bargaining. In some countries, including the United States, the brand entity has no choice but to stay at an arm's-length distance from helping franchisees set pay, through what are called "co-employment laws." This means that if McDonald's, the name most associated with the franchise model, wanted to mandate a company minimum wage of $15 per hour for all its US restaurants tomorrow, it could not easily do so. A brand that operates under a franchise arrangement, as it exists, has learned to disaggregate its responsibility for pay by outsourcing its Fair Pay Mix influence. The industry, and more so the employee, suffer as a result.

Some countries have figured this problem out and delegated power for employment conditions and pay elsewhere. One approach, practiced in Australia among others, is sectoral bargaining. We covered this concept briefly in Chapter 6, where working conditions and minimum pay are negotiated and legislated by the industry as a whole rather than the individual company. Agreements are then applied to all competitors consistently. US-based franchisors might predict a quick industry death if this model was implemented widely, but these reports would be greatly exaggerated. During my time at Yum, KFC Australia was the brand's shining beacon. The country smashed its growth targets and was known internally as a factory for outstanding management talent, producing the CEOs for both KFC and the Yum corporate entity.

Over time, I believe we'd come to see the sectoral bargaining model, or a similar shared power arrangement like an indexed and livable minimum wage, as a stage for competitive advantage. With wage-setting power better delegated, brands could focus more of their time on the employee experience, improving productivity through reduced turnover, enhanced job design, and career development. Together, these efforts would lower the cost of wage administration, improve the industry's reputation, and, most importantly, give franchise workers a fighting chance at fair pay.

THE PROBLEM WITH PLATFORMS

Where franchise workers are partially severed from the Fair Pay Mix, as many as one in five workers are kept in more arm's-length, fully separated work arrangements. This includes low-wage workers like janitorial and construction hands, but also high-wage workers classified as independent contractors and those employed by third-party staffing agencies. David Weil, a professor and former head of the Department of Labor's Wage and Hour Division, calls this the "fissured workplace" in his book by the same name. In the fissured workplace, the idea that any worker can progress from the mail room to the boardroom is now only nostalgia, not because email and instant messaging technology have eliminated mail rooms, but because the mail room rung has been cut off the career ladder.

Some types of fissured workplaces can work well, like where workers have an entrepreneurial advantage to remain separate, including doctors or freelance web designers. For jobs without obvious performance differentiation, and therefore no entrepreneurial opportunities and pay power, we see significant fair pay hurdles.

The risk of unfair pay is highest at the two ends of the employment chain, from where work is first sourced to when work is finally delivered. Starbucks refers to these end points as the *"first ten feet"* and the *"last ten feet,"* in reference to the farmer who grows their coffee plants and the barista who hands a customer their Skinny Vanilla Latte. These end points are also the most likely to be staffed through fully severed work arrangements. The business philosophy behind the ten-feet principle is that by treating the two ends of the supply chain well, the middle part, where you find full-time salaried employees with benefits, will take care of itself. More attention is needed on the first ten feet of pay, especially in global factory contexts where contractors manage subcontractors and both are kept ten legal feet (approximately ten thousand regular people feet) away from review by the company's compensation experts. We will focus on the last ten feet, specifically where the risks of unfair pay have become accelerated, concentrated, and arguably weaponized in the form of the so-called gig economy.

Gig work plays an important role in the marketplace by helping people earn irregular and supplemental income, especially where they need to smooth gaps between more traditional jobs. A gig can serve indirect purposes, too, by carving out space for innovation and allowing workers to try different types of work they are not fully ready to commit to as a profession, without giving up the stability of a day job they may not like. For others, gigs are just for fun, and we've all been roped into seeing an acquaintance's band or stand-up comedy act against our wishes. JPMorgan Chase found that for people who take up gig work, the supplemental income they earn replaces 73 percent of missing income from lost payroll jobs, which while being a positive indicator for the usefulness of gig work is also an indictment of how little most people are paid in their regular jobs.

Employers also benefit from gig experimentation, as they can use variable labor to ramp up production during peak demand seasons without carrying the extra cost of permanent employees throughout the year. By enabling opportunities for jobs to scale up and down quickly alongside business success and failure, we've made a societal trade-off that gig work can carry fewer of the long-term protections we associate with being the obligation of a traditional employer. I hope you're noticing a theme of how often flexibility is used as bait into the total rewards trap.

The controversy over gig work isn't about whether these jobs should exist—they always have and always will. Technology platforms will continue to improve matches between available workers and available work, and this will give workers more power over their own labor and a patchwork of income possibilities when the traditional employment system fails them. The two biggest problems are in how gig workers set the price of their labor, as most platforms dictate the amount, and the scale of gig work as an employment class. At a critical mass, where gig work becomes the default employment experience for anyone not paid a salary to sustain the gig platform itself, we will have gained a sense of autonomy but lost hard-fought-for stability, safety protections, and benefits. If our expectation is that all work should provide a basic standard of dignity, then we must do more to balance the inherent usefulness of new technology when the last ten feet steers into our driveways.

These losses are outlined in the "Frankfurt Paper on Platform-Based Work," released in 2016 by a network of American and European labor groups. The group stresses that gig platforms are not playing by the same sets of rules as the rest of the economy, and that this structural power imbalance is taking all workers backward. It'd be lazy to dismiss the Frankfurt group as protectionists of an old order without debating the merits of their argument, or without acknowledging they, too, see the obvious practical benefits in platform technologies. The paper closes with a call to optimism, saying that "information technology, shaped wisely, holds great promise for expanding access to good work." To achieve that great promise, the group calls on platform companies to address the power imbalance they've enabled, "instead of using technology to 'work around' the letter and spirit of existing laws."

If the FOWLs are correct and gig work becomes the future of jobs, then the track we are on now is incompatible with a future of fair pay. Businesses have to make money to pay workers, but few of the major platforms show a realistic path to profitability. Yes, losses may be rationalized as a by-product of investment in hyper-growth to capture market share. Available data on the unit economics of each transaction suggests otherwise, that the business model for many platforms may never work. Uber, the largest platform player and theoretically the furthest through its hyper-growth phase, has announced it will become profitable in 2021 but to date has only accelerated its losses on a per-transaction basis. While the technology is here to stay, and Uber may well become profitable, a day may come when shareholders force all but the biggest gig platforms to pivot into a kind of company that can generate sustained profits. Uber and its peers could one day upend their own business models to survive, licensing the platforms to other companies for logistics purposes or to municipalities for public transit, or transitioning to fully autonomous vehicles. In any of those events, the company will need a lot fewer (and possibly zero) gig workers. If this happens, Uber (and its peers) will have fulfilled Louis Hyman's belief that gig platforms are successful only as "the waste product of the service economy" that failed to provide better alternatives.

Where do gig workers, once encouraged by the FOWLs, find a paycheck in a world where gigs were already the last resort? Surely this is a question we must plan for regardless of how platform companies adapt with time, as automation will continue to transform all work. More people are seeing universal basic income (UBI) as the answer to this question, but as I said in Chapter 1, I don't think we should be so willing to trade a system capable of fair pay and robust job creation for an all-inclusive supplement that is subject to political hostage taking. Perhaps we're too far gone for any other solution, and while UBI is a useful tool to account for unpaid but necessary work like family care, or in an emergency like a pandemic, it is not a substitute for a system capable of creating good jobs with fair pay. We still have to fix the stuff that sits on top of the "basic" income to make UBI sustainable.

The legislative pressure on gig work platforms to create good jobs with fair pay can't be understated. Uber, which we'll continue to use as a proxy for all gig work as the industry's largest player, recognizes certain types of legislation as an existential threat. As a bulwark, the company has made preemptive proposals over the years, including to pay its gig workers a higher minimum of at least $21 per hour, though the company gives few details on how the calculations will play out. Platform detractors, citing their own studies, find that typical gig wages trail far behind platform company promises, with pay often netting less than minimum wage when accounting for wait times and essential vehicle maintenance.

No opposition group to gig platforms has been louder than independent restaurant owners, who have a habit of posting their transaction statements online to show how much of their already slim margins are going to the delivery platforms. Meanwhile, these platforms have been known to take a bite from the other end of the transaction, too, as delivery drivers have seen their customers' tips used to subsidize the platforms themselves, due to emphatically insincere practices that deduct tips from base pay. The old schemes of unfair pay are new again—we saw this playbook with William R. Scott's hotel manager example in Chapter 4. After countless global gig worker strikes and multipage newspaper profiles of gig drivers who have to sleep in their cars because they can't afford housing, platforms are right to be worried about their legal future.

Gig platform companies know the legislative fight is both serious and self-inflicted. In the midst of the COVID-19 pandemic and the mass US unemployment that followed, Uber CEO Dara Khosrowshahi wrote, hat in hand, to President Trump in search of federal funding to support the gig workers on his platform. The company was directly asking that gig workers be protected by the taxpayer when, as a company, it had not factored worker essentials like access to health and unemployment insurance or severance pay into its core business model (platforms would argue they are legally barred from doing so). In fact,

the company and its peers continue to fight against standard employment protections by insisting that gig workers should not be considered
eligible for these benefits on their dime under normal, nonpandemic
circumstances. If the idea of pay sincerity is still a bit nebulous for you,
think of this scenario as the opposite of what it should look like. While
raising the white flag of surrender, Khosrowshahi was also seeking to
avoid harder concessions later, specifically in classifying gig workers as
outright employees. We should read the letter as nothing less than a
landmark admission on behalf of the industry that it was culpable for
the state of its workers' affairs.

In the third paragraph of the Uber letter is a reminder that two years
prior, the company had called for a new type of portable benefits system that gig workers could use to gain access to basic employment protections. They wouldn't be standard employees, exactly, but something
in between employees and fissured freelancers, a status that remains ill
defined by law. In a *New York Times* opinion piece several months later,
Khosrowshahi called it the "third way" approach. The CEO was now
reminding legislators of the company's earlier commitment to support
legislation, because "everyone should have the option to protect themselves and their loved ones when they're injured at work, get sick, or
when it's time to retire." The company announced a pilot program and
partnership between Uber and two unlikely Washington state leaders: David Rolf, president of the local Service Employees International
Union, and venture capitalist Nick Hanauer. An outspoken critic of
corporate power imbalances, Hanauer was an early and vocal advocate
for the $15 minimum-wage movement in Seattle. Unfortunately, after
two years there has been little public progress on the portable benefits
pilot. On the legislative front, a group of the largest platform players,
including Uber, reportedly spent at least $200 million successfully lob-
bying against reform in California alone, going as far as to reimburse

gig workers directly for their expenses in protesting on the company's behalf.

From unions to platform owners to platform users, all sides agree that current legislation is insufficient to care for gig workers, making this form of work hardly ready to be our future. Platform companies are far from blameless, which, at least in Uber's case, the company readily admits. They should rightfully be derided for the insincerity of their commitments, despite episodic shoe-gazing statements about how they "know [they] need to do more." Still, platforms aren't totally making up the bind they find themselves in—gig work in the platform ecosystem is an unresolved legal gray area that will take iteration to legislate appropriately. As Khosrowshahi has said, "We are ready to do our part, but we need new laws to let us take bolder action." This sounds too similar to what we heard Jeff Bezos say in Chapter 4, where he challenged less-powerful companies to "throw the gauntlet back at us" before his company would again raise wages, as if they had no agency in their pay rates and the welfare of their employees but were being held hostage by a market that is supposed to be free for them to act at will.

The solution isn't to insist on more vertically integrated companies and get rid of the fissured workplace entirely. This would lead to a different kind of power imbalance where we expect one company to manage the entire first ten feet to last ten feet process itself. This will limit competition, stifle innovation, and distract companies from focusing on the types of work they are best at. Instead, to receive the benefits associated with flexible employment, companies must be required to do more for their regular contractors to ensure they aren't sending the societal bill to everyone else. Gig platforms need more than legislative classification updates. They also need a better-funded baseline, which Khosrowshahi has called for directly.

Some have called this flexicurity, a portmanteau of flexible and security, and the idea goes beyond the portable benefits plan proposed in various forms by Uber and its peers. There are many ways to do this, but to get us started, let me share how I interpret the problem from my seat in the compensation chair. Platform companies, consider this an invitation to fill in my blanks with your actual data and improve on the gig worker experience as presented.

All compensation programs start with design principles, and for this design we can follow the Khosrowshahi, Rolf, and Hanauer mandates that the way forward must offer flexibility, proportionality, universality, innovation, and independence. A more recent version of the plan simplifies it to three principles: proportionality, aggregation, and autonomy. To meet either set of mandates, my proposal is that all gig workers have access to a matching and portable pay-as-you-go system.

After working at least eight hours total across platforms in a week, or one standard workday, gig workers should be able to contribute matching funds up to 20 percent of their total earnings to a portable cash account. If gig workers pitch in the maximum 20 percent of their pay, then the platform must contribute 20 percent as well. This fund would vest biannually and become accessible any time thereafter, with contributions made using the same tax advantages and flexibility as a college savings plan. In addition to the matching portion of the plan, the platform would be required to contribute a baseline 10 percent of earnings into a flexible cash fund. Platform companies could choose to offer deferral bonuses for the account, which would incent workers to keep their money in the plan and allow the platform to offset administrative expenses by investing the fund for financial gains. In the States, where health insurance is far from guaranteed, gig workers who log more than sixteen hours per week (two standard days) on average would become eligible or ineligible for health insurance in line with the company's annual open-enrollment cycle, subsidized at the same rate as traditional employees. This last point is critical but would be complex for reasons I'll avoid here, which speaks to the overall efficacy of the US health-care system and its ties to employment. Platform companies, to their credit, have already made progress on health-care access despite the complexity.

In a traditional employment relationship, each employee costs about 30 percent more than their wages. The extra expense accounts for employment taxes and benefits, most of which platform companies do not currently pay. My proposal mirrors this relationship, but gives workers the power to opt out at their discretion. Gig workers can choose not to contribute to the fund, either because they have immediate need for their full paycheck or because they already have a traditional job with benefits. Here is how the math works out in three full-time scenarios: at the current US federal minimum wage of $7.25 per hour, $15.00 per hour, and the $23.25 per hour Uber says the median driver in Seattle earned in 2020.

SCENARIOS	FORMULA RATE	SCENARIO 1	SCENARIO 2	SCENARIO 3
A. Base Hourly Rate	-	$7.25	$15.00	$23.25
B. Baseline Benefit Fund	10%	$0.73	$1.50	$2.33
C. Platform Match	20%	$1.45	$3.00	$4.65
Current Annual Total Rewards	A	$15,080	$31,200	$48,360
With Baseline Benefit Fund	A + B	$16,588	$34,320	$53,196
With BBF and Full Uber Match	A + B + C	$19,604	$40,560	$62,868

At minimum, when factoring the federal minimum wage and a 10 percent basic contribution to a portable fund, additional pay is about 75 cents an hour. This is equivalent to what Uber proposed in a 2020 plan that would allow the median driver in Colorado, who works thirty-five hours per week, to accrue "approximately $1,350 in benefits funds." As shown, my plan is more generous while meeting the design principles; the plan builds in proportion to hours worked, aggregates into a portable account across platforms, and provides autonomy to the worker to use the funds at their discretion. In the third scenario, the full-time driver who earns $23.25 per hour is eligible to receive about $1,200 per month in additional pay.

The total cost to the platform company would surely be less than their 30 percent maximum commitment, as many gig workers will not fully participate in the matching portion. As a predictor, we can assume similar participation rates of retirement matching plans, which are not used by more than 40 percent of those making less than $40,000 annually, leaving a lot of "free money" on the table. By giving workers access to their money faster, perhaps a gig worker matching plan can be more successful.

If the argument made by platform companies is that the jobs they offer enable supplemental income and flexibility, and if this flexibility is true and not a total rewards trap for paying people too little, my plan keeps everyone honest and incents the company's behavior in that direction (line of sight!). If the reality of platform gig work is that contractors are using it as their primary, full-time income source, then the cost to platforms should become exponentially higher and the terms more closely resemble traditional employment.

A matching system would not by itself satisfy the full mandates of our pay sincerity model, especially if a large percentage of the economy moved to gig work, and if health insurance remains tied to the traditional employment relationship. The best use of a matching plan works as a supplement where essential benefits are available and affordable for everyone—no easy task. Other models should be tried, too. New York's Black Car Fund, which adds a 2.5 percent cost per ride to fund essential benefits, is one such approach. This model seems less equipped to meet all our design principles, especially the autonomy mandate. By making platforms themselves carry more of the direct financial obligations over time, rather than gig workers relying on user fees, the fund would be more resilient during a business downturn when gig workers need it most.

While the best approach to make pay fair for platform-based gig workers has yet to be determined, I'm encouraged in our collective recognition that the current model does not work. Our standard should be that we pursue only futures of work that improve our power to enhance the experience of work, regardless of the shape of our jobs, the hours we work, or the technology we use. The Future of Work™ must be elevated.

You know, like a platform.

(LESS) STARVING ARTISTS

I started writing Chapter 7 after an embarrassing mistake. To better understand fair pay through the lens of gender identity, I reached out to Claire Wasserman, author and founder of the career resources group Ladies Get Paid. Unfortunately, I botched the recording of our conversation due to a total lack of audio-engineering skills, leaving only my voice on the file. Desperate for professional help, I texted my friend Kyle Cox, a Nashville-based musician.

Kyle quickly told me my failure was comprehensive and none of

Claire's audio could be saved. He tried everything and expected to do so for free, not only because we're friends but because in his industry it's common to let expertise go unrewarded. Regardless of expectations, I paid him through the Venmo app, evidence that platforms *can* enable fair pay. Here's how the next exchange read between a surprised Kyle and me (and, yes, I wrote my texts in complete sentences, anticipating they would find a way into this chapter):

Kyle: GTFO, that literally took me 90 seconds. [GTFO is an acronym that does not mean "Gratitude! Totally Fair Outcome."]
Me: No, it took you a career of investing in your skills and equipment to get the work done in 90 seconds. Your expertise saved me hours.

I am not trying to pat myself on the back. I absolutely owe a debt to the art world, not just because art brings joy to my life, but monetarily for the CDs I burned throughout my teenage years. While people aren't burning CDs anymore, the business model for artists has always been ripe for unfair pay. Virginia Nicholson, in her book *Among the Bohemians*, said of artists in the early 1900s, "A minor artist with no money goes as hungry as a genius." We've all internalized the idea that by doing artistic work you shouldn't expect to make much money—being a "starving artist" is part of the deal. As a group that no doubt provides value to society, what lessons from the Fair Pay Mix can we apply to work that has no traditional access to priority, permission, process, or power structures?

In a clichéd Oscar Wilde quote, he says when bankers get together, they talk about art, and when artists get together, they talk about money. I suppose this resonates because, to pile on clichés, time *is* money. Whether work is rewarded by time, through play, or money, through pay, the same thing matters: the relative value of what one person has compared to another. The banker wishes for the entrepreneurial time of the artist, and the artist wishes for the entrepreneurial funding of the banker. Both groups want what amounts to what they see as fair, meaning more resources to live out their potential.

A difference (among many) between the banker and the artist is in the barriers to entry and exit for the artist profession, namely that there are none. If you are a terrible investment banker, you don't get to keep banking after your incompetence makes you unemployable or gets your securities license revoked. You can still do art on the side no matter how terrible it is. Successful bankers can try art, too, as demonstrated by Goldman Sachs CEO David Michael Solomon, otherwise known in nightclubs around the world as DJ D-Sol. Conversely, no artist starts a banking side hustle. When we talk about fair pay for artists, I want to talk about those who have moved through the dabbling and side-hustle phases, who have crossed an initial threshold of both commitment and skill. For those who have built enough clout to pursue their craft full-time and therefore can attempt to make a living from it, how can we make sure they are paid fairly? We'll call these people professional artists. DJ Collateralized Debt Obligation will be fine without us.

The fair-pay-for-professional-artists problem is bigger than we think. According to the National Endowment for the Arts, there are more than 2 million working artists in the United States, equivalent to the population of Nebraska. About 35 percent are self-employed. The remaining 65 percent of artists we can assume work in corporate settings like a design firm or a professional orchestra. For this 65 percent, the fair pay rules are no different than for the accountant. An artist might cringe at the thought of their work being reduced to a number and a corporate process, but I regret to inform them the same Fair Pay Mix P's and tactics found in Chapter 6 apply to designers, composers, and performers. Yes, corporate artists, we *can* put a number on your work and include it in a salary survey. For these reasons, we will momentarily expand the scope of this book and focus on the 35 percent without access to the corporate pay ecosystem.

Globally, let's assume the workforce is equally artistically inclined as in the United States, about 1 percent of the total. If the total global workforce is 3 billion people, then the total global artist population is about 30 million people. So, the 35 percent of 30 million who are self-employed equals around 10 million people globally who earn a living independently through their art. That's twice the population of Ireland, and therefore I propose the Double Irish no longer be thought of as a tax scheme and is now shorthand for independent artist count.

Pay data that includes all types of independent artists is hard to find, so I will translate the available statistics from the music industry more broadly. Within the music industry, the most successful 1 percent of artists earn 77 percent of all music revenue. While revenue is not a direct line to income, from the data available we might assume artist pay is more unequal than corporate pay. In the art world, most of the spoils go to a few victors. Steady pay for most is a fantasy at first, and many new artists experience payment for their work in something other than money, often trading exposure for exploitation. All artists have their story. Designers get asked to whip up a logo because "it will be everywhere." Photographers are told to take pictures at a friend's wedding instead of enjoying the day, because they "have the nice camera." Years ago, prior to signing with a major record label, my friend Matt played a show at a local Gap store where he was paid in jeans. This is not a sustainable living, though to be fair I have not run the numbers to see if median denim earnings over time have kept pace with productivity.

Though the art world may pay unequally, that doesn't mean artists have to rise to the Kehinde Wiley level to keep food on the table. By our definition of professional artists, most are not starving. The 2018 median wage for the Bureau of Labor Statistics category of "Fine Artists, Including Painters, Sculptors, and Illustrators," which no doubt includes a large percentage of corporate-setting artists, is a touch under $50,000, about the same as all other industries. Starting salaries in big-city US orchestras reach the six figures, or more than double the national median personal income. Also like other industries, the top 1 percent of artists are paid exponentially more than the plebs.

Unlike the executive in corporate settings, artists rarely operate in a pay environment where they get to set their own pay rules, which means those at the top can therefore be victims of unfair pay themselves. Taylor Swift held a three-year boycott of the streaming platform Spotify for fair artist royalties. Jennifer Lawrence and her female costars were found (through leaked emails) to have been paid far below their male counterparts. The United States women's soccer team (yes, athletes are artists) created such passion about their pay relative to the men's squad that chants of "Equal Pay!" rang throughout stadiums on the team's 2019 World Cup championship run. The NPR show *Planet Money* has given much consideration to the idea that LeBron James has been dramatically underpaid his entire career. Fair pay, and the processes used to set pay, are important regardless of a person's entourage size.

The economist's model for artist pay is called Baumol's Cost Disease. The idea is that while pay has historically grown in step with productivity (until the 1970s, at least), artists have less ability than most to produce work more efficiently over time. It will always take the same number of people and time to play a song by the Beatles, to paint a portrait, or to field a soccer team. Meanwhile, the administrative stuff that goes into producing the album or selling event tickets, like the legal contracts and rent at the gallery, gets more expensive as a percent of the artist's cost, leaving less for the artist over time. Major changes in the distribution models of art through the Internet have accelerated this cost pressure by lowering customer willingness to pay for art. Now, less pay is available for the creators. Artists have a first-ten-feet pay problem.

To help me understand what artists think about their pay (other than "all the time"), I called Derek Webb. Webb is a career musician with close to a million record sales in bands and as a solo artist. He's also an entrepreneur, founding several companies that help musicians make a living from their art. One company, an early Internet platform called NoiseTrade, allowed artists to give their music away in exchange for customer data like their postal code, and was later acquired by a larger company that used the data to target audiences for live events.

Webb says the biggest rewards go to artists whom people feel they can trust and with whom they resonate. I've said the same for companies—that high trust buys resilience during low times, and those who inspire a deep sense of trust in their employees (or fans) create a sustainable competitive advantage. Trust helps companies (and independent artists) withstand temporary blips like a cyclical business downturn or an experimental-phase novel. Per Webb, the power to create that trust sits with artists, assuming they don't break "rule number one, which is to be great, and rule number 1.5, to be resonant." We didn't cover how many rules exist in total or in what fractions.

Kevin Kelly, cofounder of *Wired* magazine, once wrote a piece titled "1,000 True Fans" that artists like Derek Webb have studied carefully. According to Kelly, a true fan is "a fan that will buy anything you produce." If an artist has 1,000 true fans, and every true fan spends

$100 on the artist's work each year, the artist earns a six-figure income. Webb gave me his own true fans accounting, saying, "Five percent of my fans subsidize 80 percent of my career." True fans were the insight behind NoiseTrade; artists could post their music for download as a lead generator for future sales. We could also say NoiseTrade applied the Fair Pay Mix because artists gained power over their own pricing, copyrights, and distribution, permission to contact fans with new material or when planning a tour, a process that let fans pay artists directly for the music they were downloading, and enabled artists to find the people who would make paying them a priority.

For artists, the financial points of engagement are relatively fixed. Merchandise and ticket fees don't vary much. The music streaming platforms now pay the same royalties to all artists per stream, so the artist earns their pay on volume, maybe the closest thing to a true pay-for-performance plan I've seen. This was not always the case. At first, platforms chose to keep their artists' payout calculations hidden behind an algorithmic black box, much the same as corporate compensation teams do with pay in traditional companies. After artists started posting their pay statements online, with a hard assist from power artists like Taylor Swift, a mix of transparency and shame nudged the platforms into a more equal model, at least on a relative opportunity basis. We learned the same lesson in the world of executive pay: fair pay depends on structural power, is enabled through transparency, and where insincerity makes it necessary, is catalyzed by shame.

Botched interview aside, I do remember something Claire Wasserman told me with perfect clarity: "The best thing you can do [to make pay fair] is to share what you make." Derek Webb told me something similar, saying, "Artists tend to downplay the money they make to their audience, but overstate the money they make to their friends." Regardless of your profession, earning your worth requires you to feel worthy of what you should earn, and to be open and honest when you are feeling undervalued. This vulnerability inspires a better future of work that works for everyone. In situations where power is a structural prerequisite to fair pay, find the opportunities to share what you make and what you'd like to make. Executives do it. Why not you?

You may have more power than you realize.

A Fair Pay Future

I wrote this book in the course of two extremes. When I started, all the traditional measures for the health of an economy were thriving, like employment, stock market indices, and GDP growth. The unemployment rate in particular reached near-record lows, capping more than a decade-long steady downward trend after the 2007 Great Recession. Success was being shared broadly, though unevenly, across demographic and socioeconomic lines. Organic growth was leading to abundant job creation, and minimum-wage increases passed by many cities and states ensured that as the economy grew, wages at the bottom of the scale would start to climb in a meaningful way for the first time in my compensation career.

Months later, the world and, in particular, the United States were caught unprepared for a global pandemic, followed by (and connected to) unprecedented protests for racial equality. Widespread economic pain led to calls for systemic changes to add more stability, resiliency, and equality to the employment construct. Large corporations lent their support, too, using phrases not heard from them before, like "social justice" and "white supremacy," and pledging meaningful dollars to deconstruct a social order that had always kept them afloat but disadvantaged so many. And yet.

Neither light nor dark brought fundamental change to the world of pay or how it works. In fact, almost nothing has changed in how we operate. We still participate in the same salary surveys on the same schedule, running the same policies and programs to make sure we pay the minimum amount necessary to attract, retain, and motivate the talent we need. To get through the crisis, we planned temporary policy adjustments and pay increases alongside furloughs and layoffs to account for what we assumed to be a temporary halt in business activity. We assumed the standard playbook would be enough, knowing things would go back to normal soon, seldom pausing to wonder why nothing fundamental about our industry ever seemed to change. What's that quote about the definition of insanity again?

Our outlook was and is Dickensian. It was the best of times and it was the worst of times, and we accepted both sides as inevitable. Our role would remain as stoic monitors of the free market's famed invisible hand, but not as interveners. Wild swings in the economy and the resulting welfare of those around us would have little influence on the way companies fundamentally thought about pay, because the market has limited ties to pay. The way companies pay would continue to depend on which employees they choose to prioritize, the processes they create, the permission opportunities they allow to talk about pay, and the power they share with employees in deciding pay outcomes.

At the start of the pandemic, I began meeting with a group of my peers weekly to share our reactions to the chaos and the plans that would keep the order intact. Most of the world's largest retailers and e-commerce companies participated in these meetings, which were officiated by the few vendors we all rely on as our lifeblood for market intel. Together, our companies represented a significant share of global employment, and our actions would become the bellwether for employee well-being throughout the multipronged crises. Many of us were already on a first-name basis, having worked together for many years and attended the same conferences and roundtable discussions in quieter times. If enough of us thought a temporary pay premium was a good idea and had convinced our leaders to go along with it, that would become the market norm. If some of us thought extending sick leave policies was appropriate, soon all of us would do the same. As usual, we found ourselves in a slow-moving three-legged race to make the case for change. The free market was working, but only up to a point—whatever it took to get through the month, and then the quarter, and then the year. Few of us were thinking about long-term structural change from the outset, but it wasn't long before it became clear things couldn't go back to normal.

The trace of failure some in our field had seen coming for a long time—but were feckless to fight against—was now clear to everyone. In the best of times, many of the new jobs our companies were creating were bad jobs, paying sublivable wages with limited benefits and little opportunity for economic advancement. In the worst of times, these jobs were seen as summarily disposable. Our idea of fair pay— the market's idea of fair pay—had been defined not as a decent living but as an approximation of each other's insincerity, limited to paying what we thought to be competitive rates, and monitoring for internal bias with varying degrees of seriousness. The case for changing the way pay works, for investing in employees like never before, could not have been stronger.

Fair pay requires us to have a problem solver's mindset. In our rush to make pay fair, mindset should take priority over metrics. Metrics are important, and it's critical we have rigorous data to show improvements in fair pay outcomes like equal pay, leadership representation, and investment in low-wage workers. But metrics are best served as a guide for steering us toward a higher purpose. Goodhart's law applies to pay: a measure that becomes a target ceases to be a good measure and will be manipulated to move the number. To state the obvious, manipulation and fair pay do not mix.

When we believe in fair pay as a higher purpose, when we practice pay sincerity, our mindset should be focused in four interwoven areas: building trust, creating real competition, celebrating vulnerability, and accepting no excuses for inequities. Let's consider these four mandates as our new minimum viable compensation philosophy. Here is how we'll experience the future of fair pay.

FAIR PAY BUILDS TRUST

Any movement for fair pay has to be embraced by the business leaders expected to make it happen. To you captains of industry, consider my plea. The old way of black-box pay will not solve the problems you've helped create (or ignored). Pay transparency can either come from you, where you write the narrative and are lauded for putting your company on a multiyear path to change, or it will by instigated by your employees or legislators, who will feel no such duty of care to manage the fallout. If you think your employees aren't comparing notes now, you are already behind the messaging curve. In Chapter 2, we found only one out of five employees trust they are paid fairly, which rises to two in five from the company's perspective about their own pay programs. In other words, most of your people, including the ones responsible for managing your payroll, believe you are failing them. What happens when they go public?

Harvard Business School professor Frances Frei says there are three component parts to building lasting trust: authenticity, empathy, and rigor, and that you must have all three to be successful. Building trust about pay follows a parallel path, explained by our triad of character, coordination, and cost control. High-character companies enable authenticity through diverse representation. Companies that coordinate well develop empathy by listening to all perspectives, not just those with power. And any investment in pay requires rigorous targeting and efficient cost control to be sustainable. Whichever trinity you choose, Frei's, mine, or preferably both, let me now address what I know to be your primary problem with taking a stance on fair pay and building trust with your employees: the legal consequences.

Internalize this new reality: the days of ignoring the fair-pay problem are over. By not embracing the challenge and recognizing your leadership role, you put your company in a worse competitive position. Without change, patchwork local laws that you will view as onerous will encircle your business. Consider now, at the onset of an era of legislated pay equity, how many different equal-pay methodologies exist already. How many non-revenue-generating administrative staff, like lawyers and compensation experts, will you need to hire when this scene is replicated everywhere you operate? Instead, by doing the right thing from the start, taking the time to build trust with employees, you will limit your company's litigative and public relations fire-drills caused by poor pay management. The administrative debt you build over time is the price you pay for letting real structural problems fester for too long. Your employees shouldn't be paid unfairly because your company or industry has failed to get its act together.

When you choose the fair pay path, you will find that pay regulations are rarely an added burden for your business. This doesn't mean you can totally preempt all new pay legislation or company-level litigation, though there are some reforms you should welcome. Modernizing the pay rules will make sure you can compete on an equal footing with your peers and the new entrants that design themselves to be workarounds to the old order. You will benefit from legislation that clarifies the rules of equal-pay reporting, of enhanced federal minimum-wage laws and other shared power arrangements that ensure stable wage growth for low-wage workers, of pay transparency that institutionalizes reference points for employees so they can ask questions about pay without retaliation, and of a modern foundation for employment classifications to address a future of work that is already failing so many. As a person directly responsible for applying new legislative decisions to pay, I can tell you that their threat as being existentially opposed to business success is overstated, and that effective legislation can bring clarity to your business and help you make more informed, lower-risk strategic choices.

Now, let me appeal to your legacy. For those who see themselves as values-based leaders, fair pay is what your consultants call a force multiplier, but for cultural transformation. Dan Price, in his book *Worth It*, describes what happened after his company Gravity Payments installed its $70,000 minimum wage. In the immediate years following the change, 10 percent of his team purchased their first home, the company's retirement fund contributions doubled, and a third of employees with debt paid it down by at least 50 percent. The company had a baby boom, in part due to the newfound affordability of parenthood but also because of more flexible leave policies. Gravity Payments employees reported they were eating healthier, going to the gym more often, taking family vacations, and starting new hobbies. It isn't an overstatement to say that fair pay allows people to be fully human. Consider what other social problems are solved by simply paying people what they are worth, and what people will achieve when they would walk over hot coals to work for you.

It won't be enough to make a nice speech or sign on to a toothless pledge for fair pay. In *The Peter Principle: Why Things Always Go Wrong*, the book that made famous the idea that all workers will be promoted up to their level of incompetence, the authors describe a lesser-known principle called "Peter's placebo." The idea of the placebo is that some people will mask their incompetence (and in their view everyone is incompetent) by substituting image for performance, displaying a veneer of self-importance that isn't doing much good but "at least, they would be doing no harm." Signing a pledge to create "decent jobs" would in our case be the placebo, a visual cue of wanting to do the right thing without any medicinal effect. The real prescription would involve examining company practices and allocating money toward the solutions. If your company says it values all people or dares to call its workers essential, but doesn't pay them fairly or lets unequal pay go unmonitored and uncorrected, this is not a neutral position but causing active harm. Where companies say that they want to do what is right but are "evolving" for years without accountability, their conviction shifts into complicity.

Business leaders, you should know at all times what the lowest-paid person in your company earns, why that is the case, and what processes and methodologies are in place to make sure everyone in your company is able to provide for a decent and optimistic life. To make meaningful change, you will have to build trust by making fair pay nonnegotiable and give your teams permission to do the same. If you ascribe to the maxim that company culture eats strategy for breakfast, make sure at a minimum your people can afford a breakfast table, have enough food to eat, and have time to sit down and enjoy a meal with their families.

FAIR PAY CREATES COMPETITION

There isn't a specific amount or range of pay that we can identify as being officially fair. As such, I haven't prescribed a minimum or a maximum fair wage or suggested using one of the various living-wage calculators found online. I also haven't said that we should cap or decrease executive pay at a certain value, though I believe a radically smaller gap between the top and bottom would be beneficial. I've stayed away from making these types of formal proclamations about what is and is not fair because I believe fair pay is not an achievement or a formula but that it requires constant vigilance, and the transition to fair pay will look different for every company.

Some businesses can flip the fair-pay switch now, assuming the boss has read the last section and gives the signal. These companies can amend their compensation philosophy, open their black box, reset their policies, commit sacrilege against their salary surveys, monitor their pay gaps, and make targeted investments where they have fallen behind fair pay expectations. Other businesses and industries will need time to migrate their operating model into something more sustainable, to reset their company's capability to manage fair pay, and to get the system's infrastructure in place to administer change that lasts. To transition quickly, companies will need to treat fair-pay practices not just as a compliance exercise but as a competitive mandate. Companies will not begin to compete on pay only, because as we've seen many times, raising pay alone without a supporting business and talent strategy is easily replicated and does not bring any unique strategic value to the company. Instead, the company that treats fair pay as a competitive advantage will not only have to increase pay where needed but also thoughtfully weave fair-pay practices and habits into everything it does to differentiate itself from the competition.

If fair pay is thought of as a competitive opportunity, that means a company can't outsource the task to the substrata of the human resources department. Compensation teams can only track the market as it exists, free-ish and rife with inefficiencies, not as we hope it should be, a dynamic and mutually reinforcing snapshot of supply and demand, of talent and people who have enough information and power to own the price of their labor. More transparency and a willingness of business leaders to engage in pay issues (beyond their own) will spur competition for talent and therefore force companies to get sharper in every area of the employment experience, including career development and through more responsive and representative organization design. This will help prospective employees recognize which companies are places where they can live their potential, and employers will become more agile as their business environment changes. Fair pay, when thought of as more than a minimum viable number, creates a reciprocal competitive advantage on both sides of the paycheck.

Few companies view pay as a competitive opportunity because they have a limited understanding of what pay is meant to do, which is to signal not only a person's immediate work value but also their potential. So much effort is put into the first part, paying the minimum amount required for the present job, that the second part about potential goes underserved. Employees are left to manage their own career prospects, without recognition that they may not have a viable pathway to do so. This leads to the commonly held view that in matters of fairness, what counts is not equality of outcome, but equality of opportunity. This idea is correct in principle but can be problematic in practice, notably where opportunity *for* opportunity is not equitably available.

Take note of who usually makes this argument—those who have already won the pay game because they have had opportunities to reach their potential. Equality of outcome can't be ignored if its fullness is prevented by inequality of opportunity; outcome absolutely matters when women are not promoted to senior roles, or when paychecks aren't enough to provide for a person's essential needs or more education.

We can celebrate the anecdotal cases of those who, against all odds, blazed their own pathways, but this Lone Ranger mentality isn't how most people who reach the corporate summits got there. By intentionally creating more avenues of opportunity, examining and removing the barriers to competition, we will see greater equality of outcomes. As Martin Luther King Jr. said, with my added parentheticals, "What does it profit a man to be able to eat at an integrated lunch counter [opportunity] if he doesn't have enough money to buy a hamburger [outcome]?"

Here is a simple test to see how much competitive opportunity exists in your workplace. If you manage people, think about what will happen if you ask for a pay raise for yourself. If you expect to experience fewer barriers to yes than if one of your direct reports had done the same, your company has a competitive opportunity problem and is potentially limiting its people's work value and potential. Where these problems exist, an unexamined fair-pay "P" is the likely culprit. The process for lower-level workers may be more cumbersome, the company may not prioritize the request or take it seriously, requesters may not have permission to apply for a raise or a promotion because the job requirements are artificially high or exclusionary, or they might have less power to press the issue. Creating more opportunity through more competition makes for more fair pay outcomes.

FAIR PAY CELEBRATES VULNERABILITY

The workplaces of the future, however we choose to trademark them, will have two defining features: they will operate with an ingrained expectation of transparency, and they will recognize the abundant possibilities of all people through open systems of opportunity. Successful companies will understand that when people can bring their full selves to work, the organization is pushed forward and in new directions. They will find the capability of people to be their most renewable resource, as they will choose to expand the definition of what people can do in their careers and take down any barriers in the way. In an era of possibility, companies that create bad jobs that box people in will fall too far behind to survive.

Giving people abundant possibilities starts with being transparent, which assumes vulnerability. As Brené Brown says, "Vulnerability sounds like truth and feels like courage." How we pay says everything about how we value a person's potential, and transparency gives everyone the tools to bring accountability to the system. As companies become more transparent, they should welcome the sharper questions they'll get about pay, especially if those questions expose a weakness in the company and an opportunity to get better.

Consider the differences in these two statements:

"I'd like a raise."

"I'm 14 percent below the pay range midpoint for our communications specialist job, and the work I'm doing is closer to the senior communications specialist criteria found in the company leveling guide. Can we come up with a plan to fix my pay and job level starting at the pay review next quarter?"

The second version is possible only through pay transparency, and the sharpness of the question demands specific answers that require sincerity. By making it obvious that something has gone wrong with your pay, and proposing specific adjustments and timelines, the request can't be easily dismissed. Giving your manager ways to frame the conversation, like how you see your performance compared to your true peers and the expectations for your job outlined in the company's job-leveling guide, makes it more likely you'll get that raise. If we're honest, both employees and managers would like to avoid these uncomfortable, vulnerable conversations about pay, but managers should be prepared to respond well when they get called out. Setting clear expectations for pay through transparent resources and processes, which, yes, makes us vulnerable, then becomes automatic and secondary to conversations about career development, which we'd all prefer to have.

According to Harvard professors Alison Wood Brooks and Leslie K. John, asking better questions is an underused way to balance power dynamics. They've found that a good question achieves two goals: learning, through information exchange, and liking, through impression management. As much as we think pay is entirely about performance, the "what" of the job, the "how" you do the job matters, too. In some companies both factors are tied to the annual performance rating. This means to get to the leadership ranks, you have to be effective in your work but also in managing relationships. Unfortunately, many people, including 83 percent of the LGBTQ+ community, 78 percent of Black workers, and 45 percent of heterosexual white men, manage their work relationships through what is called "covering," masking a part of their identity to blend in. There are inherent power dynamics associated with being vulnerable, and for those on the margins who feel like they can't bring their full selves to work, leaning in will always feel more like holding out.

If you are in a position of power and recognize these imbalances, make a habit of asking questions about pay not only for yourself but for others who have less power. What process will increase pay for support staff, and who has decision-making authority? How does the company make fair pay for underrepresented groups a priority? When are the career moments your team should be most focused (permission) on pay? What power do I have to change a practice that I think is unfair? Be sure to celebrate the fair-pay wins. As Brooks and John say,

"Sustained personal engagement and motivation—in our lives as well as our work—require that we are always mindful of the transformative joy of asking and answering questions."

Companies, whether you choose to be vulnerable about pay or are forced to be by legislation or irate employees, you are absolutely going to mess this up. Regardless of your starting place, you will need persistence and consistency. The first year will be hard. You'll get good questions and fumble lots of answers, but you'll get credit for trying to do the right thing. The second year will be easier and you'll get more confident in your answers, but the idea of fair pay still won't click for many people, and some (well-paid people, naturally) will still be outright antagonistic. By the third year, pay sincerity becomes your company culture, and those who aren't sold on the new ways of working will have self-selected out of the company. Wish them well and don't think twice.

By taking your first steps toward vulnerability on pay, you are committing to the long road. It's your role to build the right ecosystem and venues for allowing pay questions to be asked and answered without retaliation. Here are a few ideas to get you started:

- Create fair-pay training for all employees, with advanced modules specific to managers and HR.
- Empower managers and line HR leaders to adjust pay as needed within common guidelines.
- Share your pay ranges and let employees see where they fit in compared to their true peers.
- Publish not only your pay-equity numbers but your pay-gap results, too.
- Eliminate outdated (and often illegal) pay-secrecy clauses in employment policies and contracts.
- Assign pay-coaching responsibilities to your internal sponsorship program.

- Establish "red teams" dedicated to rooting out process bias in the same way you have teams dedicated to finding holes in your network security.
- Set up confidential resources for employees who worry about discrimination or retaliation.
- Aggressively fund pay adjustments through a centrally held funding pool to circumvent rogue, penny-pinching managers.

Once you get started, you'll find there are abundant possibilities for improvement.

FAIR PAY MEANS EQUAL PAY. NO EXCUSES

That unequal pay exists is not a debatable point, but the problem is not equally applicable to all companies. Many companies take their mandate to provide equal pay for equal work seriously (not perfectly) and are focused now on closing systemic representation gaps. Other companies are earlier in the process of transformation or do not yet realize what equal-pay problems they may have. Sadly, some are hostile to the idea, though they will not say so publicly. In all cases, if we want to make sure all people can reach their full potential, this means doing the hard work of rectifying injustices that were purpose-built into the economy and whose remnants linger with us today. The moral case for equal pay is unassailable (and to be clear, the moral case should be enough), but the business case goes under-acknowledged.

Paying your employees fairly makes them smarter, literally. When employees experience financial insecurity, these thoughts never escape them during the workday, and the corresponding mental strain reduces their functional IQ by thirteen points. When companies build cultures that respect the dignity of all employees, they deliver 20 percent higher returns to shareholders than comparable companies. When companies treat men and women equally at work, they see a sixfold increase in innovation. Where companies have representation of 50 percent women in senior operating roles, they see a 19 percent higher return on equity than their peers. Gains in equality for one company or one person do not come at the expense of another but improve the entire system by setting a more competitive bar.

Over a ten-year period, if women participated in the economy in identical ways to men, we would add up to $28 trillion to annual global GDP. This number assumes a more equitable sharing of responsibilities within the unpaid labor of home life, creating space for both men and women to participate in higher-productivity jobs. When we don't recognize the opportunity for fair pay, we forgo the growth equivalent of putting a second United States on the map, or ten United Kingdoms. A more conservative estimate from the same McKinsey study found that where local standards are raised only to the best performer in each region, we would add $12 trillion in annual GDP. In geographic terms, this approaches the size of the Chinese economy over the ten-year period, or ten Mexicos. Now expand these findings beyond representation for women to include all underrepresented groups, considering the visible and unseen trade-offs made by limiting the potential of all people. When we enlarge the pool of talent to represent all people across all job levels, broadening the set of experiences and perspectives of decision makers, the positive business effects won't be additive but exponential.

Equal pay will not arrive as happenstance but through the recruitment criteria, hiring policies, promotion practices, and performance-management systems companies design. To think bigger, companies can start with the smaller things by resetting each stage of this employment life cycle. Simplify the problem into immediate next steps and pursue the most direct action. Reducing the complexity bias is essential to building momentum on making pay fair. The best companies learn from their initial, awkward fair-pay baby steps and then create simple processes that allow for rapid change, at scale. While large companies will need to use a vendor or hire a statistics team to calculate enterprise pay and representation gaps, individual managers at any company can look at their rosters and find opportunities for improvement without much effort. And yes, managers, it's your responsibility, not HR's, to make sure your team is paid fairly.

While under renovation, companies should also create intentional pathways to "hack" their own infrastructure. Let Disney's innovative CODE:Rosie program be our model. The program offers any woman in the company, from headquarters to theme park workers, the opportunity to learn the hard-to-find technical skills that the company expects it will need in the future. On completion of the program, graduates become eligible for jobs that can theoretically more than double their pay overnight. Instead of whining about a supposed lack of pipeline for diverse talent, and the trailing pay gaps this creates, Disney has decided to build its own pipeline. These types of programs can be created for all business functions, because we only need so many coders. They can help underrepresented and socioeconomically disadvantaged groups move past the myth of the skills gap, which is CODE:Lazy for the ways businesses blame their workforce for the bad jobs they create. The standard models used by most companies for talent sourcing, career pathing, and promotional pay increases are not built to foster the kind of rapid acceleration we need in representation or pay, and they often lock out workers in low-wage parts of the company entirely.

Central to the equal-pay experience is the belief that all people have inherent capability and potential, and that we can build many (and faster) paths to the same summit. As long as we view equal pay as some-one else's problem to solve or as a box to tick, we limit not only the potential of others but of our companies and the broader economy, too. We should not be overwhelmed; we can do more and we can do better.

YOU DESERVE FAIR PAY

The stories we tell ourselves about what is fair and what we deserve are often a product of our own experiences and expectations. Too often, we fixate on managing expectations with ourselves, and that makes us too exhausted to talk about pay with others. The added pressure of a promotion or pay raise, and the negative self-talk that starts instantly after the slightest bit of success becomes overwhelming. *Did I deserve this? Should I have asked for more money? A better office? When will I be found out as an impostor and be forced to repay my raise and individually apologize to each member of the leadership team for thinking I was worthy?* Instead of celebrating, you come to work wearing a mental hair shirt as penance.

We have to celebrate pay—louder, more often, and with greater transparency. Finding a better story for why fair pay matters helps us check ourselves when we fall into traps about our self-worth and the worth of others. We should share not just our current story—what we want out of our career this year before the next annual performance review—but our past stories about how we got here and our future stories about where we want to go. Those who come up behind us will need to know how we did it. Those ahead of us will need to clear the way so we can keep going.

As we move through our careers, we need different stories about our pay at different times. For the new parent, the story you need might be more scheduling flexibility without fear of punishment, including lost promotion and pay opportunity. For the midcareer executive, the story might be controlling your anxiety, reminding yourself that you are more than your team's deliverables and year-end bonus, and that you deserve a paid vacation that doesn't involve checking email. For the late-career line worker, the story could be about the loyalty you've shown throughout your career and wanting to feel secure in a dignified job with decent pay as you approach retirement. And for the boss, you might have a legitimate cash crunch because your last product launch failed while the rent has increased and your bankers are calling you every day—giving anyone a raise is the last thing on your mind. No one has a complete picture of another person's career motivations and struggles, which means we all have room to grow, to learn, and to empathize.

Now is the time to redeem the idea of fairness. We teach playing fair to our children and make it the basis of our legal system, but at work, fair remains an enigmatic four-letter word. Seeing workers fight for fair pay is not new, but a sincere attempt at codification by companies is only now taking shape.

So how will we recognize fair pay when we see it? In 1906, the Catholic priest John Augustine Ryan wrote of this same question in a treatise called "A Living Wage." He described the difficulty of pinning our hopes on a specific outcome, yet stressed the importance of keeping a watchful eye, of having a fair-pay mindset:

> We can distinguish twilight from darkness, although we cannot identify the precise moment when the one merges into the other. Though we cannot say just when artificial light becomes more effective than that of the waning day, we usually call it into service before the approaching darkness proves notably inconvenient.

It's time to shine more light into the way we pay, calling ourselves and our companies into service. We do this by relentlessly showing up to advocate for ourselves and others, in our work and in our personal lives, by anticipating and participating in solving our shared pay problems, by recognizing that dignity and sincerity matters for everyone, and, yes, by being paid fairly for our efforts. Adam Smith, recognizing that fair pay is at the root of so many of our problems, said it with more concision: "The great affair, we always find, is to get money."

Let's help each other get more money—it's only fair.

Acknowledgments

For the three years I worked on this book, there were two questions I couldn't shake: "Can I do this?" and "Should I do this?" Navigating the book process was new for me, and the logistics of logging writing hours around a day job and a family were not easy. I worried constantly about what sort of career risk I was taking by questioning the foundations of my own field. But the alternative question—"What if I *don't* do this?"—always felt worse to me. I believe deep down that we need to fix pay, and that now is the time to do it.

Thank you to my lovely wife, Kallie, for helping me sort through these questions and for being the first editor of every chapter. On many occasions, you spared me the embarrassment of sending incoherent ideas to my actual editor. To my dearest daughter, Tova, thank you for encouraging me always and forgiving me when I was too tired to be fun.

Thank you to my editor, Rebecca Raskin. You are brilliant, and you shaped so much of this book for the better. I appreciate your maturity in walking back my many bad jokes. Any bad jokes that remain are on me alone. To the whole Harper Business team, thank you for making this book real and for letting Tova raid your offices for new books.

To my agent, Laurie Abkemeier, thank you for believing in me and this project. This book would not exist without you. I am eternally grateful for your guidance, advocacy, and encouragement.

To my parents, thank you for setting an example by always having a stack of books nearby. I learned from you that readers are leaders and leaders are readers. To my big sisters, thank you for your support and

I guess also for your relentless teasing over the years that turned me to the inner life of writing.

Thank you to Todd Sattersten and the rest of the crew in our Portland writing group. Your reassurance kept me going. Speaking of reassurance, thank you to my friends who sent kind notes and read drafts along the way. A special point of gratitude to those who went the extra mile, like Sarah and Chris Odell, Sarah and Kyle Cox, and Rachel and Matt Hires. I'd also like to thank Claire Wasserman and Derek Webb for telling me their stories.

This book started as an entry essay for the Bracken Bower Prize through the *Financial Times* and McKinsey & Company. Thank you to Andrew Hill of the *Financial Times* and the Bracken Bower judges for seeing the potential in these ideas. Your validation gave me the confidence to turn this into more than a stuffy-sounding essay.

To the reader, thank you for trusting me. I hope this book lets you see inside the black box of pay, and that I've helped bring less anxiety and greater prosperity to you and your family. I'd love to hear from you on how this book has affected your life and career.

Finally, to my team at Nike, and my past teams at Starbucks and Yum! Brands, thank you for teaching me not only how to improve my work but also to become a better person. Many of you have invested deeply in me personally and in my career, and I am grateful. This book would no doubt have been better if I had let any of you read it ahead of time. To my peers in the compensation industry, I know we all see the opportunities to make our field better, and I look forward to your calls. Let's get to work.

Notes

Chapter 1: What We Know about Pay Is Wrong

3   series of increases starting at $11: "Minimum Wage Ordinance," City of Seattle Office of Labor Standards, accessed August 17, 2020, http://www.seattle.gov/labor standards/ordinances/minimum-wage.

4   twenty-two counties across five states: Andrew Aurand, Dan Emmanuel, Diane Yentel, Ellen Errico, Jared Gaby-Biegel, and Emma Kerr, "Out of Reach: The High Cost of Housing," National Low Income Housing Coalition, 2018, https://reports.nlihc.org/oor/2018.

4   half are over age twenty-five: "Characteristics of Minimum Wage Workers, 2018: BLS Reports," U.S. Bureau of Labor Statistics, March 1, 2019, https://www.bls.gov/opub/reports/minimum-wage/2018/home.htm.

5   below the $15 threshold: Irene Tung, Yannet Lathrop, and Paul Sonn, "The Growing Movement for $15," National Employment Law Project, November 2015, https://www.nelp.org/publication/growing-movement-15/.

5   "Can Starbucks Save the Middle Class?": Amanda Ripley, "The Upwardly Mobile Barista," *The Atlantic*, May 1, 2015, https://www.theatlantic.com/magazine/archive/2015/05/the-upwardly-mobile-barista/389513/.

5   Partner Experience Investments: "Starbucks Announces New Partner Experience Investments," Starbucks, October 16, 2014, https://stories.starbucks.com/stories/2014/starbucks-announces-new-partner-experience-investments/.

7   brain reactions of seeing marginalized people: Pia Dietze and Eric D. Knowles, "Social Class and the Motivational Relevance of Other Human Beings," *Psychological Science* 27, no. 11 (2016): 1517–27, https://doi.org/10.1177/0956797616667721.

10   well-being climbs with their income: Daniel Kahneman and Angus Deaton, "High Income Improves Evaluation of Life but Not Emotional Well-Being," *Proceedings of the National Academy of Sciences* 107, no. 38 (2010): 16489–93, https://doi.org/10.1073/pnas.1011492107.

10   shaped by his childhood experiences: Dan Price, *Worth It* (Seattle: Gravity Payments, 2020).

11   80 percent pay cut to join from Yahoo: Karen Weise, "The CEO Paying Everyone $70,000 Salaries Has Something to Hide," *Bloomberg Businessweek*, December 1, 2015, https://www.bloomberg.com/features/2015-gravity-ceo-dan-price/.

12   90 percent of Americans owned only 12 percent: Robin Wigglesworth, "How America's 1% Came to Dominate Equity Ownership," *Financial Times*, February 10, 2020, https://www.ft.com/content/2501e154-4789-11ea-aeb3-955839e06441.

13   America's fastest-growing major city: Gene Balk, "114,000 More People: Seattle Now Decade's Fastest-Growing Big City in All of U.S.," *Seattle Times*, May 24, 2018, https://www.seattletimes.com/seattle-news/data/114000-more-people-seattle-now-this-decades-fastest-growing-big-city-in-all-of-united-states/.

13   "The conflict between security and progress": John Kenneth Galbraith, *The Affluent Society,* 40th Anniversary Edition (New York: Mariner Books, 1998), 94.

13   "economic death wish": Danny Westneat, "Local Facts No Match for National Fiction on $15 Minimum-Wage Issue," *Seattle Times*, January 25, 2016, https://www.seattletimes.com/seattle-news/local-facts-no-match-for-national-fiction-on-15-minimum-wage-issue/.

13   "The most impressive increases": Galbraith, *The Affluent Society*, 94.

16   wages for physicians have stagnated: "2019 Physician Compensation Report," Doximity, March 2019, https://s3.amazonaws.com/s3.doximity.com/press/doximity_third_annual_physician_compensation_report_round4.pdf.

16   entry copilots close to minimum wage: Dennis Schaal, "The U.S. Airline Pilots Who Barely Make Minimum Wage," *Skift*, December 4, 2013, https://skift.com/2013/08/28/the-u-s-airline-pilots-who-barely-make-minimum-wage/.

17   similar in adjusted terms to what pilots made in the 1990s: Peter Gall, "The US Is Facing a Serious Shortage of Airline Pilots," CNN, July 16, 2018, https://www.cnn.com/travel/article/airline-pilot-shortage-united-states/index.html.

20   The bottom 50 percent of American households: Michael Batty, Jesse Bricker, Joseph Briggs, Elizabeth Holmquist, Susan Hume McIntosh, Kevin B. Moore, Eric Reed Nielsen, Sarah Reber, Molly Shatto, Kamila Sommer, Tom Sweeney, and Alice Henriques Volz, "Introducing the Distributional Financial Accounts of the United States," FEDS Working Paper No. 2019-017, Board of Governors of the Federal Reserve System Finance and Economics Discussion Series, March 22, 2019, https://ssrn.com/abstract=3358906.

20   one-third from differences within companies: Jae Song, David Price, Fatih Guvenen, Nicholas Bloom, and Till Von Wachter, "Firming Up Inequality," June 17, 2016, https://doi.org/10.3386/w21199.

20   increasing within countries but decreasing between countries: Jos Verbeek and
     Israel Osorio Rodarte, "Increasingly, Inequality Within, Not Across, Countries Is
     Rising," World Bank, October 2, 2015, http://blogs.worldbank.org/development
     talk/increasingly-inequality-within-not-across-countries-rising.

21   the "supermanager" accounts for much of the increase in pay inequality: Thomas
     Piketty and Arthur Goldhammer, *Capital in the Twenty-First Century* (Cambridge,
     MA: Belknap Press of Harvard University Press, 2017), 397–98.

21   increase in national income share: Jon Bakija, Adam Cole, and Bradley Heim,
     "Jobs and Income Growth of Top Earners and the Causes of Changing Income
     Inequality: Evidence from U.S. Tax Return Data," U.S. Department of the Treas-
     ury, April 2012, https://web.williams.edu/Economics/wp/BakijaColeHeimJobs
     IncomeGrowthTopEarners.pdf.

22   28 percent of patents: Jay Shambaugh, Ryan Nunn, and Becca Portman, "Eleven
     Facts about Innovation and Patents," *Hamilton Project*, December 2017, https://
     www.brookings.edu/wp-content/uploads/2017/12/thp_20171213_eleven_facts
     _innovation_patents.pdf.

23   "most common human occupation": Louis Hyman, *Temp: The Real Story of What
     Happened to Your Salary, Benefits, and Job Security* (New York: Penguin Books,
     2019), 37.

23   jobs available now has not yet been reduced by automation: Jacques Manyika, Su-
     san Lund, Michael Chiu, Jacques Bughin, Jonathan Woetzel, Parul Batra, Ryan
     Ko, and Saurabh Sanghvi, "Jobs Lost, Jobs Gained: Workforce Transitions in a
     Time of Automation," McKinsey Global Institute, December 2017.

23   "more human work than our ancestors": Hyman, *Temp*, 315.

24   "everybody was finally equal": Kurt Vonnegut, "Harrison Bergeron," *Welcome to
     the Monkey House* (New York: Dial Press, 2010).

24   "The best-performing companies": "Toward Common Metrics and Consistent Re-
     porting of Sustainable Value Creation," World Economic Forum, January 2020,
     http://www3.weforum.org/docs/WEF_IBC_ESG_Metrics_Discussion_Paper
     .pdf.

25   120,000 deaths in the United States each year: Jeffrey Pfeffer, *Dying for a Paycheck:
     How Modern Management Harms Employee Health and Company Performance—
     and What We Can Do About It* (New York: Harper Business, 2018), 38.

25   four times the number of people who die in car accidents: "Motor Vehicle Crash
     Deaths," Centers for Disease Control and Prevention, accessed August 17, 2020,
     https://www.cdc.gov/vitalsigns/motor-vehicle-safety/index.html.

25 $1 per hour increase in minimum wage equates to lower suicide rates: John A. Kaufman, Leslie K Salas-Hernández, Kelli A Komro, and Melvin D Livingston, "Effects of Increased Minimum Wages by Unemployment Rate on Suicide in the USA," *Journal of Epidemiology and Community Health* 74, no. 3 (January 7, 2020), https://jech.bmj.com/content/74/3/219.

26 two-thirds of the region's higher homicide rates: "Income Inequality and Violent Crime," *Equality Trust Research Digest*, 2011, https://www.equalitytrust.org.uk /sites/default/files/research-digest-violent-crime-final.pdf.

27 Three-quarters of US jobs: Naema Ahmed, "Most Jobs Created Since the Recession Have Been Low-Paying," *Axios*, September 7, 2018, https://www.axios.com/most -jobs-created-since-recciu-1536269032-13ccc866-5fb0-44e8-bd14-286ae09c296f.html.

27 restaurant and personal-care workers dominate: "Occupations with the Most Job Growth," U.S. Bureau of Labor Statistics, accessed August 17, 2020, https://www .bls.gov/emp/tables/occupations-most-job-growth.htm.

Chapter 2: A New Way of Pay Sincerity

31 America's first space station: "Saturn V at Rocket Park," Space Center Houston, accessed August 17, 2020, https://spacecenter.org/exhibits-and-experiences/nasa -tram-tour/saturn-v-at-rocket-park.

33 believe they are paid below market: Dave Smith and Amy Gallo, "Most People Have No Idea Whether They're Paid Fairly," *Harvard Business Review*, November 30, 2017, https://hbr.org/2015/10/most-people-have-no-idea-whether-theyre -paid-fairly.

33 their own employees would say they are paid fairly: "The Corporate Chasm: Why Communication in Today's Workplace Is Fundamentally Broken," PayScale, 2017, https://www.payscale.com/hr/why-workplace-communication-is-broken.

34 nearly half of all global pay: "Just 10 Per Cent of Workers Receive Nearly Half of Global Pay," International Labour Organization, July 4, 2019, https://www.ilo.org /global/about-the-ilo/newsroom/news/WCMS_712234/lang--en/index.htm.

35 American companies dominate: Elvis Picardo, "10 of the World's Top Companies Are American," Investopedia, May 30, 2019.

36 "lunatic of all lunatics": Nicholas Kristof, "The $70,000-a-Year Minimum Wage," *New York Times*, March 30, 2019, https://www.nytimes.com/2019/03/30/opinion /sunday/dan-price-minimum-wage.html.

40   more than twenty states: Mark Trumbull, "With 21 States Raising Minimum Wage, 2015 Is a Tipping Point," *Christian Science Monitor,* January 1, 2015, https://www .csmonitor.com/USA/2015/0101/With-21-states-raising-minimum-wage-2015-is -a-tipping-point.

40   50 percent faster wage growth: Elise Gould, "Wage Growth for Low-Wage Workers Has Been Strongest in States with Minimum Wage Increases," Economic Policy Institute, March 5, 2019, https://www.epi.org/publication/wage-growth-for-low -wage-workers-has-been-strongest-in-states-with-minimum-wage-increases/.

42   "a little sincerity is a dangerous thing": Oscar Wilde, "The Critic as Artist," 1891.

44   "better, freer way of life": "193. Paper Prepared by the Assistant Secretary of Defense for International Security Affairs (McNaughton)," *Foreign Relations of the United States, 1964–1968*, Volume II, Vietnam, January–June 1965, https://history .state.gov/historicaldocuments/frus1964-68v02/d193.

46   the banking industry is pretty good on a relative basis: Max Zahn and Andy Serwer, "Jamie Dimon Backs Minimum Wage Hike: 'We've Got to Give People More of a Living Wage,'" Yahoo! Finance, July 1, 2019, https://finance.yahoo.com /news/jamie-dimon-backs-minimum-wage-hike-weve-got-to-give-people-a-living -wage-175636833.html.

47   in a better position than about 20 percent of the local population: "American Community Survey," filtered on Irvine City, California, US Census, accessed August 17, 2020, https://data.census.gov/cedsci/table?q=DP03&g=1600000US 0636770&tid=ACSDP5Y2017.DP03.

48   "a good one and the real one": Owen Wister, *Roosevelt, the Story of a Friendship, 1880–1919* (New York: Macmillan, 1930).

48   "it will often become *the* issue": Rodd Wagner, *Widgets: The 12 New Rules for Managing Your Employees as if They're Real People* (New York: McGraw-Hill Education, 2015), 55.

50   half the positive effect on profit: Michael V. Marn, Eric V. Roegner, and Craig C. Zawada, "The Power of Pricing," *McKinsey Quarterly,* no. 1 (2003), https:// www.mckinsey.com/~/media/McKinsey/Business%20Functions/Marketing%20 and%20Sales/Our%20Insights/The%20power%20of%20pricing/The%20 power%20of%20pricing.pdf.

51   nearly $2 trillion of cash reserves: "U.S. Corporate Cash Reaches $1.9 Trillion but Rising Debt and Tax Reform Pose Risk," *S&P Global,* May 25, 2017, https://www .spglobal.com/en/research-insights/articles/us-corporate-cash-reaches-19 -trillion-but-rising-debt-and-tax-reform-pose-risk.

51 "that would be terrible for the stock market": Dion Rabouin, "The 1% Has So Much Money They Literally Don't Know What to Do with It," *Business Insider*, June 7, 2019, https://www.businessinsider.com/the-1-percent-dont-know-what-to -do-with-money-2019-6.

52 record profits of $2.3 trillion: "National Income and Product Accounts, Table 6.16D, Corporate Profits by Industry," National Income and Product Accounts, Bureau of Economic Analysis, accessed August 17, 2020, https://apps.bea.gov/iTable/iTable .cfm?reqid=19&step=3&isuri=1&1921=survey&1903=239&utm_source=news letter&utm_medium=email&utm_campaign=newsletter_axiosmarkets&stream =business#reqid=19&step=3&isuri=1&1921=survey&1903=239.

52 "commitment to the countries, regions, and communities": Larry Fink, "Larry Fink's 2019 Letter to CEOs: Purpose & Profit," BlackRock, accessed August 17, 2020, https://www.blackrock.com/corporate/investor-relations/2019-larry-fink-ceo -letter.

Chapter 3: What's Old Is New Again

54 "*the* turning point": Arch Patton, *Men, Money, and Motivation: Executive Compensation as an Instrument of Leadership* (New York: McGraw-Hill, 1961), v.

56 among the first to reprice its own stock options: Bruce R. Ellig, *The Complete Guide to Executive Compensation* (New York: McGraw-Hill Education, 2014), 481.

57 "perpetual motion machine": Duff McDonald, *The Golden Passport: Harvard Business School, the Limits of Capitalism, and the Moral Failure of the MBA Elite* (New York: HarperBusiness, 2017), 538.

57 Americans believing CEO pay should be capped: David F. Larcker, Nicholas Donatiello, and Brian Tayan, "Americans and CEO Pay: 2016 Public Perception Survey on CEO Compensation," Stanford Graduate School of Business and the Rock Center for Corporate Governance, 2016, https://www.gsb.stanford.edu/sites/gsb /files/publication-pdf/cgri-survey-2016-americans-ceo-pay.pdf.

58 raises went almost exclusively to the lowest-paid workers: Claudia Goldin and Robert A. Margo, "The Great Compression: The U.S. Wage Structure at Mid-Century," *Quarterly Journal of Economics* 107, no. 1 (February 1992): 1–34.

59 Truman signed a new executive order: Paul G. Pierpaoli, "Truman's Other War: The Battle for the American Homefront, 1950–1953," *OAH Magazine of History* 14, no. 3 (Spring 2000): 15–19.

60   Adolf Hitler had banned labor unions: Justin Fox, "Why German Corporate Boards Include Workers," *Bloomberg*, August 24, 2018, https://www.bloomberg .com/opinion/articles/2018-08-24/why-german-corporate-boards-include -workers-for-co-determination.

61   Henry Ford notoriously doubled the rate of pay: Daniel M. G. Raff and Lawrence Summers, "Did Henry Ford Pay Efficiency Wages?," *Journal of Labor Economics* 5, no. 4 (October 1987), https://doi.org/10.3386/w2101.

61   "thrift, cleanliness, sobriety, family values, and good morals in general": Raymond Fisman and Tim Sullivan, *The Org: The Underlying Logic of the Office* (Princeton, NJ: Princeton University Press, 2015), 9.

63   "unwise to have a large proportion of executive pay consist of incentives": William Herman Newman, *Administrative Action: The Techniques of Organization and Management* (New York: Prentice-Hall, 1951).

63   superior effort and inherent intelligence: Michael Young, *The Rise of the Meritocracy* (New Brunswick, NJ: Transaction Publishers, 1994).

68   worker productivity rose 72 percent and real wages just 9 percent: Josh Bivens and Lawrence Mishel, "Understanding the Historic Divergence Between Productivity and a Typical Worker's Pay: Why It Matters and Why It's Real," Economic Policy Institute, September 2, 2015, https://www.epi.org/publication/understanding -the-historic-divergence-between-productivity-and-a-typical-workers-pay-why-it -matters-and-why-its-real/.

70   Executives have been able to time buybacks at a lower share price: Amy Dittmar and Laura Casares Field, "Can Managers Time the Market? Evidence Using Repurchase Price Data," *Journal of Financial Economics*, May 7, 2014, http://dx.doi .org/10.2139/ssrn.2423344.

71   again played the role of executive champion: Michael C. Jensen and Kevin J. Murphy, "CEO Incentives—It's Not How Much You Pay, But How," *Harvard Business Review*, 1990, https://hbr.org/1990/05/ceo-incentives-its-not-how-much-you-pay -but-how.

72   The new rules exempted additional performance-based pay: Steven Balsam, "Taxes and Executive Compensation," Economic Policy Institute, August 14, 2012, https://www.epi.org/publication/taxes-executive-compensation/.

73   the number was 10 million: Zvi Bodie, Robert S. Kaplan, and Robert C. Merton, "For the Last Time: Stock Options Are an Expense," *Harvard Business Review*, March 2003.

73   the ratio quadrupled: Steven Clifford, *The CEO Pay Machine: How It Trashes America and How to Stop It* (New York: Blue Rider Press, 2017), 78.

74   Buffett has been said to stay true to this belief: Gretchen Morgenson, "Stock Options Are Not a Free Lunch," *Forbes*, May 18, 1998.

74   address society's needs not at the periphery: Michael E. Porter and Mark R. Kramer, "Creating Shared Value," *Harvard Business Review*, January–February 2011.

76   the Roundtable gave stockholders the keys once again: Jay Lorsch and Rakesh Khurana, "The Pay Problem: Time for a New Paradigm for Executive Compensation," *Harvard Magazine*, May–June 2010.

76   the 2019 version made five commitments: "Business Roundtable Redefines the Purpose of a Corporation to Promote 'An Economy That Serves All Americans,'" Business Roundtable, August 19, 2019, https://www.businessroundtable .org/business-roundtable-redefines-the-purpose-of-a-corporation-to-promote-an -economy-that-serves-all-americans.

77   "good jobs with decent wages": "Business Pledging Against Inequalities at the G7 Summit 2019," Organisation for Economic Co-operation and Development, August 23, 2019, https://www.oecd.org/inclusive-growth/businessforinclusive growth/.

78   "the world where we were preeminent": Atossa Araxia Abrahamian, "The Rise of the Inequality Industry," *The Nation*, September 17, 2018, https://www.thenation .com/article/the-inequality-industry/.

80   managers had badly abused his survey: Dana Canedy, "Arch Patton, 88; Devised First Survey of Top Executives' Pay," *New York Times*, November 30, 1996, https:// www.nytimes.com/1996/11/30/nyregion/arch-patton-88-devised-first-survey-of -top-executives-pay.html.

80   "You get cocker spaniels": Clifford, *The CEO Pay Machine*, 75.

80   fifteen hours per week: John Maynard Keynes, "Economic Possibilities for Our Grandchildren," *Essays in Persuasion* (New York: W. W. Norton, 1963), 358–73.

81   "The past decade and a half seems to be different": Christian Zimmermann, "Corporate Profits versus Labor Income," FRED Blog, Federal Reserve Bank of St. Louis, August 9, 2018, https://fredblog.stlouisfed.org/2018/08/corporate-profits -versus-labor-income/.

Chapter 4: How Your Company Thinks about Pay

86   "no acts of Parliament": Adam Smith, *An Inquiry into the Nature and Causes of the Wealth of Nations* (London: Oxford University Press, 2008), 65.

89   Walmart's CEO Doug McMillon: Lauren Thomas, "Walmart CEO Says Congress Should Fix the 'Lagging' Federal Minimum Wage," CNBC, June 5, 2019, https://www.cnbc.com/2019/06/05/walmart-ceo-federal-minimum-wage-is-lagging-congress-should-act.html.

95   increase its waiting list: Eric Ries, "How DropBox Started as a Minimal Viable Product," *TechCrunch*, October 19, 2011, https://techcrunch.com/2011/10/19/dropbox-minimal-viable-product/.

95   companies should try to fail quickly: Eric Ries, *The Lean Startup* (New Yok: Crown Business, 2011), 97–99.

96   "algorithm that determined the lowest possible salary": Mike Isaac, *Super Pumped: The Battle for Uber* (New York: W. W. Norton, 2019), 135.

99   "top of their personal market": "Netflix Culture," Netflix, accessed August 20, 2020, https://jobs.netflix.com/culture.

103   "frequent acts of deception": Lenny Bernstein and Katie Zezima, "Lawsuit Claims Sackler Family Disregarded Safety, Opioid Addiction in Purdue Push to Profit from OxyContin," *Washington Post*, February 2, 2019, https://www.washingtonpost.com/national/lawsuit-claims-sackler-family-disregarded-safety-opioid-addiction-in-purdue-push-to-profit-from-oxycontin/2019/02/01.

103   millions of fake accounts: Matt Levine, "Wells Fargo Opened a Couple Million Fake Accounts," *Bloomberg*, September 9, 2016, https://www.bloomberg.com/opinion/articles/2016-09-09/wells-fargo-opened-a-couple-million-fake-accounts.

103   Facebook stopped paying commissions: Emily Glazer and Jeff Horwitz, "Facebook Curbs Incentives to Sell Political Ads Ahead of 2020 Election," *Wall Street Journal*, May 23, 2019, https://www.wsj.com/articles/facebook-ends-commissions-for-political-ad-sales-11558603803.

104   direct assault on the value of human life: William R. Scott, *The Itching Palm: A Study of the Habit of Tipping in America* (Philadelphia: Penn Publishing Company, 1916).

105   Elements of this legacy continue: Michael Lynn, Michael Sturman, Christie Ganley, Elizabeth Adams, Mathew Douglas, and Jessica McNeil, "Consumer Racial Discrimination in Tipping: A Replication and Extension," *Journal of Applied Social Psychology* 38, no. 4 (2008): 1045–60, https://doi.org/10.1111/j.1559-1816.2008.00338.x.

106 Netflix, which ended its cash bonus plan: Alicia Ritcey and Jenn Zhao, "Netflix's Cash Bonuses Become Salary Thanks to New Tax Plan," *Bloomberg*, December 28, 2017, https://www.bloomberg.com/news/articles/2017-12-28/netflix-s-cash-bonuses-become-salary-thanks-to-new-tax-plan.

106 the bank got to off-load toxic assets: Matt Levine, "You Can Pay Credit Suisse Not to Work There," *Bloomberg*, May 29, 2020, https://www.bloomberg.com/opinion/articles/2020-05-29/you-can-pay-credit-suisse-not-to-work-there.

Chapter 5: How Much Are You Worth?

115 more popular than YouTube: Ricardo Perez-Truglia, "The Effects of Income Transparency on Well-Being: Evidence from a Natural Experiment," University of California, Los Angeles, 2019, https://doi.org/10.3386/w25622.

125 Job titles with the word "ninja": "Weird Job Titles 2018: The Year in Review," Indeed Blog, December 14, 2018, http://blog.indeed.com/2018/12/14/weird-job-titles-year-in-review/.

142 The results weren't close: Emily Price, "Warren Buffett Won a $1 Million Bet, But the Real Winner Is Charity," *Fortune*, December 30, 2017, https://fortune.com/2017/12/30/warren-buffett-million-dollar-bet/.

143 "knowledge from one problem or domain and apply it in an entirely new one": David Epstein, *Range: Why Generalists Triumph in a Specialized World* (New York: Riverhead Books, 2019), 53.

143 "often while working in groups": Epstein, *Range: Why Generalists Triumph in a Specialized World*, 93.

144 five elements to its total rewards model: "What Is Total Rewards?," WorldatWork, accessed August 19, 2020, https://www.worldatwork.org/total-rewards-model/.

144 "Club Bureaucracy": Aaron Dignan, *Brave New Work: Are You Ready to Reinvent Your Organization?* (New York: Portfolio/Penguin, 2019), 164.

146 capping base pay: Graef S. Crystal, *What Are You Worth?* (Knoxville: Whittle Direct Books, 1992), 28.

Chapter 6: What to Expect When You're Expecting (a Raise)

169 women do ask as often as men: Benjamin Artz, Amanda Goodall, and Andrew J. Oswald, "Research: Women Ask for Raises as Often as Men, but Are Less Likely

to Get Them," *Harvard Business Review*, June 25, 2018, https://hbr.org/2018/06/research-women-ask-for-raises-as-often-as-men-but-are-less-likely-to-get-them.

173 "They recognize we're investing in their futures": Courtney Reagan, "Target Raises Its Minimum Wage to $13 an Hour, with Goal of Reaching $15 by End of 2020," CNBC, April 5, 2019, https://www.cnbc.com/2019/04/04/target-raises-its-minimum-wage-to-13-an-hour-aims-for-15-by-2020.html.

182 prominent conservatives: "Conservatives Should Ensure Workers a Seat at the Table," American Compass, September 6, 2020, https://americancompass.org/essays/conservatives-should-ensure-workers-a-seat-at-the-table/.

182 a "cool model": Kara Swisher and Scott Galloway, "Pivot Schooled #3," *New York Magazine and the Vox Media Podcast Network* (Interview with Uber CEO Dara Khosrowshahi, September 8, 2020).

183 setting working conditions: Adam Smith, *An Inquiry into the Nature and Causes of the Wealth of Nations* (London: Oxford University Press, 2008), 65.

183 "union workers receive larger wage increases": George I. Long, "Differences Between Union and Nonunion Compensation, 2001–2011," Monthly Labor Review, Bureau of Labor Statistics, April 2013, https://www.bls.gov/opub/mlr/2013/04/art2full.pdf.

183 Union workers are also less likely to be paid unequally: Elise Gould and Celine McNicholas, "Unions Help Narrow the Gender Wage Gap," Economic Policy Institute, April 3, 2017, https://www.epi.org/blog/unions-help-narrow-the-gender-wage-gap/.

184 relationship between peak years of union membership and consistent wage growth: Steven Greenhouse, *Beaten Down, Worked Up: The Past, Present, and Future of American Labor* (New York: Alfred A. Knopf, 2019).

Chapter 7: Mind the Gap

191 believe that the gender pay gap is a myth: Jillesa Gebhardt, "On Equal Pay Day 2019, Lack of Awareness Persists," SurveyMonkey, accessed August 17, 2020, https://www.surveymonkey.com/curiosity/equal-pay-day-2019/.

192 semantic two-step: Carrie Gracie, *Equal: A Story of Women, Men and Money* (London: Virago Press, 2019), 80.

204 "literally didn't know": Tina Fey, *Bossypants* (New York: Reagan Arthur/Back Bay Books), 141.

206 full diversity data: Grace Donnelly, "Fortune 500: Diversity by the Numbers," *Fortune*, June 7, 2017, https://fortune.com/2017/06/07/fortune-500-diversity/.

210 single reform of the minimum wage: Ellora Derenoncourt and Claire Montialoux, "Minimum Wages and Racial Equality," November 5, 2018, https://scholar.harvard.edu/elloraderenoncourt/publications/minimum-wages-and-racial-inequality.

211 "tap dance recital in a minefield": Fey, *Bossypants*, 256.

211 wage penalty per child: Michelle J. Budig, "The Fatherhood Bonus and the Motherhood Penalty: Parenthood and the Gender Gap in Pay," Third Way, September 2, 2014, https://www.thirdway.org/report/the-fatherhood-bonus-and-the-motherhood-penalty-parenthood-and-the-gender-gap-in-pay.

212 peak earning potential: Teresa Perez, "Earnings Peak at Different Ages for Different Demographic Groups," Payscale, June 4, 2019, https://www.payscale.com/data/peak-earnings.

212 participate in paid work: "Employment Characteristics of Families Summary," U.S. Bureau of Labor Statistics, April 21, 2020, https://www.bls.gov/news.release/famee.nr0.htm.

212 gender-wage gap in childhood allowances: "2011 Teens & Money Survey Findings," Charles Schwab, 2011, https://www.schwabmoneywise.com/public/file/P-4192268/.

214 "Pay is a power relationship": Gracie, *Equal*, 80.

215 "When decision makers know": Emilio J. Castilla, "Accounting for the Gap: A Firm Study Manipulating Organizational Accountability and Transparency in Pay Decisions," *Organizational Science* 26, no. 2 (March–April 2015): 311–33, https://doi.org/10.1287/orsc.2014.0950.

217 found through a personal connection: Gina Belli, "How Many Jobs Are Found Through Networking, Really?," Payscale, April 6, 2017, https://www.payscale.com/career-news/2017/04/many-jobs-found-networking.

218 gain little to nothing: Brooke A. Shaughnessy, Alexandra A. Mislin, and Tanja Hentschel, "Should He Chitchat? The Benefits of Small Talk for Male Versus Female Negotiators," *Basic and Applied Social Psychology* 37, no. 2 (March 18, 2015): 105–17, https://doi.org/10.1080/01973533.2014.999074.

218 "whiten" their résumés: Sonia K. Kang, Katherine A Decelles, András Tilcsik, and Sora Jun, "Whitened Résumés," *Administrative Science Quarterly* 61, no. 3 (March 17, 2016): 469–502, https://doi.org/10.1177/0001839216639577.

218   Emily and Greg: Marianne Bertrand and Sendhil Mullainathan, "Are Emily and Greg More Employable Than Lakisha and Jamal? A Field Experiment on Labor Market Discrimination," National Bureau of Economic Research, Working Paper 9873, July 2003, https://doi.org/10.3386/w9873.

218   formal sponsors: Joanne Barsh and Lareina Yee, "Unlocking the Full Potential of Women at Work," McKinsey & Company, 2012, https://www.mckinsey.com /business-functions/organization/our-insights/unlocking-the-full-potential-of -women-at-work.

219   marches won't end until 2068: "Women in Iceland to Leave Work at 2:38 PM," *Iceland Review*, October 24, 2016, https://www.icelandreview.com/news/women -in-iceland-to-leave-work-at-238-pm/.

Chapter 8: When Your Pay Gets Disrupted

225   the resulting composite image: Joshua Conrad Jackson, Neil Hester, and Kurt Gray, "The Faces of God in America: Revealing Religious Diversity Across People and Politics," *PLoS ONE* 13(6): e0198745, https://doi.org/10.1371/journal.pone.0198745.

226   thirty times as much: Sorapop Kiatpongsan and Michael I. Norton, "How Much (More) Should CEOs Make? A Universal Desire for More Equal Pay," *Perspectives on Psychological Science* 9, no. 6 (2014): 587–93, https://doi.org/10.1177/17456916 14549773.

226   half its size: Lucian Bebchuk and Yaniv Grinstein, "The Growth of Executive Pay," National Bureau of Economic Research, Working Paper 11443, June 2005, https://doi.org/10.3386/w11443.

232   CEO pay had declined: Ricardo Correa and Ugur Lel, "Say on Pay Laws, Executive Compensation, Pay Slice, and Firm Valuation Around the World," *Journal of Financial Economics*, January 20, 2016, http://dx.doi.org/10.2139/ssrn.2430465.

236   "choice between only a handful of employers": Thomas Philippon, *The Great Reversal: How America Gave Up on Free Markets* (Cambridge, MA: Belknap Press of Harvard University Press, 2019), 280.

239   supplemental income: Diana Farrell, Fiona Greig, and Amar Hamoudi, "Bridging the Gap: How Families Use the Online Platform Economy to Manage Their Cash Flow," JP Morgan Chase Institute, October 2019, https://institute.jpmorganchase .com/content/dam/jpmc/jpmorgan-chase-and-co/institute/pdf/institute-bridging -the-gap-report.pdf.

241 "waste product": Louis Hyman, *Temp: The Real Story of What Happened to Your Salary, Benefits, and Job Security* (New York: Penguin Books, 2019), 298.

243 "third way" approach: Dara Khosrowshahi, "I Am the C.E.O. of Uber: Gig Workers Deserve Better," *New York Times*, August 10, 2020, https://www.nytimes.com/2020/08/10/opinion/uber-ceo-dara-khosrowshahi-gig-workers-deserve-better.html.

245 design principles: "Building a Portable Benefits System for Today's World," Uber Newsroom, Uber, January 24, 2018, https://www.uber.com/newsroom/building-portable-benefits-system-todays-world/.

245 A more recent version: Uber Newsroom, "Working Together: Priorities to Enhance the Quality and Security of Independent Work in the United States," Uber, August 10, 2020, https://ubernewsroomapi.10upcdn.com/wp-content/uploads/2020/08/Working-Together-Priorities.pdf.

246 median driver in Seattle: Uber Newsroom, "Working Together."

247 median driver in Colorado: Uber Newsroom, "Working Together."

250 35 percent are self-employed: "NEA Announces New Research Note on Artists in the Workforce," National Endowment for the Arts, October 28, 2011, https://www.arts.gov/news/2011/nea-announces-new-research-note-artists-workforce.

251 the most successful 1 percent: Mark Mulligan, "The Death of the Long Tail: The Superstar Music Economy," MIDiA Consulting, March 2014.

252 about the same as all other industries: "Occupational Employment and Wages, May 2019: 27-1013 (Fine Artists, Including Painters, Sculptors, and Illustrators)," U.S. Bureau of Labor Statistics, March 29, 2019, https://www.bls.gov/oes/current/oes271013.htm.

Conclusion: A Fair Pay Future

260 authenticity, empathy, and rigor: Frances Frei, "How to Build (and Rebuild) Trust," TED, April 2018, https://www.ted.com/talks/frances_frei_how_to_build_and_rebuild_trust.

262 what happened after: Dan Price, *Worth It* (Seattle: Gravity Payments, 2020), 202–4.

263 substituting image for performance: Laurence J. Peter and Raymond Hull, *The Peter Principle: Why Things Always Go Wrong* (New York: HarperBusiness, 2011), 150.

268   a good question achieves two goals: Alison Wood Brooks and Leslie K. John, "The Surprising Power of Questions," *Harvard Business Review*, May–June 2018, https://hbr.org/2018/05/the-surprising-power-of-questions.

268   masking a part of their identity: Christie Smith and Kenji Yoshino, "Uncovering Talent: A New Model of Inclusion," Deloitte, 2019, https://www2.deloitte .com/content/dam/Deloitte/us/Documents/about-deloitte/us-about-deloitte -uncovering-talent-a-new-model-of-inclusion.pdf.

270   reduces their functional IQ: Anandi Mani, Sendhil Mullainathan, Eldar Shafir, and Jiaying Zhao, "Poverty Impedes Cognitive Function," *Science* 341, no. 6149 (August 30, 2013): 976–80, https://doi.org/10.1126/science.1238041.

270   cultures that respect the dignity: Alex Edmans, "Does the Stock Market Fully Value Intangibles? Employee Satisfaction and Equity Prices," *Journal of Financial Economics* 101, no. 3 (September 2011): 621–40, https://doi.org/10.1016/j .jfineco.2011.03.021.

271   sixfold increase in innovation: John M. Bremen, Carole Hathaway, and Amy DeVylder Levanat, "High-Impact Total Rewards: Sustainable. Fair. Inclusive," *Journal of Total Rewards* 29, no. 1 (First Quarter 2020), https://www.worldatwork .org/journal/2aur020/q1/pdfs/f9.pdf.

271   higher return on equity: Mark Misercola, "Higher Returns with Women in Decision-Making Positions," Credit Suisse, March 10, 2016, https://www.credit -suisse.com/about-us-news/en/articles/news-and-expertise/higher-returns-with -women-in-decision-making-positions-201610.html.

271    $28 trillion to annual global GDP: Jonathan Woetzel, Anu Madgavkar, Kweilin Ellingrud, Eric Labaye, Sandrine Devillad, Eric Kutcher, James Manyika, Richard Dobbs, and Mekala Krishnan, "How Advancing Women's Equality Can Add $12 Trillion to Global Growth," McKinsey & Company, September 2015, https:// www.mckinsey.com/featured-insights/employment-and-growth/how-advancing -womens-equality-can-add-12-trillion-to-global-growth.

275   "The great affair": Adam Smith, *An Inquiry into the Nature and Causes of the Wealth of Nations* (London: Oxford University Press, 2008), 276.

Index

Page numbers of illustrations or tables appear in italics.

Levitical law and, 79
low-wage earners and, 32–33, 112–14,
  174–75, 179, 183, 263,
as a maintenance activity, 48, 209–10,
  213–14, 263–64
as a mindset, 24, 259
outside factors influencing, 84–85
pay ranges and, 138
pay transparency and, 21, 25, 88, 116,
  151, 232, 267
process by which pay is determined,
  35–36, 45, 49, 51–52, 54–56, 60, 65,
  66, 79, 85, 95–101
pushing everyone toward, 40
repercussion-free dialogue and, 32,
  41, 66, 204, 215
resetting assumptions and, 15
salary surveys inhibiting, 87–88
shared-value model and, 74–75
steps for companies to take, 269–70
"three-legged race problem" of pay,
  88, 94, 173, 182, 236
trust of employees and, 260–63
as two-way pursuit, 28
valid but explainable concerns about,
  121–23
vulnerability celebrated by, 266–70
wage growth opportunity and, 18
what your job is worth and, 115–47
World Economic Forum white paper
  (2019) on, 24–25
your personal fair-pay strategy, 143
See also business leadership; pay
  equity; pay transparency; wage gaps
Fair Pay Mix (and Four P's), 154–81,
  189, 222, 266
for artists, 249
for executives, 227, 228–29, 231
for franchise workers, 233–37, 238
permission case for more pay, 164–72,
  180, 181, 228
power case for fair pay, 177–81

priority case for low-wage work, 174–75
priority case for more pay, 172–77, 180
process case for more pay, 154,
  157–64, *159–60, 163,* 180, 181, 229
Fast Company, "Why We Hate HR," 176
Fey, Tina, 204, 211
Fight for $15 movement, 3, 5, 7, 9, 10, 11,
  12, 13, 17, 40, 187, 243
calculating the cost of, 36–37, 39
companies responding to, 39–40, 90
workplace power and, 186
financial services industry, 34
fissured workplaces, 238, 243, 244
Flynn Restaurant Group, 235
Follet, Mary Parker, 178
food service industry, 236
franchises and, 233–37
international compensation, 234–35
minimum wage and, 4, 105
sectoral bargaining and, 182
tips and, 104–5
Forbes, "Science Reveals the Face of God
  and It Looks Like Elon Musk," 225
Ford, Henry, 61
France, 193
franchises, 233–37
"co-employment laws" and, 237
disaggregation of pay and, 237
free-market economy, 86–90
compensation philosophy and, 91
competition for workers, 88–91, 94
decentralized decision making, 86–87
global pay growth as a metric, 29
interventions and, 79, 86, 87
pay rates and supply and demand,
  15–19, 26, 33
tension between government and
  private enterprise and, 67
wage-gap problems and, 210
wage growth, causes of, 40
war effort, New Deal, and, 57–58
worker protections and, 185

About the Author

David Buckmaster is a corporate compensation expert. He has led teams responsible for compensation design and equitable pay practices at companies all over the world, including Nike, Starbucks, KFC, and Pizza Hut. A graduate of the University of Florida, he was shortlisted in 2018 for the *Financial Times* and McKinsey & Company Bracken Bower Prize, given to emerging business writers under the age of thirty-five. Buckmaster lives with his wife and daughter in Portland, Oregon. This is his first book.